▪ MONOPOLISTIC COMPETITION THEORY

MONOPOLISTIC COMPETITION THEORY

Origins, Results, and Implications

JAN KEPPLER

The Johns Hopkins University Press ▪ *Baltimore and London*

10-31-96

This book has been brought to publication with the generous assistance of the Karl and Edith Pribram Endowment.

© 1994 The Johns Hopkins University Press
All rights reserved. Published 1994
Printed in the United States of America on acid-free paper
03 02 01 00 99 98 97 96 95 94   5 4 3 2 1

The Johns Hopkins University Press
2715 North Charles Street
Baltimore, Maryland 21218-4319
The Johns Hopkins Press Ltd., London

Library of Congress Cataloging-in-Publication Data
will be found at the end of this book.
A catalog record for this book is available
from the British Library.

ISBN 0-8018-4813-X

This essay in the history of economic thought is dedicated to Melina Georgitsis and Professor Peter K. Newman. For very different reasons it would have never been written without either of them.

▪ CONTENTS

The customary claim that the author is solely responsible for faults and omissions goes further than usual in a work on the history of economic thought. The nature of the subject makes the attempt to establish irrefutable truths even more futile than is the case in other areas of economic theory. The hermeneutic act of the historian necessarily implies a certain degree of openness. The selective process of gathering and arranging facts in order to formulate meaningful hypotheses makes omission not only inevitable, but a central technique in the work of historians. I hope the facts selected, arranged, and interpreted here make for fruitful hypotheses that are not prima facie refutable by those facts omitted. Yet any historical analysis is preliminary and open to challenge. Ideally, this book will be considered open enough to inspire further research and complete enough to be taken as a point of departure.

This view of the work of the historian as part of a continuing research project is in keeping with the contribution of monopolistic competition theory to economic thought, past and present. Monopolistic competition theory showed itself to be a hybrid characterized at the same time by analytical rigor and by a desire to reflect the multidimensional nature of economic reality. It reemphasized the openness of economic theory to considerations of practical economic life, policy, and ideology, and at the same time insisted on the consistency of the complete analytical framework it employed. The effort to bridge the gap between theoretical completeness and openness to all facets of economic practice proved highly attractive to researchers during the heyday of monopolistic competition theory; nevertheless, it was ultimately considered a failure. This was largely because it was unable to keep its balance under the ever more stringent methodological requirements of the profession. Ironically, it thus became a victim of a development it had itself vigorously propelled. Yet despite its failure to establish itself as the general foundation of modern economic theory, monopolistic competition theory retained an attraction that in the meantime has helped reestablish elements of its theoretical corpus at the center of some of the most exciting contemporary research. It has always preserved its relevance for practical economic policy making.

This book redraws the outlines of the research project and its determinants that focused professional attention in the 1930s. It shows the underlying motives of the original project that are relevant to today's research. It also justifies its choice of wording, talking about "monopolistic" rather than "imperfect" competition. At the time, this language implied theoretical allegiances that from today's point of view seem to be characterized more by style than by substance. Finally, it hopes to satisfy the curiosity and to deepen the understanding of the reader who is interested in an economic theory that tries to combine relevance with consistency.

This ambition is shared by the following people, to whom I am deeply grateful; it is this legacy that is their most important contribution to this work. My most sincere thanks go to Professor Peter K. Newman of the Johns Hopkins University for his creative suggestions and his continuing support during the completion of this study. Professor Alan A. Walters, also of Johns Hopkins, offered helpful comments. I further wish to thank Professor Jan Kregel of the Università di Bologna for continuing theoretical and academic advice over many years; he set me on the path of the study of economic theory. Professor M. Ali Khan of Johns Hopkins has also proven to be an invaluable mentor, guiding through encouragement and example; I offer my most sincere thanks to him as well. Without him the observations on methodology would have been considerably less concise. I am further indebted to several referees, Giovanna Davitti of Macmillan Press, Scott Parris of Cambridge University Press, and, in particular, Henry Tom of the Johns Hopkins University Press, for their contributions. On a more personal note I would like to thank Francesco Mongelli for his friendship and continuing intellectual companionship during my years as an economist and Nelly Wong Tin Niam for her patience and gentle support during the writing of this book.

Translations of quoted material are mine, except where indicated.

·PART I

Introduction

CHAPTER 1

Overview

At the height of its influence, monopolistic competition theory provided a unique combination of theoretical progress, practical relevance, and desirable policy prescriptions. It constituted a coherent whole, a scientific endeavor based on common questions and techniques. During a relatively short period of time (1926–41), monopolistic competition theory dominated international economic science. It was an intensely debated topic that elicited contributions from leading economic thinkers. The most notable exception was John Maynard Keynes, whose work was decisive in shifting scientific attention to new subjects in the second half of the 1930s. This essay in the history of economic thought presents an analysis of the theoretical work on monopolistic competition, the political, economic, and ideological forces that shaped its development, and its implications for today's research.

In marked contrast to the intensive interest in monopolistic competition theory during a limited period of time stands the sudden loss of interest in the late 1930s. Today, after a period of almost total neglect, monopolistic competition is a topic for specialists in various areas, not a unified field of research. The temporary and fragmented character of monopolistic competition theory stands in opposition to its original claim of being a general representation of economic behavior, encompassing the two extreme cases of perfect competition and monopoly. The dominance and sudden demise of monopolistic competition theory have hitherto been unexplained phenomena; they will be analyzed below.

Monopolistic competition theory arose from dissatisfaction with Alfred Marshall's treatment of increasing returns to scale in perfectly competitive industries. The theory eventually stood in marked contrast to the Walrasian concept of perfect competition, although it could claim to encompass perfect competition as a special case. The emphasis of the theory, though, was clearly on situations in which single firms exerted some degree of monopoly power due to the absence of complete substitutes for its products.

Piero Sraffa's critique, in his seminal 1926 article "The Laws of Returns under Competitive Conditions," of Marshall's unsatisfactory treatment of Cournot's dilemma (the incompatibility of perfect competition and increasing returns to scale internal to the firm) contains a first sketch of a theory of monopolistic competition. It initiated a theoretical debate leading to comprehensive elaborations in the work of Joan Robinson, Nicholas Kaldor, and Roy F. Harrod. Sraffa's non-mathematical but rigorous general-equilibrium reasoning completed the process, which was defined as "The Erosion of Marshall's Theory of Value" by Peter K. Newman in his 1960 article of that title. Monopolistic competition theory developed amid claims by a majority of economic thinkers that economics was developing into a positive predictive science, having emancipated itself from its roots in history and moral philosophy and having been rigorously developed from generally agreed-upon premises. Ironically, this newfound rigor sometimes went hand in hand with fervent political advocacy.

Monopolistic competition theory was fed from a second source as well: American theorists attempting to increase the relevance of economic theory to a changed economic environment. This was done by concentrating on hitherto unanalyzed concepts such as product variation, selling costs, advertising, and brand names. Allyn A. Young and his student Edward H. Chamberlin were the most important theorists in this field. Despite differences in emphasis, this strand of economic theory merged with European research in the early 1930s to form a unified and clearly demarcated area of research that dominated economic theory until the beginning of World War II.

Denying the optimality results of perfect competition, monopolistic competition theory was always linked to politically motivated criticisms of liberal capitalism—whether in the form of the corporatist critique in Germany and Italy or the thought experiments of social reformers in Great Britain and New Deal America. Without taking into account this political and economic background, much of its extraordinary hold on the economics profession for the period in question cannot be understood. The crisis of liberal capitalism following the stock market crash in 1929 was perceived also as a crisis of traditional economic theory, which failed to deliver convincing explanations of the events and was unable to outline possible remedies.

Economic theory necessarily enters into a dialectic relationship with the political and economic events of its time insofar as it attempts to understand them and to provide possible answers to the most pressing problems. This does not mean that theoretical developments can be wholly explained by extratheoretical motivations. In the development of economic theory one can identify an underlying tendency toward mathematical abstraction and internal consistency and away from historical and institutional considerations, a shift from inductive to deductive reasoning. This tendency toward greater analytical rigor has played a major role both in promoting the ascendance of monopolistic competition theory and in hastening its decline. Yet the urge for analytical rigor is not a satisfying enough explanation to exclude the political, ideological, and economic events and concepts surrounding the theorists interested in monopolistic competition. The particular interplay of intra- and extratheoretical motives and developments needs illumination.

In Italy, and to a lesser degree in Germany, political transformations during the 1920s and 1930s were accompanied by fully developed institutional frameworks that promised to transform the economy along corporatist lines. In order to justify these projects theoretically, economists in Italy and Germany pointed out the destabilizing elements of monopoly power and rejected the common assumption of perfect competition. Monopolistic competition theory thus also served as a rationale for a higher degree of state intervention in private markets.

Although corporatism never took hold in Great Britain or in the United States (which were the centers of theoretical research on monopolistic competition), the events in Germany and Italy had repercussions in these countries as well. In the United States, the advances in monopolistic competition theory were propelled by empirical observations of new forces shaping capitalist enterprise: the advent of huge, impersonal corporations and the increasing use of advertising and other marketing devices (thus establishing artificial monopolies exploiting the newly created demand inelasticities). This was cause for widespread popular concern; it undermined the trust in perfect-competition economics, and thus reinforced further the effect of the economic crisis.

In Great Britain, concern for social welfare and the work of groups of highly engaged intellectuals had created a climate in which people were attentive to the shortcomings of the existing economic order.

Monopolistic competition theory also provided arguments for market intervention and income redistribution. Classical economic theory had little to say about economic practice, which provided a strong incentive to find a higher degree of realism in economic theory. Monopolistic competition promised to deliver this realism. In its heyday, monopolistic competition theory thus combined theoretical progress, practical relevance, and the hope for political solutions to the pressing problems of economic instability and social inequality.

The sudden loss of interest in monopolistic competition theory can only be understood as the result of several mutually reinforcing factors. First, researchers in monopolistic competition theory had become increasingly dissatisfied with their inability to come up with a rigorous model of comparative statics that could be quantitatively tested, while at the same time recognizing the desirability of such a positivist model. Due to this theoretical shortcoming, monopolistic competition theory was considered unscientific by those who felt that the empirical testability of previously formulated predictions was the only possible procedure in science. The effect of this perceived shortcoming was amplified by the loss of attractiveness of economic interventionism along corporatist lines with the onset of the political events leading to World War II. Theoretical work motivating political alternatives was not popular in times of national crisis. These factors combined to increase the vulnerability of monopolistic competition theory when it was attacked by proponents of the resurrection of the original dichotomy of perfect competition and monopoly.

Keynes's *General Theory of Employment, Interest, and Money* also played a role in the demise of monopolistic competition theory. Keynes's seminal work brought about a loss of interest in microeconomic theory for economists interested in policy in general, and created confusion concerning monopolistic competition theory in particular. Nearly all researchers in Great Britain shifted from monopolistic competition theory to Keynesian macroeconomics. Although monopolistic competition is ultimately the only microeconomic theory fully compatible with Keynesian macroeconomics, Keynes's own reluctance to renounce the Marshallian tradition, combined with his attitude (which seemed to imply that microeconomics did not really matter), was decisive in diverting attention.

The frustration with the inability to develop a model of comparative statics was heightened because the theory of monopolistic competition had never shed its connection with partial-equilibrium theory. Although the theory of monopolistic competition discarded the concept of a competitive industry, it did not at the time attempt to develop comprehensive models of general equilibrium, but rather pursued results in a framework that could best be described as extended partial equilibrium. The influence of competitors outside the single firm was taken into account, yet attempts to link the analysis to factor markets remained sporadic. Sraffa's original and decisive foray had been followed in its implications, not in its technique (rare but notable exceptions apart).

This was due largely to the technical difficulties involved in the mathematical modeling of monopolistic competition. This made it unattractive in a science that was being formalized and extended into general equilibrium. The legitimacy of the claim of the theory of monopolistic competition to be an alternative to perfect-competition theory was thus severely restricted by a lack of mathematical tractability. Suddenly, the theory of monopolistic competition, which had begun as a rebellion against Marshall's economic thought, appeared fundamentally Marshallian, exhibiting concerns with partial equilibrium, descriptive realism, and vaguely formalized dynamics. This stood in marked contrast to the developments in perfect-competition theory at the time. Starting with J. R. Hicks in 1939, theorists of perfect competition managed to extend economic theory in a meaningful way to general equilibrium. This set research on a road that led to the successful proof of the existence of general equilibrium by Kenneth J. Arrow and Gerard Debreu in 1954. Once at the forefront of theoretical progress, the theory of monopolistic competition had been overtaken and had fallen behind.

In this situation it was easy for advocates of perfect-competition theory, such as the theorists of the Chicago school, to claim victory. In 1949, one of their leading theorists, George J. Stigler, gleefully published an article titled "Monopolistic Competition Theory in Retrospect." But just as monopolistic competition theory had served in some circumstances as a rationale for a priori preferences for increased government intervention, its rejection was often motivated by an unquestioned belief in the optimality of free markets. Microeconomic theory thus became subjected to the twin dominance of the Chicago school and general-equilibrium theory. The former rejected monopolistic competition theory for ideological, methodological, and—purportedly—empirical reasons, the latter for its mathematical intractability.

This development relegated monopolistic competition theory for several decades to second rank in terms of the time and effort devoted to it by neoclassical mainstream economists. The most notable exception here, as in many other cases, is Paul A. Samuelson, who on numerous occasions returned to the unanswered questions and unsolved problems of monopolistic competition theory. Despite the rather bleak picture concerning academic acceptance of the theory during the years after World War II, it remained a relevant reference for practical economic policy making and a host of empirical studies. The conceptualists of the German social market economy around Walter Eucken were deeply influenced by the results of monopolistic competition theory, of which one of their peers, Heinrich von Stackelberg, had earlier been a protagonist. The lack of theoretical interest in monopolistic competition theory compared to its relevance for policy making also hints at a deficiency in the relationship between mainstream economic theory and actual economic life, including public discussion and political dispute.

Recently, monopolistic competition theory has gained fresh theoretical credibility. New mathematical techniques have been employed to prove the existence of general equilibrium under monopolistic competition—so far without a convincing proof, but also without being able to definitively disprove it. In addition, competition under increasing returns has provided the microfoundations for newer models of the macroeconomy capable of explaining the real effects of monetary policy. Similarly, the model of monopolistic competition has reappeared in trade theory, spatial economics, and endogenous growth theory. Game theory, which shares with monopolistic competition theory a lack of interest in perfectly competitive markets, but little else, has in itself become an important field of study. Despite these significant developments, monopolistic competition theory as a coherent field of research has remained an interlude in the history of economic thought. So far its once-accepted claim to represent the general economic behavior of single agents has not been taken up again.

Yet the new theoretical interest stems from a desire to add relevance to mainstream economic theory developed from the neoclassical synthesis. An analysis of the reasons for the extraordinary impact of monopolistic competition theory in the period under discussion, and for its sudden demise, will illuminate the potency of the combination of theoretical progress and policy relevance. Monopolistic competition was not a chance contribution of a few outstanding theorists at the beginning of the 1930s but the result of an intense effort by a large number of economists over an extended period of time to make economic theory pertinent to the economic issues of the day. The abandonment of monopolistic competition theory meant the abandonment of the quest for the practical relevance of a general theory of microeconomics. As dissatisfaction with economics based on the unrealized optimality results of perfect competition increases, monopolistic competition theory becomes again the natural point of departure for economists engaged in the search for a policy-relevant theory.

CHAPTER 2

Elements of Monopolistic Competition Theory

Without, at this point, inquiring extensively into the historic development of the field, I offer an overview here of the theoretical notions connected with monopolistic competition theory. (For modern work on the theory, see chapters 15 and 19.) While no single contemporary source gives a complete account of all the theoretical problems discussed, textbooks such as Kenneth E. Boulding's *Economic Analysis*, first published in 1941, provide an introduction to monopolistic competition theory as it was understood at the time.

The theory of monopolistic competition is dominated by the vision of single firms producing under conditions of increasing returns, competing with their products against other firms with similar yet nonidentical products. In its most complete formulation there is only one market for the whole economy, in which each firm faces its own downward-sloping demand curve. The shape of the demand curve is determined by marginal utilities and the cross-price elasticities with all other products. As average costs decrease, each firm is a monopolist; it would like to sell as much of its product as the market will bear, unconstrained by considerations of decreasing returns. It is also a competitor, however, inasmuch as its share of the market is constantly contested by rivals who offer close substitutes to its own product. It has been well established since 1838, when Antoine Augustin Cournot wrote *Recherches sur les principes mathématiques de la théorie des richesses*, that a profit-maximizing producer, facing a downward-sloping demand curve, will produce at the point where marginal cost equals marginal revenue. During the late 1920s a series of writers independently rediscovered this forgotten result, regarding it as a crucial step in the development of a theory of imperfect or monopolistic competition. The same pricing rule also applies to a firm that enjoys a position hitherto known as a monopoly. This clear analytical link to the concept of monopoly is also the reason to talk about *monopolistic* competition as opposed to *imperfect* competition, which implies a less clearly defined concept.

Although there have been numerous historical misunderstandings, it is ultimately of no relevance whether the phenomenon of a downward-sloping demand curve for a single firm and the related monopoly power are brought about by genuine differences in product design and quality or by frictions in the market. The latter considerations were usually of concern to researchers talking about imperfect competition; the former concerned those talking about monopolistic competition. Product differentiation can be real or perceived, as in cases where consumer loyalty is increased through advertising of minor distinguishing traits or the insistence on different brand names. Frictions can be caused by imperfect information, differences in location, or consumer inertia. Analytically there is no difference between the two approaches, as each proceeds from the assumption that some consumers will still buy a certain product even if the producing firm raises its output price slightly vis-à-vis its competitors. It is equivalent whether this monopoly power is created by genuine consumer loyalty, the cost of covering additional distance, or inertia (the unwillingness to incur additional information costs).

Researchers in both lines also agreed that monopoly power, the power—however limited—to ask prices higher than marginal cost, is essentially linked to production under increasing returns to scale. Under constant or decreasing returns to scale the possibility of replication would inevitably push prices toward marginal cost. However, the question whether increasing returns to scale were the cause or the effect of a downward-sloping demand curve was hotly debated. Researchers of imperfect competition usually assumed that increasing returns were due to indivisible capital goods combined with labor of constant marginal cost, whereas researchers of monopolistic competition often assumed traditional U-shaped cost curves, where competition through similar products pushed the production below the optimal quantity corresponding to full capacity exhaustion. Thus the first line of research saw monopolistic competition as cost-determined, while the second line saw consumer behavior as the final cause; however, this was an ultimately meaningless distinction, since falling average cost and a falling demand curve for the single firm are intrinsically linked.

Production did not take place in either case at the point of equalization of marginal and average cost; this was considered to imply the existence of excess capacity. In the first case, the concept of capacity is not defined, whereas in the second case it becomes meaningless because marginal cost is always lower than average cost over the relevant range of production. Each assumption reflects a different historical tradition and different personal concerns, yet the two are completely interchangeable with regard to their analytical implications, their technical formulation, and their results, including those pertaining to welfare considerations. The question whether the downward-sloping demand curve is due to production under increasing returns to scale or vice versa is moot; one immediately implies the other.

The theory of monopolistic competition was opposed to different concepts of industrial organization, particularly to the Walrasian theory of perfect competition. In order to understand the fascination with monopolistic competition theory, one must keep in mind that it claimed not only to provide an alternative to these concepts, but to be sufficiently general to be able to include all their essential features in one analytical framework. All that was necessary to reformulate an industrial organization was to specify suitably the characteristics of the firms analyzed. In the Walrasian world, producer/traders offer negligible quantities of well-defined homogeneous commodities in frictionless auction markets—one for each separate industry—where prices are called out by an impersonal auctioneer until supply and demand are equated. The implications are well known: each producer can potentially sell unlimited amounts of its product, constrained only by rising marginal costs, which, as a profit-maximizing agent, it will equate to the price offered by the market. There is one market for every "industry" in which all producers offer identical goods. Free entry guarantees that excess profits are reduced to zero at a point where price equals average cost and both equal marginal cost. Monopolistic competition theory breaks with the conventional premise that this analytical representation resembles reality to a reasonable degree. Together with the concept of perfect competition, the concept of industry as hitherto understood was discarded.

Monopolistic competition also differs from the concept of monopoly in that the monopoly power of the single firm is constantly in danger of being eroded by competitors with similar products. In particular, a firm's monopoly power is threatened by the entrance of firms carving out new niches in the market and being able to create new consumer loyalties. One of the most important insights of monopolistic competition theory was that no position of monopoly is absolute; all products are substitutes to greater or lesser degrees, and the potential or actual entry of new competitors, or output expansion by existing competitors, will lead to a loss of monopoly profits due to shifts in the demand curve. The possibility of new entrants, always on the minds of researchers in monopolistic competition theory, also draws attention to the implicit dynamic component in monopolistic competition. Although it was rarely explicitly modeled, this remains an essential feature of monopolistic competition, as distinct from a set of clearly demarcated monopolies of the traditional variety. It also lies at the basis of the most frequently featured single result of monopolistic competition theory, the "tangency solution," which will be discussed further below.

Monopolistic competition theory originally also distinguished itself from oligopoly theory. Oligopoly could be described as monopolistic competition in a Marshallian industry. Under oligopoly, different firms compete with identical products in a clearly demarcated market, an assumption that under monopolistic competition theory was considered absurd, since different firms would automatically produce different goods, even if the only difference between the goods was the labels on their packages. Any situation of oligopoly was considered a situation of monopolistic competition, as two or more firms with some (limited) monopoly power competed for market share. Purely static oligopoly theory has always proved vulnerable to the suggestion of collusion, because even under the most advantageous constellation (the Cournot duopoly), combined profits are inferior to the profits of a single monopolist. Implicit product differentiation (e.g., in terms of location), and the dynamic quest for a more advantageous position by forcing the rival into ruin (Bertrand) or submission (Stackelberg), have served to motivate it. Oligopoly thus shares many features with monopolistic competition, and it ceased during the 1930s to be an independent field of research. It was reestablished as a separate field after World War II as a corollary of the reestablishment of the concept of industry.

The last distinction to be drawn between monopolistic competition and other forms of industrial organization is the most difficult one, since it concerns a concept intimately connected with monopolistic competition itself—the Chamberlinian "large group." This distinction is necessary because the concept of the large group continues to confuse researchers and is sometimes even hailed as a central result of monopolistic competition theory, although it contradicts an essential feature of that theory (the nonexistence of industry boundaries in the quest for market share) and employs dubious rationality assumptions. The large group is essentially a Marshallian industry in which firms behave like small, isolated monopolies, although they produce slightly differentiated goods with strong elasticities of substitution. Each firm assumes that its profits are dependent only on total group demand, not on its own behavior, and thus optimizes with respect to a more inelastic perceived-demand curve. Due to this misperception of the demand curve, firms do not fully optimize, and thus they avoid potentially ruinous competition. This allows the establishment of a symmetric group equilibrium. The concept is neither consistent with other parts of Chamberlin's analysis nor particularly revealing, and it was consequently abandoned by Chamberlin himself. Its appeal is exclusively due to its attempt to model an equilibrium beyond that of the single firm. It is a valiant but ultimately unsuccessful attempt, because monopolistic competition theory does indeed focus on the single firm potentially interacting with *all* other firms.

Three aspects of monopolistic competition deserve more detailed attention. These are the *tangency solution*, the concern of researchers with optimal product differentiation, and welfare considerations. The tangency solution is the best-known single result of monopolistic competition theory, since it integrates its main elements into a single-firm equilibrium. It is no coincidence that the tangency solution was published simultaneously in 1933 by the two most important researchers in imperfect and monopolistic competition theory respectively, Joan Robinson and Edward Chamberlin. This result postulates a static equilibrium in which a monopolistic competitor produces at a point at which the average-cost curve and the demand curve (average-revenue curve) are tangent. This is the result of the double equilibrium condition that marginal cost equals marginal revenue, and, in addition, that average cost equals average revenue. The last condition implies that a firm operates with zero excess profits, although prices are above marginal cost. The zero-excess-profit condition is always motivated by the continuing entrance of new competitors, the continuing expansion of production by existing rivals, or both.

The partial equilibrium of the firm under monopolistic competition is thus essentially unstable, because each firm continues to have an incentive, due to its declining average costs and the size of its potential market, to disrupt it. This feature distinguishes the tangency solution from the single-firm equilibrium under both perfect competition and monopoly, where no inherent forces to upset the equilibrium remain. Under perfect competition, the single producer becomes passive once the *tâtonnement* process is concluded, since the producer has no incentive to change the amount of production; taking advantage of the limitless market would be impossible because any additional revenue would not cover the additional cost. Similarly, the single-industry monopolist has no incentive to expand production, since its market is limited, and expanding production would limit the possibility of extracting consumer surplus for profit. The equilibrium of the tangency solution is not a Cournot-Nash equilibrium in the sense that it is the result of a priori formulated equilibrium requirements and not of the interaction of competitors with clearly defined objective functions. Only one of the equilibrium conditions— marginal revenue equals marginal cost—is derivable from the principle of profit maximization; the zero-profit condition is largely assumed. On the other hand, it does not contradict a potential Cournot-Nash formulation, because it is conceivable that the desire for profit by new entrants would bring about just such an equilibrium.

The zero-profit condition itself is based on rather far-fetched additional assumptions, a point not always adequately acknowledged. For instance, the postulate of freedom of entry (necessary in order to bring about zero profits) clashes with the indivisibilities inherent in the existence of increasing returns; furthermore, freedom of entry faces restrictions by less-than-infinite cross-price elasticities and limited aggregate demand. That firms may earn positive profits due to finitely small firm sizes under limited demand is also called the "integer problem." The tangency solution is indeed the product of "heroic assumptions" (to use Edward Chamberlin's expression). The implication is that, by coincidence, market capacity and output at the profit-maximizing point match perfectly. If they do not match, then excess profits are also made under monopolistic competition. Another reason for monopoly profits is the existence of gaps in the chain of substitutes, a circumstance applying in all cases traditionally defined as monopolies. There is room for continuing monopoly rents even under monopolistic competition. To whom those rents accrue depends on the bargaining process between the owners of the firm and the providers of the factors of production. Only as long as the factors of production are in sufficiently elastic supply, and barriers to entry such as indivisibilities are absent, is a long-run no-profit equilibrium theoretically possible.

Another important, and more descriptive, line of inquiry went beyond the search for equilibrium under monopolistic competition to an investigation of product differentiation between firms, thus beginning a comprehensive integration of empirical observations and economic theory. Advertising, marketing, design, selling costs, the importance of brand names, and the like were recognized as part of the efforts of monopolistic competitors to extend their markets by increasing demand, at the cost of either their direct competitors or producers of more-distant substitutes. An important part in these profit-maximization strategies, involving many more parameters than the usual two, quantity and price, is the attempt to increase consumer attachment to one's own product in order to increase monopoly power. This line of research had originally also been fed by general concerns about the changing nature of capitalism, independent of theoretical considerations. This does not imply, however, that no analytically valuable results were reached.

In the quest for markets, one tendency is to stay close to mainstream taste, trying to enlarge marginal differences in order to distinguish oneself from one's competitors, a result that became known as the *principle of minimum differentiation*. Another argument suggested that firms develop products at the opposite ends of a spectrum in order to be able to exploit the market monopolistically, a result called, not surprisingly, the *principle of maximum differentiation*. In practice, which of the two principles yields a higher profit if implemented depends on the particular circumstances.

As it is ultimately of little analytical importance which of the parameters—price, quantity, or quality—is employed strategically, these competitive struggles bear strong resemblance to the results furnished by oligopoly or duopoly theory. Heinrich von Stackelberg's instability result for duopoly, for instance, is directly linked to the idea that two competitors producing under increasing returns to scale compete for a limited demand by using output (not marketing) as their strategic parameter. This struggle would eventually lead to continuing instability, and eventually even ruinous competition and welfare losses, which could only be overcome by state intervention. Theorists of monopolistic competition tended to have a less negative view of the strategic interaction between competing firms, interpreting it as a struggle for the marginal consumer in a setting that would tend toward the tangency solution, rather than a Darwinian struggle in which firms are willing to risk their existence in order to win an optimal market share.

Welfare considerations were of great concern to theorists of monopolistic competition. The welfare gains of existing product differentiation, which matched individual tastes more precisely, were weighed against the inefficient allocation of resources implied by excess capacity. Furthermore, product differentiation was often seen to be linked only to artificially emphasized detail, which did not take into account the real spread of tastes. Advertising and marketing expenses were generally regarded as a waste of resources, at least to the extent that their cost was considered to be substantially higher than their contribution to a fulfillment of human wants and needs (Boulding 1948a, 575). Often, the rationale behind this reasoning was that advertising programs by different firms would ultimately cancel each other out.

The biggest welfare problem connected with monopolistic competition concerned the existence of excess capacity, whose losses were emphasized especially by British theorists such as Roy Harrod. The existence of excess capacity implied that production was taking place at a point where increasing returns to scale prevailed, and this was seen as paradoxical. Why would an entrepreneur choose a firm size that would reach its point of minimum average cost only at an output higher than that actually sold? The solution to this paradox proposed at the time was to involve abnormal demand conditions, such as those prevailing in times of depression. With normal demand, output could increase again up to a point of constant average cost. But this solution is only relevant so long as it remains tied to the usual assumption of rising marginal costs. When marginal costs are constant or decreasing, the existence of excess capacity is no longer a paradox. Production under increasing returns then becomes the inevitable consequence of the combination of some fixed and indivisible factor of production (e.g., a specific capital good) with a variable factor in sufficiently elastic supply in order to impute a constant cost to the single firm (e.g., labor). An alternative explanation for excess capacity remained product differentiation and the resulting downward-sloping demand curve due to imperfect substitutability among the products of different firms.

The link between indivisibilities and excess capacity led to a heated debate between Nicholas Kaldor and Edward Chamberlin, in which it was not always made sufficiently clear that the existence of excess capacity, for instance through the technically fixed size of equipment, does not constitute a welfare loss so long as it is the most cost-effective means of production. The production of output whose quantity is limited by demand conditions at the lowest average cost is by no means identical to the production of a given firm at the point of lowest possible average cost. There can be many reasons for excess capacity. The cost of running excess capacity has to be equated at the margin to the cost of tailoring each piece of fixed equipment to the minimum average cost of the firm. This cost of tailoring contains costs for calculation as well as for the lack of standardized equipment. The minimal-input vector needed for production always has to be at least large enough to produce the desired quantity; that is, the desired quantity of output is a lower bound of the set of all quantities possibly produced.

For the historical period under consideration, monopolistic competition as a theoretical endeavor followed two lines of thought. First, it arose out of the theoretical discussion of the implications of increasing returns to scale at the level of the individual firm, and their consequences for the existence of perfect competition. The chief contributors to this line of reasoning were Piero Sraffa, Joan Robinson, and Roy Harrod, all of whom took the writings of Marshall and Cournot as their point of departure. Second, monopolistic competition theory included the attempt to broaden the relevance of theoretical economics for a changed environment, in which firms with substantial market power could be observed outside isolated monopolistic markets, and new techniques of market extension had become the order of the day. In this field Edward Chamberlin made the most important contributions; he was later joined by Nicholas Kaldor and other British economists, who began to link their discussion about increasing returns to the same phenomena. The theory of monopolistic competition thus combines logical deduction with extensive empirical observation in order to develop a full-fledged alternative to the Walrasian model, and to provide a new analytical representation for industrial organization.

The combination of analytical ambition and the drive for realism and relevance was at once the greatest strength of monopolistic competition theory and the decisive condition for its demise. As long as circumstances and preferences favored such a combination and monopolistic competition theory was able to integrate important new elements, it thrived. The theory began losing its appeal when it became clear that it was increasingly difficult to handle new aspects at an analytical level considered sufficiently rigorous by a profession leaning ever more strongly toward mathematical tractability. When Keynesianism also promised to contribute realism and relevance to economic theory, monopolistic competition theory disintegrated again into the single elements it had managed to combine into a unified field of research.

·PART II

Historical and Ideological Background

CHAPTER 3

Germany

In the late 1920s and early 1930s, monopolistic competition theory constituted the intellectual point of reference for the most progressive analysts of the fundamental shifts taking place in the economic and political organization of much of the industrialized world. It thus stood at the center not only of theoretical debates, but also of ideologically motivated discussions about the character and results of modern capitalism and the appropriate policy responses to its perceived shortcomings. The development of monopolistic competition theory cannot be fully understood without taking into account the political, ideological, and economic realities of the time after World War I. This holds true for all four countries analyzed herein: Germany, Italy, Great Britain, and the United States. However, the specific form of the relationship between economic theory and social practice on the one hand and economic theory and ideological preference on the other varies widely among the four countries in question.

A pervasive sense of the instability of capitalism was typical of the mood in all Western industrialized nations in the late 1920s and early 1930s. Because it denies to free-marketeers in all countries the claim that laissez faire would adjust the economy to a socially desirable state of perfect competition guaranteeing full employment of resources, monopolistic competition theory is as much the product of this mood as its reinforcer.

In Germany and Italy there was no way in which the preoccupation with monopolistic competition could have been independent of the debate about corporatism. Corporatist ideology defined the questions of political economy during most of the 1920s and 1930s for the whole of continental Europe. Corporatist theorists proclaimed a "revolutionary third way" between capitalism and communism. This claim was supported by an organic vision of a society in which the common weal would be put ahead of individual gain, while at the same time preserving private property. Corporatist theorizing developed into a debate that concentrated on the legitimation of and the degree of state intervention in a capitalist economy. In this context, the question of the stability or instability of free markets became of prime importance. In Italy and Germany, corporatism became in differing degrees part of official doctrine with the rise to power of fascist parties. Theorists in these countries such as Heinrich von Stackelberg (1905–46) and Luigi Amoroso (1886–1965) viewed themselves as taking part in a broad public debate, connecting their theoretical elaborations with statements concerning policy preferences.

The link between politics and economic theory in Germany and Italy was tight; in Great Britain and the United States monopolistic competition theory was more strongly determined by academic discussions. In Great Britain monopolistic competition theory took its original impulse from Sraffa's attack on Marshall's unsatisfactory treatment of Cournot's dilemma (see chapter 7). This sparked a debate involving the whole of Great Britain's economic-theory establishment, with the notable exception of J. M. Keynes. In the United States, monopolistic competition theory seemed to spring from the efforts of Edward Chamberlin to create single-handedly a "new theory of value." Yet the nonacademic debate about big corporations was a strong indication that perceptions of capitalism were changing and new modes of representation were deemed necessary. Nevertheless, it would be altogether wrong to view the Anglo-Saxon economists as working in a social and political vacuum. The British theorists, especially Joan Robinson (1903–83), Richard F. Kahn (1905–88), and Roy Harrod (1900–1978), were keenly aware of the relevance of their work for economic policy. This holds true only to a lesser degree for the American Edward Chamberlin (1899–1967).

German economic history during the first thirty years of the twentieth century was full of dramatic instability. In rapid succession there followed a quasi-corporatist "war socialism" during World War I, the reinstatement of an essentially liberal economy, hyperinflation, an unprecedented boom, and a deep crash after a devastating banking crisis in 1930–31. During the whole period, the German economy witnessed a strong tendency to cartelization of industry (a rise from 233 to 1,539 cartels in the period from 1905 to 1925, according to one estimate [Kellenbenz 1981, 411]). Given a traditionally activist state and a history of corporatist thought, a debate about the implications and the desirability of competition was inevitable.

This debate took place in an environment characterized, according to the British historian Harold James, by "the politicisation of the economy and the creation of a committedly interventionist state" (James 1986, 1). He identifies five major areas in which these processes took place: first, the high degree of industrial organization and the increasing cartelization of the economy, especially in heavy industry; second, the de facto cartelization of agricultural output by price fixing due to the disproportionate political influence of the East Elbian Junkers; third, the cartelization of the labor market and the setting of wages according to political instead of economic priorities; fourth, the high level of taxes and social contributions; and fifth, the high reparation payments agreed to in the Treaty of Versailles (ibid., 17–21). One statistic will illustrate the increase in the importance of the state sector, and thus the primacy of politics over the economy: government expenditure as a proportion of national income rose from 14.5 percent in 1910 to 24 percent in 1925.

In Germany, unlike in Italy, there never existed a coherent framework in which these different trends of politicization were discussed and implemented. There was no one well-defined period of corporatist experimentation. The fascist regime used parts of corporatist ideology as propaganda. One of the central claims of corporatism, the overcoming of class conflict by placing labor and capital under state control, was effectively used by the National Socialists as a pretext for suppressing internal opposition in the labor movement, while private capital remained largely free of state interference; capital controls were mild at worst. National Socialist attitudes toward the economy were part of a long series of ad hoc attempts to reconcile a private-enterprise economy with political prerogatives. Gustav Stolper explicitly emphasized the continuity of economic development after 1933 (Stolper 1940, 133). (Obviously, this does not detract from the sharp distinction between National Socialism and its predecessors in other respects, in particular its peculiarly vicious character.)

Throughout the first half of the twentieth century, discussions about economic policy in Germany were intrinsically linked to ideological argument. Economists such as Ludwig von Mises, Albert Weber, and Gustav Stolper severely criticized the high degree of state intervention and argued that the supersession of market forces (e.g., in the labor market) was the prime cause for the enduring crisis after 1929. These authors frequently associated themselves with economic theorists in the Anglo-Saxon countries, to whose neoclassical economics they largely subscribed. Increasing importance was attached to the discussion of monetary policy. Authors such as J. M. Keynes,

Gustav Cassel, and Albert Hahn tried to shape public opinion in favor of monetary expansionism to differing degrees. Originally, their position had also been shared by Wilhelm Lautenbach, "the German Keynes" (James 1986, 339). Yet it was partly Lautenbach's change of mind regarding monetary policy that was responsible for the enactment of a deflationary monetary regime under Chancellor Brüning at the end of 1931. These policies contributed to the eventual rise in the number of unemployed to six million.

These theoretical economists must be contrasted with the so-called political economists, who integrated their analyses with institutional and legal considerations. All of the political economists participated to varying degrees in the debate on a German form of corporatism. Their economic theory did not present a coherent corporatist approach, but instead offered a mix of justifications of state control. Their work was linked closely to the German historical school, and had originated during the nineteenth century with the visions of Fichte and Hegel of an "organic society" based on a system of guilds, largely in opposition to modern industrialization.

The most coherent attempt at theoretical corporatism had been presented in the aftermath of World War I by Walter Rathenau and his close collaborator Wichard von Moellendorff. Walter Rathenau had been responsible for a restructuring of the German war economy on the basis of *Kriegswirtschaftsgesellschaften*, huge semiprivate combines, in which the state participated as a majority stockholder. His widely discussed attempt to implement similar structures in peacetime included the creation of corporations that would be supervised by boards consisting of workers, capital owners, consumer representatives, and state delegates. It failed, because of political resistance, shortly before it was to be put up to public debate as an official outline of government policy.

Two other influential names in this context are Werner Sombart and Erwin von Beckerath. In *Deutscher Sozialismus*, published in 1934, Sombart embraces economics as only part of a wider vision of society. He emphasizes the responsibility of the state in curtailing the potentially negative activities of big monopolies. His approach distances itself from capitalism as well as from "proletarian socialism," which are both rejected as "hedonistic." His idealistic stand, emphasizing community values, is similar to that of many political economists of the time. In his 1927 book *Der moderne Kapitalismus*, he identifies the declining importance of the single entrepreneur to the benefit of larger corporatist structures as typical of the era of *Spätkapitalismus* (latter-day capitalism).

Beckerath, on a more institutionally oriented level, reviews positively the "economic constitution" of Italian fascism, which regulated the economy in the form of bilateral monopolies under state supervision, with the aim of creating "artificial equilibria." In contrast to the rhetorical fervor of Italian corporatists, Beckerath emphasizes the continuity between the new regime and the old. His antirevolutionary stance stresses that state intervention is a means of regulating and improving a private enterprise system rather than an attempt to abolish it. Not coincidentally, his student Heinrich von Stackelberg was the most original German contributor to monopolistic competition theory. Stackelberg's 1934 habilitation thesis *Marktform und Gleichgewicht* links the instability of his oligopoly analysis to his preference for the establishment of bilateral monopolies under the supervision of a corporatist state.

Stackelberg had been educated in the neoclassical tradition. During a prolonged study trip to Vienna he had met the members of the Austrian school around Gottfried Haberler and Friedrich A. von Hayek. Nevertheless, he was an early supporter of the National Socialists and their policies. Later he and Beckerath joined the antifascist Freiburger Kreis around Walter Eucken. Stackelberg's views on competition and state intervention gradually approached the ideas of Eucken concerning competition control, which were to become the basis for the postwar economic order (see chapters 12 and 18).

It is not entirely clear what induced Stackelberg's gradual shift from convinced corporatism to support for neoliberal positions. But it is clear that in the later stages of his life, Stackelberg favored forms of economic organization close to a social market economy. Instead of imposing the prerogatives of the state on single productive entities, the neoliberals wanted to use the forces of competition for the benefit of society; hence their insistence on the state as a guarantor of the competitive order. This is reflected also in their credo as formulated by Eucken: "State planning of forms—Yes; state planning and control of the economic process—No! The essential thing is to recognize the difference between form and process, and to act accordingly" (Eucken 1951, 96). The discussion about the degree of state intervention in the economy went on until the early 1950s. The emphasis had changed, yet the political relevance of any analysis of the virtues or faults of free unregulated competition remained.

In this context, Erich Schneider and Frederik Zeuthen were also important contributors to monopolistic competition theory. Schneider, a German, emphasized the gains of free competition more than its potential shortcomings, but made contributions to the unification of the terminology regarding imperfect markets (e.g., Schneider 1948). Schneider later gained international recognition in different fields, one being the theory of the producer in perfect competition. Zeuthen, a Dane, developed early conceptions of monopolistic competition under product differentiation independently of Chamberlin (see chapters 9 and 10). But despite their work, they did not receive the same degree of international attention as did Stackelberg, at least as far as monopolistic competition theory is concerned. Stackelberg's work remained the only form in which theoretical economists in Great Britain and the United States were exposed to an ideological and political discussion relevant to German public opinion.

CHAPTER 4

Italy

Italy was the country in which the interdependence among politics, economic practice, and economic theory was greatest. Corporatist ideology was intrinsically linked to the rise of Mussolini's fascist party, where it had become a major part of official doctrine. In the early 1920s the conflict of interest between capital and organized labor had brought Italy to the brink of civil war. In this politically unstable situation the fascists had seized power in a coup d'état in 1922, carrying with them a program for a corporatist restructuring of the economy. Important pieces of corporatist legislation were enacted in 1925 (establishing a bilateral monopoly under state supervision in the labor market) and in 1926 (establishing the corporate state, albeit at this point without any corporations). At all times, corporatism had a strong rhetorical element whose fervor contrasted with actual practice, which was characterized by compromise and cautious maneuvering between different interest groups. In its heyday Benito Mussolini would address the National Council of Corporations with the following words: "When we dealt a death-blow at all that had been the theory and practice of liberalism . . . we entered definitely upon the road of Revolution. Today we are burying economic liberalism" (Mussolini 1935, 23).

Theoretical corporatism in Italy arose in the first two decades of the twentieth century as a blend of revolutionary syndicalism and authoritarian nationalism. It proclaimed a "third way" between communism and capitalism in order to overcome class conflict. Its main hallmark was the gathering of industries into cartels that would be organized and supervised by boards containing representatives of all the parties involved. These cartels were then to be integrated into nine corporations, which would supervise the relationship of bilateral monopoly among the cartels. Most important was the idea of bilateral monopoly under state supervision in the labor market. Capital and labor were to be united under the principle of *produttivismo*, furthering the well-being of the nation as an organic whole.

Theoretical corporatism came in many forms. It probably received its most extreme formulation in a 1932 essay by Ugo Spirito, "Individuo e stato nella concezione corporativa." Spirito pushed corporatism to its logical conclusion by attacking its most critical element—private property. His idealist concept of the ultimate unity of state and individual, designed to overcome "pathological individualism," was immediately rejected by more-pragmatic fascists, yet it retained its function as a point of reference in the debate. A similar statement can be made in the case of Edmondo Rossoni, who represented the syndicalist branch of corporatism. His attempts to increase workers' influence on the shop-floor level and to integrate the powerful employers' organization Confederazione Generale degli Industriali Italiani into the corporations prolonged the attachment of syndicalists to fascism, yet his efforts were ultimately thwarted.

These two cases exemplify the tendency of the fascist regime to stop well short of implementing its own propaganda. In practice, private property and free enterprise were generally left untouched, except when strategic goods for the war effort were concerned. Tight control over the labor market and independent workers' organizations was opposed by a rather tentative control of production. Hugh Dalton's cutting remark that fascism was "middle-class liberalism with a spiritual element" also fits corporatism, once it is stripped of its forceful rhetoric (Dalton 1923, 69). This dichotomy between theory and practice has been formulated by the historian Eugenio Zagari: "Corporatism . . . had two faces in the Italian experience: it was an attempt to transform the respective relations of production, which did not succeed in its original intent; and it was an ideological phenomenon that intrigued Italian culture for twenty years and also had repercussions abroad" (Mancini, Parillo, and Zagari 1982, 13). Despite the limited influence of corporatism in practice, the theoretical contributions of Italian and German economists have to be read in the light of the corporatist experience.

This holds especially for the work of Luigi Amoroso, which reflected the internal contradictions of corporatism in an exemplary manner. His 1930 article "La curva statica di offerta" was an ingenious, though incomplete, attempt to come to terms with Marshall's legacy. In spite of its final equilibrium results, his work reflects the tendency of economists with corporatist sympathies to emphasize the inadequacy of the assumption of perfect competition for an analysis of modern economic life (as Stackelberg did). The preoccupation with monopoly elements and a frequent insistence on their negative welfare results and potential instability are the bases for arguments that ultimately justify a higher degree of state intervention in the economy. Even though on a purely analytical level the connections (apart from the ones in Amoroso's article) are scant, this opposition to the model of perfect competition links the corporatist literature to monopolistic competition. In addition, there is an element of diffidence toward an unregulated capitalist economy also seen in the writings of many British economists.

Amoroso, the most well known Italian writer of the period, reveals the neoclassical base of much of actual corporatist theorizing behind the attacks on liberalism. The main theoretical influence on Amoroso was Vilfredo Pareto. Initially, Amoroso had even adopted the Pareto's theory of indeterminacy of the outcome in situations of duopoly, but he later refuted it in favor of Cournot's solution. All of Amoroso's purely theoretical writings are strictly in the marginalist tradition, promoting the notion of general economic equilibrium under perfect competition. Yet there is another vein in his writing in which he violently attacks economic liberalism and embraces the corporatist ideal of state intervention. Amoroso tried to combine the two aspects in the paper he wrote with A. de' Stefani, "La logica del sistema corporativa," published in 1933. The combination of neoclassical notions with a touch of the German historical school and a little state interventionism makes this "authoritative synthesis" of neoclassical theory and corporatist critique surprisingly unexciting. Both aspects of his work can be found—often in the same books—standing seemingly unconnected side by side.

No Italian economist at the time could escape discussion with the corporatists. The formerly liberal economist Maffeo Pantaleoni took part—at an advanced age—in the adventurous occupation of Fiume under the command of Gabriele D'Annunzio, thus displaying his fascist sympathies. Luigi Einaudi and Francesco de Vito as confirmed liberals held their ground against the theoretical assaults of the corporatists, but were mostly restricted to defending known results, unable to push knowledge further. Yet it is surprising how vehemently de Vito would limit the benefits of state intervention to areas outside the purely economic sphere. In his article with the telling title "Sui fini dell' economia corporativa" (On the limits of corporatist economics), he cites state intervention "for every other objective, except to bring about the outcome of competition" (de Vito 1935, 433), and elsewhere says "it is absurd that governmental activity should and could bring about the result of perfect competition" (de Vito 1934, 474).

This open attack on the claims of a totalitarian regime is surprising at first sight, yet it does not constitute an isolated case. The relative freedom of speech it illustrates was due less to the generosity of the regime than to the regime's inherent balancing act between the ideological aspirations of its syndicalist followers and the economic demands of its corporate sponsors. There followed a split in corporatist theory between pure corporatists, such as Spirito, and fundamentally neoclassically oriented technicians with strong fascist ties, such as Amoroso, with a third faction composed of liberals such as de Vito, who did away with all but the most superficial formal adherence to the corporatist state. Just as corporatists in practice were unable or unwilling to make a clear break with the tenets of a liberal economy— private property and essentially free enterprise—corporatist economic theorists found it increasingly difficult to draw a clear line of demarcation between the neoclassical legacy and the results of the corporatist theory. This gave the liberals around Einaudi and de Vito considerable leverage.

Umberto Ricci's counterattack on corporatism is similar; it warns of a world of monopolies controlled by syndicalized workers (*polipolio di lavoratori*), which would diminish welfare because output would be restricted as each syndicate tried to maximize profits. In *Dal protezionismo al sindacalismo*, his broad defense of political economy, which was identified with free trade and economic liberalism in the tradition of Vilfredo Pareto, Ricci speaks out surprisingly frankly against any attempt to improve on the outcomes of free markets along corporatist lines. Although he avoids mentioning the fascists by name, it is clear that when he lashes out against Sorel's revolutionary syndicalism and G. D. H. Cole's evolutionary guild socialism, his objects of attack include a large group of fascist followers. His booklet, which is a collection of three public speeches, is a good indicator of the relative freedom of discussion allowed in economic matters as long as the fascist party was not directly attacked.

But only Amoroso's contribution survived as part of the theoretical legacy of monopolistic competition. This is all the more significant since he emerged as the authoritative voice of the fascist regime with regard to economic theory. His contradictions are typical in that they reflect the larger underlying contradictions of the whole fascist movement, which in the economic sphere was driven by the desire to improve on the standard tools prescribed by neoclassical analysis. As far as more technically oriented economic writing is concerned, corporatism reveals parallels to mainstream monopolistic competition theory in its attempt to shake off its neoclassical legacy, while being at the same time largely determined by it. In analyzing the Italian economic theory of the time, it is impossible to escape the massive ideological phenomenon lurking behind it, which gave the whole debate about monopolistic competition, at least in Europe, a special political relevance.

CHAPTER 5

Great Britain

The British economic experience in the interwar years was different from that of the United States in that the economy experienced no "golden twenties." After a short postwar boom in 1918, Great Britain experienced a crisis more devastating than the one following the stock market crash in 1929. The abandonment of the gold standard in combination with low interest rates led in the years 1918–19 to a short-lived, purely demand-induced boom that caused strong price increases after capacity levels had been reached. In order to curb inflation and regain control over the money market, the dollar/pound exchange rate was again fixed at prewar parity at the end of 1919; at the same time, interest rates rose to 7 percent. The sudden decline in aggregate demand induced such a severe recession that in 1921 real output was 14 percent lower than in 1914, unemployment had risen to 22 percent, and prices fell to such an extent that real wages rose significantly. Weekly real rates were 23 percent higher in 1921 than in 1914. This experience sheds light on the motivations for theoretical contributions such as the "Pigou effect," which otherwise seem of little practical relevance from today's perspective.

The hoped-for recovery set in slowly in 1923, and unemployment stayed at 10 percent and above. Reintroduction of the gold standard in 1925 and the ensuing general strike of 1926 further disrupted economic life. In this situation, the events of 1929 and after were seen as a confirmation of existing tendencies rather than as an unforeseen crash. Great Britain also experienced a strong tendency to monopolization of industry, to such an extent that in 1939 nearly every industry had a monopolistic or oligopolistic structure (Arndt 1944, 128).

Great Britain was largely dependent on exports, and it maintained a positive trade balance throughout the 1920s. Discussions about monetary policy received a great deal of attention. The question of keeping or abandoning the gold standard was of prime importance. With the reestablishment of the gold standard in 1925 and the advent of the world economic crisis, the trade balance deteriorated; in 1931 Great Britain once again abandoned the gold standard. In this context, the debate over internal monetary policy also played a big role. Advocates of a loose monetary policy in order to reflate the economy usually protested in vain against the notorious "Treasury view," which was put forward by, among others, Winston Churchill: "It is orthodox Treasury dogma, steadfastly held, that whatever might be the political and social advantages, very little additional employment can, in fact, and as a general rule, be created by State borrowing and expenditure" (Aldcroft 1986, 1:27).

This conservative approach to economic problems is reflected in the structural policies undertaken by the government in order to overcome the structural inadequacies of some British industries. In the absence of grand corporatist designs for the economy, of laws favoring cartelization under state control, or of New Deals of any kind, the only notable interventions were the Coal Mines Act of 1930, the "scrap and build" schemes in the iron and shipping industries, and the attempts to "rationalize" the cotton industry. The immediate goal of the Coal Mines Act—to stabilize employment, prices, and wages—was met to a degree, yet the quota system introduced could, given its own inefficiencies, only retard the decline of an increasingly uncompetitive industry. Similar contradictory goals were pursued in the steel and shipping industries, where programs for reducing capacity were supplemented by rationalization schemes. Despite extensive price fixing and subsidies, none of the attempts was successful, and the industries were ultimately saved only by the war. Speaking of British industrial policy in the late 1920s and the 1930s, H. W. Arndt says dryly: "The great depression did not lead to any marked increase in state interference in, or control of, the economic system" (Arndt 1944, 122). There were no broad attempts at cartelization, but neither were there any attempts to counter the trend toward monopolization in the manufacturing industries in order to increase competition.

British economic policy was characterized by restraint and little or no excitement. This contrasts with the extremely lively theoretical discussion of matters economic during the same period. The prolonged crisis in an essentially liberal market economy had intensified the search for new solutions. Intellectual groups that attempted to find such solutions ranged from the left-leaning New Fabian Research Bureau to the more esoteric Bloomsbury Group (which counted John Maynard Keynes and Gerald Shove among its members) to the Political and Economic Planning Group around conservative M.P. Harold Macmillan. In addition, British intellectuals were during the late 1920s and the 1930s increasingly fascinated by the economic experiments in the Soviet Union. These "political pilgrims" contributed to the intensity of the debate. Foremost among them were Sidney and Beatrice Webb.

Their conversion to Stalinism was the last turn in the lives of two highly committed social reformers, who had created with Fabianism their own brand of moderate socialism and who had for many years exerted an extraordinary influence over the British intellectual scene. There were many seriously committed leftist or left-leaning intellectuals in the Great Britain of the first half of the twentieth century. The spectrum reached from the leftist Labour politicians John Strachey and Oswald Mosley to the moderate conservatives of the Next Five Years Group (originally named the Liberty and Democratic Leadership), who advocated a mixed economy with strong state responsibilities.

In many ways the Webbs were representative of the general approach to social reform, combining upper-class paternalism with an emphasis on "scientific" procedures and results to form a modern utilitarianism. Education and lobbying efforts ("permeation") were stressed. The "inevitability of gradualism" was a slogan; it reflected their abstention from revolutionary fervor as well as their conviction that they stood on the right side of history. In order to explain their great influence, Donald Dewey resorts to a "sociology of the intellectual," attempting to make the common cultural and educational background of the members of Great Britain's small intellectual elite responsible for its receptiveness to the Webbs' ideas: "This . . . will, I think, serve to make more comprehensible the type of 'educational' work carried out with such incredible success by Sidney and Beatrice Webb. The people whom they wined and dined, maneuvered, and alternately flattered and badgered had a common cultural background . . . the Fabian Society could be a power of the first order in Britain, when its counterparts in the United States were fated to be impotent" (Dewey 1950, 205).

To a large extent, the famous public schools and the three major universities, Oxford, Cambridge, and London, were responsible for this cultural homogeneity. In the sphere of economics, Cambridge was the leading university; in the 1920s and 1930s it had assembled an extraordinary number of first-rate economists. A. C. Pigou and J. M. Keynes were the authorities in a scientific community that included Joan and Austin Robinson, D. H. Robertson, Gerald Shove, Richard F. Kahn, Colin Clark, and Piero Sraffa. Moreover, two Oxford economists each spent an academic year at Cambridge: Roy Harrod in 1925–26 and James Meade in 1930–31. With additional visiting scholars such as Michael Kalecki and frequent visitors such as Nicholas Kaldor, Cambridge provided a historically unique intellectual environment for theoretical economics (see accounts in Kahn 1984 and Shackle 1967). At the same time, all of those mentioned were keenly aware of the potential social relevance of their work, whether in monopolistic competition theory or in the creation of the theory of effective demand.

This by no means implies that all or even most of these economists were convinced Fabians. Nevertheless, the conviction that scientific research by an intellectual and social elite was not only relevant but necessary to improve living conditions is typical of many British economists of the period. Scientific effort that concerned itself with social relevance was as characteristic of liberals such as Keynes, who was aesthetically disgusted with the state of contemporary capitalism, as it was of researchers directly involved with labor causes, such as Colin Clark, not to mention Piero Sraffa, who combined more than ten years of messenger services for the exiled leadership of the Italian Communist party with the placid life of an English gentleman.

Perhaps the most distinguished personality to combine theoretical achievement and social engagement was Joan Robinson herself. The daughter of a Christian Socialist family, she displayed all her life a passionate advocacy for the disadvantaged, whether as a member of the Capital Supply subcommittee of the New Fabian Research Bureau or as a diligent and gratefully acknowledged proofreader of and collaborator on several books by the Labour politicians John Strachey and Hugh Dalton. Yet her leanings to leftist policy prescriptions and later her professed openness to Marxist economists were countered by the foundation of her analytical apparatus in neoclassical Marshallian economics. At the same time, her book *The Economics of Imperfect Competition*, published in 1933, helped establish monopolistic competition theory as a focus of scientific attention. Although later she was interested principally in macroeconomics, she exemplifies the interdependence of academic discussion in the Marshall-Sraffa vein and the actual political and economic problems of the day.

CHAPTER 6

The United States

The economic history of the United States in the first half of the twentieth century is put in historical focus by the economic crisis beginning in 1929 and the policy reactions to it. The United States came out of World War I as the world's biggest lender and the technologically most advanced nation. After a short slump in 1920–21, it experienced an unprecedented boom during the 1920s. From 1921 to 1929, real income rose by 40 percent and exports by 28 percent. The big slump triggered by the stock market crash in October 1929 hit the United States hard. Prices fell by 30 percent, foreign trade was reduced to a third of its former size, and real income was halved in the period from 1929 to 1932.

After a series of small-scale measures under Hoover, the new Roosevelt administration started the massive recovery program known as the New Deal in 1933. The core piece of New Deal legislation was the National Industry Recovery Act (NIRA), designed to give American industry an essentially corporatist structure. The cartelization of industry was supposed to assign quotas and to fix wages in order to break the deflationary spiral. Despite massive propaganda and a huge bureaucratic effort, the NIRA did not fully live up to its promise. It was already considered a failure, due to business resistance and lack of enforcement, when it was declared unconstitutional in 1935. Yet it remains the single most coherent attempt of American policymakers to improve on the outcome of laissez faire.

During the early 1930s, several writers in the United States expressed concern that the structure of the American economy had profoundly changed. They were responding to objective structural changes as well as to a huge increase in popular interest in matters economic as the reasons for the ongoing economic depression were explored. In an opinion poll taken in January 1930 that asked what people considered the paramount problems of the United States, "Farm Relief" was the only economic problem to occupy a place among the leading twenty entries. In January 1932, the picture had dramatically changed; of the first thirty entries, twenty-seven were concerned with economic problems ranging from "Coordination of Production" to "Anti-Trust Laws" (Arnold 1937, 106).

In search of the underlying causes for the collapse of the American economy, several books were published that, although largely descriptive, were as much contributions to theoretical analysis as they were expressions of common fears and preoccupations. Without referring to it directly, many writers implicitly identified "the decline of competition" (which was the title of a book by Arthur R. Burns published in 1933) with the existing economic crisis. The increasing size of firms, especially of common-stock corporations with widely dispersed (and hence impersonal) ownership, in opposition to the mythical individual entrepreneur, was a recurring theme in these attempts to come to terms with the new situation. The question of general interest was, in the formulation of Harry W. Laidler, "Are we living in an era of 'rugged individualism,' or of monopolized industry, or are we in some twilight zone between the two extremes?" (Laidler 1931, 3). Later in the same book (*Concentration of Control in American Industry*), he provides the answer: "Everywhere, in manufacturing, distributing, retailing, competition has given way in some degree to industrial monopoly" (ibid., 434). Many writers at the time, among them Adolf A. Berle and Gardiner C. Means, Arthur R. Burns, Thurman W. Arnold, and Alfred L. Bernheim, agreed that firm size in itself had become an increasingly important factor in economic life. In addition, most authors corroborated their statements with extensive statistical data. For instance, Gardiner Means states in "The Growth in the Relative Importance of the Large Corporation in American Economic Life": "Between 1909 and 1927 the assets of the 200 largest [corporations] increased more than twice as fast as the assets of other non-financial corporations . . . If recent rates of growth were to continue, 80% of non-financial corporate wealth would be in the hands of 200 corporations by 1950" (Means 1931, 10). This trend toward the concentration of economic power in the hands of a few megacompanies was a commonly observed phenomenon. *Big Business: Its Growth and Its Place* cites the following facts: in 1933, in industries such as cigarettes, sewing machines, and typewriters, more than 90 percent of output was produced by six or fewer firms; in forty-six of eighty-two analyzed industries, more than half of the wage earners were concentrated in the six largest firms (Bernheim 1937a, 46). The revenue of sixty-nine firms was equal to 30 percent of total corporate income (ibid., 69). Berle and Means estimated for 1930 that the two hundred largest firms owned half the corporate wealth (Berle and Means 1940, 9). The most significant result might be the strictly positive relationship between size and profitability established for all businesses in the critical years 1931–33 in *How Profitable Is Big Business?* (Bernheim 1937b, 31).

Although the quality of this statistical data is not always completely above suspicion, the results reflect in their selection and presentation not only objective phenomena but also the widespread concern of the American public that the pure size of economic entities had changed the fundamental assumptions of economic life. In working through masses of single-industry data, these writers stripped the assumption of perfect competition of its claim to be the relevant model for economic analysis by statistical argument.

Different writers came up with different explanations for these new phenomena. Arthur Burns cites indivisibilities and the resulting increasing returns to scale as the main reasons for bigger and bigger units, the phenomenon of excess capacity being due to cyclical fluctuations and overly optimistic expectations. His second explanation, although not immediately obvious, is shared by at least one other writer, the idiosyncratic Thurman Arnold. Both writers see the United States antitrust laws, such as the Sherman Act of 1890 and the Clayton Act of 1914, as major culprits in the tendency toward monopolization of industry. Arnold argues that the purely legalistic approach of treating individual trespassers as "bad" clouded the larger welfare issues at stake connected with a general trend toward monopolization, furthered by technology and patent law. "The antitrust laws became the great myth to prove by an occasional legal ceremony that great industrial organizations should be treated like individuals, and guided by principle and precept back to the old ways of competition and fair practices, as individuals were" (Arnold 1937, 221). A further point regarding the counterproductive effects of the antitrust laws was made by Burns. With the interdiction of tacit collusion, de facto collusion, as in takeovers, became the only alternative for firms that wanted to avoid eroding profit margins under cutthroat competition. This supposedly contributed further to the growth of the single productive establishment (Burns 1933, 34).

A classic explanation is that offered by Berle and Means in *The*

Modern Corporation and Private Property; they argue that the separation of ownership and management was not only responsible for the increasing monopolization of America's industry but ultimately for a loss of competitiveness: "Growing out of this separation are two characteristics, almost as typical of the quasi-public corporation as the separation itself—mere size and the public market for its securities" (Berle and Means 1940, 5). They continue: "The explosion of the atom of property destroys the basis of the old assumption that the quest for profits will spur the owner of industrial property to its effective use" (ibid., 9). The book displays a strong concern about what today would be called principal-agent problems. The fear that managers might have their own prerogatives and might put size (and its corresponding power) before profits underlies the whole analysis. This concern is combined with a latent disdain for the dispersion of ownership in a stock market. Their contention that size and profitability are somewhat contradictory objectives is understandable, considering that in their minds the contemporary growth of firms, the recent experience of the stock market crash of 1929, and the subsequent collapse of American industry go together, according to the logic of *post hoc ergo propter hoc*. Yet this analysis is not backed up by statistical evidence, as the biggest corporations fared best in the crisis.

Berle and Means agree with most of their colleagues about the implications of their findings. Although ostensibly the main concern of all the writers cited above (with the exception of Arnold) is increased realism, they do not demand changes in the legal or societal framework of the economy, but instead want a radical overhaul of traditional economic theory:

> Private property, private enterprise, individual initiative, the profit motive, wealth, competition,—these are the concepts which . . . if given free play would lead to the optimum satisfaction of human wants. Most writers of the Nineteenth Century built on these logical foundations, and current economic literature is, in large measure, cast in such terms.
>
> Yet these terms have ceased to be accurate, and therefore tend to mislead in describing modern enterprise as carried on by the great corporations . . . New terms, connoting changed relationships, become necessary. (Ibid., 345)

This work was first published in 1932. Monopolistic competition theory in the United States was, to a degree, a response to these descriptive approaches, which maintained that the small privately owned company at the basis of a strongly competitive system was no longer an adequate representation of economic reality. Monopolistic competition theory was developed against this background, which accounts for its frequently professed concern with realism, in contrast to the (mainly British) research that arose out of either a theoretical debate or political concern, and sometimes out of both.

One of the few economic theorists who had before 1930 taken up the issue of the rationalization of industrial organization and the resulting greater size of the single economic entity was the Austrian Joseph Schumpeter, soon to be a professor at Harvard and at the time a professor at the University of Bonn. In his 1928 article "The Instability of Capitalism," he voices the concern that the tendency to "trustification" of capitalism with its division of ownership and entrepreneurship might ultimately cause its demise by stifling its dynamic elements: "Capitalism whilst economically stable, and even gaining in stability, creates, by rationalising the human mind, a mentality and a style of life incompatible with its own fundamental conditions, motives and social institutions, and will be changed, although not by economic necessity and probably even at some sacrifice of economic welfare, into an order of things which it will be merely [a] matter of taste and terminology to call Socialism or not" (Schumpeter 1928, 385–86).

This implies, with a typical twist on conventional wisdom, that capitalism is threatened by too much stability, not by too little. He explicitly excludes increasing returns to scale as a sufficient causal factor for any serious degree of instability. The only cause for instability, and thus for progress, is the introduction of new methods of production by the entrepreneur, a feat that can assume almost heroic dimensions. It was left to Allyn Young to combine those two lines of thought brilliantly in another article in the same edition of the *Economic Journal* (see chapter 8).

Another widely read publication in the United States that explicitly took account of the widespread discussion about contemporary economic problems, their remedies, and the fears about the future of capitalism was the little booklet *The Economics of the Recovery Program* (Brown et al. 1934). Edited as a joint project by some Harvard professors, among them Joseph Schumpeter, Wassily Leontieff, and Edward Mason, it was designed to explain some economic concepts in connection with the New Deal in a form understandable to a wider public. The small entry "Purchasing Power" was written by Edward Chamberlin, whose 1933 book *The Theory of Monopolistic Competition* was to become the major work establishing monopolistic competition theory as a generally recognized approach to industrial organization.

Frank H. Knight, the influential chairman of the Department of Economics of the University of Chicago, had discussed as early as 1923 (in "The Ethics of Competition") the links between the concept of perfect competition, its underlying assumptions about production functions, information, and individual behavior, and the desirability of policy prescriptions derived from it. "A clear formulation of the postulates of theoretical individualism [perfect competition] will bring out the contrast with practical *laissez-faire* and will go far to discredit the latter as a policy . . . in the conditions of real life no possible social order based upon a *laissez-faire* policy can justify the familiar ethical conclusions of apologetic economics" (Knight 1976a, 49). Thus, inside the profession of theoretical economics, the concept of perfect competition had outlived its unquestioned validity as the basis for economic reasoning.

Monopolistic competition theory in the United States lacked a distinct tradition of theoretical formulation. In this respect, Edward Chamberlin's *Theory of Monopolistic Competition* stood largely alone. Most theoretical economists in the United States remained for a long time uninfluenced by the dramatic developments in practice as well as in popular reaction to political changes. Chamberlin's approach is explicitly concerned not with monopoly but with the blending of monopolistic elements and competitive elements. In its emphasis on the positive welfare effects of monopolistic competition, it is a reassuring answer to the concerns voiced in the books and articles mentioned above, rather than a theoretical extension of their mainly descriptive and statistical approaches. Yet it vigorously takes up their challenge for a greater degree of realism in economic theory.

Despite this continuity and its own concern with realism, *The Theory of Monopolistic Competition* does not contain any reference to actual events or to the discussion about current structural changes in the American economy (although a 1941 book by Edward Chamberlin's student Robert Triffin, *Monopolistic Competition and General Equilibrium Theory*, does make such references). Chamberlin is silent on this point; his book started as a Ph.D. dissertation submitted in April 1927. The book was meant to stand on its own in the debate about monopolistic competition, yet it reflected much of the research done in the period from 1927 to 1933. Its great influence was due less to its originality than to its synthesis of many ongoing research topics.

According to Chamberlin's account (Chamberlin 1962, 292ff.), his teacher and thesis supervisor, Allyn Young, had contributed to the discussion the essential concept of product differentiation by trademarks and brand names and the ensuing monopoly elements (ibid., 302). Young also provided the link to the ongoing debate on increasing returns in Great Britain. He had been educated at the University of Wisconsin by the founder of the Wisconsin school, Richard T. Ely, for whose brand of institutionalist economics he maintained a lifelong ideological, if not intellectual, sympathy. Significantly, *The Theory of Monopolistic Competition* contains several references to Ely's *Monopolies and Trusts* concerning patents and trademarks.

Young's own work concerning the organization of industry is best represented in his famous presidential address to the British Association for the Advancement of Science, "Increasing Returns and Economic Progress" (Young 1928). Presenting a dynamic version of monopolistic competition under increasing returns to scale as the basis of economic progress, Young elaborates on how technical progress must be viewed as part of a dynamically evolving equilibrium. The address constitutes a major theoretical extension of the problem concerning the compatibility of increasing returns to scale and competition; it is also a comment on the perceived instability of capitalism, allaying the fears of those who associated technical progress and change with dangerous instability. After his early death in 1929, it remained for his pupil Edward Hastings Chamberlin to give the theory of monopolistic competition its most widely acclaimed form, albeit again in a static version. The latter's synthesis of monopolistic competition theory is far less isolated than might appear at first glance.

· PART III

The Development
of Monopolistic
Competition Theory

CHAPTER 7

Origins

The theory of monopolistic competition originates in Marshall's discussion of Cournot's dilemma: the incompatibility of increasing returns to scale internal to the individual firm and perfect competition. This result had been stated in 1838 by Cournot in his *Recherches*, when he discussed the conditions for perfect competition (*concurrence indéfinie*):

> It is, moreover, plain under the hypothesis of unlimited competition, and where, at the same time, the function Π_k' (D_k) [the marginal-cost function of firm k] should be a decreasing one, that nothing would limit the production of the article. Thus, wherever there is a return on property, or a rent payable for a plant of which the operation involves expenses of such a kind that the function Π_k' (D_k) is a decreasing one, it proves that the effect of monopoly is not wholly extinct, or that competition is not so great but that the variation of the amount produced by each individual producer affects the total production of the article, and its price, to a perceptible extent ... all the functions Π_k' (D_k) are supposed to increase with D_k. (Cournot 1960, 91–92)

This statement stands in opposition to Marshall's results concerning the same problem, which had defined the issue for almost all economic scientists in the late nineteenth and early twentieth centuries. As in so many areas of economic thought, in this one Marshall's *Principles of Economics* was the authoritative voice of received truth. A clear break with Marshall's vision came only after Sraffa's intervention in 1926. Marshall's influence barred the evolution of thought along alternate lines for some time and motivated some ill-fated attempts at defense once a more coherent framework had been developed. Nevertheless, from the outset there had been a certain uneasiness in the theoretical literature concerning Marshall's treatment of a competitive industry's supply curve under conditions of increasing returns to scale.

Marshall's discussion centers, curiously, on a severe criticism of Cournot for allegedly not having noticed Cournot's dilemma: "Some [economists], among whom Cournot himself is to be counted, have before them what is in effect the supply schedule of an individual firm; representing that an increase in its output gives it command over so great internal economies as much to diminish its expenses of production; and they follow their mathematics boldly, but apparently without noticing that their premises lead inevitably to the conclusion that, whatever firm first gets a good start will obtain a monopoly of the whole business of its trade in its district" (Marshall 1961, 459n). This is a well-written polemic, but its main victim is innocent—Cournot had already made much the same observation.

It seems odd that Marshall sees the need for a clear break with previous theorists, at least on a rhetorical level, precisely in a case where his own analysis just barely avoids falling into the same trap that he says has ensnared others. Although he points out Cournot's dilemma, he subsequently develops three different concepts that allow the compatibility of increasing returns to scale with perfect competition, in order to circumvent the dilemma. None of these concepts was—even at the time—entirely convincing, but together they exerted sufficient influence to delay alternative approaches until after his death in 1924.

The three concepts developed by Marshall to circumvent the incompatibility of perfect competition with production under increasing returns are (1) the fear of spoiling the market, (2) the irreversibility of long-run industry supply curves, and (3) increasing returns due to effects external to the individual firm but internal to the industry as embodied in the representative firm. Of these three concepts only the last one is fully compatible with standard assumptions of economic analysis, but it is empirically difficult to verify.

The first concept implies a straightforward renunciation of short-run profit maximization. Marshall argues that individual establishments producing under increasing returns to scale will limit output (and thus the exploitation of scale economies) in order not to upset a given market structure. On behalf of technologies with high fixed costs in combination with relatively low variable costs (technologies with increasing returns to scale over a wide range of output), he writes: "This increases the intensity of those fears of spoiling the market, or incurring odium from other producers for spoiling the common market; which we have already learnt to regard as controlling the short-period supply price of goods, when the appliances of production are not fully employed" (ibid., 458–59). Depicting a typical situation of monopolistic competition under excess capacity, Marshall assumes this kind of behavior as typical for short-period drops in demand. In effect it implies an informal cartelization in which firms abstain from attempts to gain market share out of a sense of civic responsibility. This argument has two drawbacks. First, it restricts the phenomenon of increasing returns to scale to being a short-run phenomenon of depressed demand for the output of competitive industries. Second, it is unclear how this kind of behavior is compatible with long-run profit maximization for the single firm. It seems that Marshall implies such a link without further reference to analytical reasoning.

Marshall's abandonment of comparative-statics reasoning constitutes a second attempt to keep the incompatibility of increasing returns and perfect competition in static equilibrium. In order to understand the problem, one must realize that increasing returns had been historically linked to Adam Smith's fundamental insight into the gains from the division of labor. But in order to construct a static industry supply curve, these effects would have to be excluded from analysis as accruing over time with a changing structure of industries and firms alike. Efficiency gains due to general technical progress and inventions would also have to be excluded. These factors can only be applied in a dynamic framework, and thus do not contribute to an analysis of the relationship between output and costs. Instead of doing so, Marshall moves in the opposite direction, emphasizing these factors and elaborating a concept thoroughly incompatible with most of his previous analysis, which was couched in terms of comparative statics. He writes: "In fact we are here [with the phenomenon of increasing returns] verging on the high theme of economic progress; and here therefore it is especially needful to remember that economic problems are imperfectly presented when they are treated as problems of statical equilibrium, and not of organic growth" (ibid., 461).

This is certainly correct. The problem with Marshall in this case is that he is not clear about where he makes the break between adjustment to a static equilibrium and dynamic economic progress. In the body of the text he is in favor of an approach interested in the characteristics of static equilibria: "with this caution, the risk may be taken" (ibid.). But in the famous appendix H he sees increasing returns inevitably linked to the long-run historical growth of an industry, which constitutes an irreversible process through time as opposed to a reversible relationship between output and cost of production. This view, which was later convincingly outlined as a vision of the actual workings of the economy by Allyn Young, is puzzling, since the dynamic approach would have made obsolete the whole elaborate construction of the representative firm, which constituted his final attempt to avoid Cournot's dilemma.

Marshall's third attempt around Cournot's dilemma was the one best known, and it subsequently became identified with his name. It is the only one that is entirely compatible with static equilibrium and standard economic assumptions, such as profit maximization, at the same time. It is identified with the concept of the representative firm and the effects external to the firm and internal to the industry. The main problem with this approach is that it does not involve the existence of increasing returns to scale at the level of the individual firm and thus loses much of its inherent appeal.

The notion of increasing returns to scale is formally maintained, but in the new context it applies only to the industry as a whole, not to the individual firm. It assumes the existence of efficiency-enhancing effects internal to the industry but external to the individual firm. These effects are then projected onto the representative firm. Thus, the representative firm is able to have internal effects, which in the case of a real firm would make the existence of a competitive industry impossible. Marshall writes: "Let us call to mind the 'representative firm,' whose economies of production, internal and external, are dependent on the aggregate volume of production of the commodity that it [the industry] makes" (ibid., 342). Thus, internal economies of scale of the representative firm are just a reflection of industry growth, and as such pose no danger to its competitive structure. It is important at this point not to see the representative firm as some kind of average firm, which it is not. It is basically an industry in miniature. Marshall's construction satisfies the intuition ("internal economies of scale exist"), and at the same time the analytics ("these internal economies do not endanger our construction of competitive industry"). Confusion sets in when the internal effects of a real firm (which still are not allowed to exist) are not cleanly separated from those of the representative firm. Marshall seems to be talking about something highly interesting but difficult: the compatibility of increasing returns with perfect competition. What he actually talks about is something much less interesting, but technically feasible: the compatibility of efficiency gains accruing to the industry as a whole with perfect competition.

This confusion also obscures the observation that admissible factors that are external to a real firm but internal to the industry "constitute precisely the class which is most seldom to be met with" (Sraffa 1926, 540). However, these effects are the only ones to be taken into consideration when Marshall writes "But we . . . expect a gradual increase in demand to increase gradually the size and the efficiency of this representative firm; and to increase the economies both internal and external which are at its disposal" (Marshall 1961, 460). Arthur Pigou later corrected this picture by pointing out that there is no necessary link between the increase in size of the representative firm and the increase in industry size (see also Newman 1960, 596–97). Indeed, if increases in firm size were in any way linked to efficiency gains, then Marshall's firm, representative or not, would immediately be caught again in Cournot's dilemma.

In order to evaluate comprehensively Marshall's complex and ambiguous attitude toward the phenomenon of increasing returns, one must distinguish between his own writing and the concepts that subsequently became connected with his name. Marshall himself did not emphasize the idea of the representative firm throughout the *Principles of Economics*, yet it was ready for use. By his followers and also by his critics, especially Pigou and Sraffa, it was read as an unequivocal endorsement of a static (and thus reversible) downward-sloping supply curve. It seems that Marshall himself was more inclined to take the dynamic view of an irreversible supply curve:

> It must however be admitted that this [static] theory is out of touch with real conditions of life, in so far as it assumes that, if the normal production of a commodity increases and afterwards again diminishes to its old amount, the demand price and the supply price will return to their old positions for that amount . . . there are not many cases in which two positions of stable equilibrium would stand out as possible alternatives [for different outputs] at one and the same moment, even if all the facts of the market could be ascertained by the dealers concerned. (Marshall 1961, 807–9)

It seems that Marshall's fear that the equilibrium side of his approach (including the marginal analysis) would break down if he were to push this dynamic view too far was the main reason for his reluctant conservation of the static analysis.

In the light of the theoretical discussions that were to come, it is unfortunate that Marshall never specified his opinions unequivocally. It would probably have made comments like this one by Paul Samuelson superfluous: "much of the work from 1920 to 1933 was merely the negative task of getting Marshall out of the way" (Samuelson 1967, 111). Although this harsh remark can be justified from the viewpoint of an analysis interested only in comparative statics, it must be qualified. Marshall did not have the same concept of equilibrium as Pigou, Sraffa, and others did. Samuelson does not sufficiently take this into account when he discusses the merits of Marshall's contributions. As shown by Peter Newman, Marshall's view of long-run equilibrium is a "macroscopic" equilibrium in which supply and demand are equated, but in which the single firm does not necessarily have to be in equilibrium (Newman 1960, 590). Unfortunately, in this case a gain in realism has to be paid for with a loss in mathematical tractability—at least considering the mathematical tools available at the time (ibid., 593).

One should regard similarly the Latin motto that introduces Marshall's *Principles of Economics: Natura non facit saltum*. It is more than a habitual display of erudition; it is an expression of an intuitive aversion to comparative-statics analysis, which proceeds with the idea of frictionless and instantaneous adjustment. Marshall is indeed often closer to the idea of an equilibrium evolving through historical time, as later outlined by Allyn Young in his 1928 presidential address to the British Association for the Advancement of Science. Unfortunately, Marshall never makes a clear distinction between the two approaches. Thus his "irreversible supply curve" runs the risk of seeming more the product of ad hoc reasoning in order to save the concept of competitive industry under any circumstances than a coherent extension of his underlying economic principles.

None of the ways around Cournot's dilemma outlined above was satisfying. Typically, in his discussion of increasing returns to scale many pertinent questions either are not addressed at all or are addressed in a spirit that runs counter to scientific rigor. Marshall again faces the question of Cournot's dilemma: "The remedy for such difficulties as these is to be sought in treating each important concrete case very much as an independent problem, under the guidance of staple general reasonings . . . The 'principles' of economics must aim at affording guidance to an entry on problems of life, without making claim to be a substitute for independent study and thought" (Marshall 1961, 459n). Marshall himself must have felt that his treatment of the question of increasing returns was unsatisfactory. This quotation can be interpreted as an admission of his failure to deliver a closed theory of value, as far as the question of increasing returns is concerned. In the end, Marshall's own words must be taken seriously. He did indeed insist both on the compatibility of the empirically obvious phenomenon of increasing returns and on the theoretical concept of a perfectly competitive industry in static equilibrium. Whereas Marshall and his older contemporaries were unwilling to discard perfect competition as a necessary assumption, even at the price of inconsistency, in the following years that concept was replaced by the new theory of monopolistic competition.

Monopolistic competition theory as a self-conscious field of research began with Piero Sraffa's 1926 article "The Laws of Returns under Competitive Conditions." Until then, the six years between the most recent edition of Marshall's *Principles of Economics* and the appearance of Sraffa's article had showed that the problem of increasing returns to scale remained an uneasy concept for several economists, among them J. H. Clapham, who would have preferred to do away with it completely. In his humorous article "On Empty Economic Boxes," published in 1922 in the *Economic Journal*, Clapham challenges the concept of different kinds of returns to scale on the ground that their empirical determination proves difficult or impossible. His contention that "analysis has . . . outrun verification" (Clapham 1922b, 312) leads to the advocacy of a more descriptive, more historically oriented economic science. Although Clapham's approach is not analytic, his proposal to discard increasing returns to scale as a category for industries shows an intuitive awareness of the problems connected with it. He writes:

> As to Increasing Returns: if we are to restrict the conception . . . to the increased efficiency resulting from the improved organization which generally accompanies an increase of capital and labour in any industry . . . to the exclusion of the efficiency flowing from invention . . . then, I think, we should on principle avoid even the suggestion that we know that particular industries come into the "increasing" category, because we never can know what proportion of their efficiency is due to organization resulting from mere size and what to invention. (Ibid., 314)

True enough, but the economics profession had irreversibly decided to become an analytic rather than a descriptive science. Pigou, after Marshall's death and before Keynes's rise to stardom the leading authority of British economic thought, swiftly responded to Clapham's remarks in "Empty Economic Boxes: A Reply" (Pigou 1922). He emphasized that the laws of returns are part of an "intellectual machinery," and that descriptive realism is not necessarily the objective of economics. Twenty-seven years later, George Stigler came surprisingly close to Pigou's stand on methodology when he pointed out that the aim of economic science is to generalize, not to particularize (Stigler 1949, 24; see chapter 13 below). Pigou's remarks concerning the way economics works set the laws of returns in a prominent place in the analytic structure of the whole science. His remarks also prepared the way for Sraffa's article, enabling it to appear immediately as an important contribution concerning essential questions.

In a different way, D. H. Robertson's 1924 article "Those Empty Boxes" fulfills the same task. The title is misleading, for Robertson is not concerned with a debate on methodology, even though he refers to the debate and imitates its forcedly playful tone. One of Robertson's objects of attack is the curve of "marginal supply price," Pigou's construct from his 1912 *Wealth and Welfare* that had led him to the erroneous belief that taxation of decreasing-returns industries and subsidization of increasing-returns industries would necessarily lead to an improvement in welfare. The error had been corrected much earlier by Allyn Young and J. M. Clark in their reviews in 1913, yet Robertson has a more ambitious objective in mind: he wants to develop his own interpretation of the laws of returns, particularly of the law of increasing returns to scale.

His final statement gives an expositionally improved version of Marshall's irreversible downward-sloping supply curve in a competitive industry: "I am content with an old-fashioned supply-curve, the locus through time of the end-points of a number of 'particular expenses curves' [average-cost curves], each of them indicating the conditions of production in a given state of organization. And I am content to suppose that at each point on the locus competition . . . is on the whole securing the best results at that time and in that state of organization attainable" (Robertson 1924, 25). But on the way to this statement, Robertson developed a view of industry under increasing returns to scale due to indivisibilities, which was the first attempt to describe equilibrium under monopolistic competition— an equilibrium quite similar to the one described by the tangency solution. It contrasts favorably with the unfortunately conservative position he was to take in 1930, in his contribution to the symposium on increasing returns in the *Economic Journal*. Robertson writes, referring to himself as David battling the two Goliaths Clapham and Pigou, "he [David] knows . . . his Class (I) industries [with increasing returns due to indivisibilities] exist, and that they do not all exercise monopoly powers, but that in their case, as in others, normal competitive price must in the long run cover supplementary as well as prime costs. He is even prepared to invent for his own use a meaning of the term 'competition,' which shall imply that producers are not in a position to make monopoly profits, but are free, and determined, in the long run to cover their standing charges" (ibid., 20).

This passage has not been quoted in order to right any injustice that the history of economic thought might have done to D. H. Robertson as an early contributor to monopolistic competition theory. His formulations are too vague and his final position is too ambiguous for that. Yet they are evidence that Sraffa's article could only exert the influence it did because of a lingering need among economists to come to terms with the problem of increasing returns to scale. Inconsistency and ambiguity were signs of a conflict between the logical consistency of a pure comparative-statics approach, in which the equilibrium of supply and demand would imply the equilibrium of each firm, and the intuitive realism of the Marshallian approach, backed up by the *Hilfskonstruktion*, as Nicholas Kaldor would put it, of the representative firm.

▪ CHAPTER 8

Sraffa and Young

Piero Sraffa, in "The Laws of Returns under Competitive Conditions," elevated the treatment in the pages of the *Economic Journal* of the problem of increasing returns to scale to a rigorous application of logical reasoning. By ultimately rejecting, on logical and empirical grounds, the concept of perfect competition, he freed the way for an approach that was able to include the empirically obvious tendency to increasing returns to scale in most manufacturing establishments. It is worth discussing this article and its Italian predecessor at length; not only does it contain the first outline of monopolistic competition as an alternative to perfect competition, but it also exemplifies how monopolistic competition theory evolved out of the "erosion of Marshall's theory of value."

Sraffa's article applied rigorous comparative-statics reasoning to economics at a time when this kind of reasoning was becoming the dominant form of economic analysis. In this respect, Sraffa does not stand alone. Other economists, such as Frank Knight in Chicago and Arthur Pigou, were pushing similar agendas at about the same time. But "The Laws of Returns under Competitive Conditions" is the first example of general-equilibrium reasoning employed not only to describe abstract systems of equations, but to analyze the concrete interplay between the supply conditions in factor markets and the resulting cost conditions for several industries that recruit the same factors. In this aspect Sraffa was surprisingly modern, integrating considerations that were followed up at the time only by Allyn Young.

The first half of Sraffa's seminal paper consists of the summary of a discussion of the different laws of returns as undertaken in its

Italian precursor, "Relazioni fra costo e quantità prodotta," published in *Annali di economia* in 1925. The Italian article and its English counterpart constitute two steps in the same direction, the rejection of the downward-sloping supply curve of a competitive industry and its replacement by an alternative concept of industrial organization. But this direction is not immediately obvious, especially in the case of the original Italian article. This is due to Sraffa's unwillingness to confront orthodox authority, especially that of Marshall, head-on. This tendency to downplay the radical nature of his results had already led Joan Robinson to observe even on behalf of the second, more explicit, version: "Mr. Sraffa, whose article of 1926 took such an important part in the work of emancipating economic analysis from the tyranny of the assumption of perfect competition, was not himself completely aware of the freedom that he was winning for us" (J. Robinson 1935, 104–5).

It seems futile to speculate whether Robinson's assessment is correct, and whether Sraffa was aware of the importance of his results. The intensity of the debate concerning the compatibility of the laws of returns and the assumption of perfect competition was certainly not unknown to Sraffa, who was well acquainted with developments in British theory. Yet he displayed a tendency to avoid provocative statements wherever possible. Tatjana Schucht, the sister-in-law of Sraffa's close friend Antonio Gramsci, for instance, wrote to the latter in reference to their common friend: "Before, you always rebuked Piero for his excessive scientific scruples, which forbade him to write anything; it seems that he never got cured of this bad habit" (Gramsci 1965, 483).

The Italian article of 1925 is a long and scholarly discussion of different opinions concerning the existence of a supply curve in a competitive industry. In this context the different laws of returns assume a crucial importance. Sraffa restricts himself largely to a presentation of the work of various authors on this subject, among them Ricardo, Mill, and Wicksteed. Of prime interest in this context is his discussion of Marshall.

Considering the eventual theoretical developments, it comes as no small surprise that Sraffa begins by reaffirming Marshall's authority concerning the industry supply curve. Marshall's unjustified criticism of Cournot in the *Principles of Economics*, "the work . . . which has cleared the question [of the compatibility of increasing returns to scale and perfect competition] in a definite way and has eliminated any possibility of doubt" (Sraffa 1925, 304), is fully accepted. Indeed, his compatriot Barone, who denied the possibility of a downward-sloping static supply curve in a competitive industry, is harshly criticized: "Instead, Barone is the one who persists in believing that the error [of Cournot] has not been righted, even after the publication [of the *Principles*] . . . forgetting that the theory of 'external econo- mies' allows the perfectly correct construction of such a curve, at least from the formal point of view" (ibid.). Subsequently, Sraffa presents Marshall's theory without any major caveats.

It is only in the conclusion of this 1925 Italian article—which is the part on which he draws most heavily for the 1926 English article— that he proceeds to reveal the industry supply curve as a fudge of different, inconsistent theoretical constructs not comparable to the upward-sloping demand curve, which is solidly based on the law of diminishing utility. At this point the last part of the 1925 article and the first part of the 1926 article become virtually indistinguishable. In each of them Sraffa arrives through identical reasoning at the identical conclusion: that only constant returns to scale are compati- ble with a perfectly competitive supply curve. In the 1925 article, Sraffa writes: "There are therefore strong reasons . . . due to which in a system of static perfect competition nonproportional cost curves cannot be part of the determination of the particular equilibria of single commodities" (ibid., 328).

This leaves only industries with constant returns to scale to be considered under perfect competition. There are two significant as- pects to this important result: its derivation and its implication. Its implication turns out to be nothing less than the founding of monopolistic competition theory, and will be discussed below. The derivation of the nonadmissibility of nonconstant returns to scale as the basis for perfect competition is characterized by a new approach combining empirical facts with stringent general-equilibrium reason- ing. The exclusion of decreasing returns to scale provoked a revealing criticism by Paul Samuelson.

Concerning the law of decreasing returns, Sraffa only considers the declining productivity of each unit of a variable factor subsequently applied to a fixed factor. He had already limited decreasing returns to scale (without the existence of a fixed factor) in his Italian article to cases in which replication is impossible—a restriction he consid- ered "un artificio" (ibid., 301). He argues that usually the cost effects of an expansion in production in a particular industry are not trans- mitted only "when a variation in the quantity produced by the indus- try under consideration sets up a force which acts directly, not merely upon its own costs, but also upon the costs of other industries; in such a case the conditions of the 'particular equilibrium' which it was intended to isolate are upset, and it is no longer possible, without contradiction, to neglect collateral effects" (Sraffa 1926, 539). But usually, Sraffa argues, factor supply is sufficiently elastic for growing industries to avoid decreasing returns. The general-equilibrium reasoning he employs leads to the result that "the imposing structure of diminishing returns is available only for the study of that minute class of commodities in the production of which the whole of a factor of production is employed" (ibid., 539). Thus, industries with decreasing returns are not sufficiently frequently encountered to warrant study as a form of economic behavior.

This is plausible. But in the light of Sraffa's conclusion that only constant returns to scale are compatible with perfectly competitive industries, Paul Samuelson writes concerning this part of Sraffa's article, "This is plain wrong" (Samuelson 1987, 458). Samuelson is correct in pointing out that rising marginal-cost curves (i.e., decreasing returns to scale) are fully compatible with perfect competition. Yet at no point does Sraffa attempt to demonstrate the (false) conclusion that the law of increasing cost is technically incompatible with the concept of perfect competition. Sraffa's "error" warrants closer analysis. Samuelson reads a reasoning into Sraffa's article that it does not contain. Sraffa does not reject decreasing returns on logical grounds (as Samuelson implies), but on empirical grounds. Earlier— in a purely abstract and theoretical discussion—he had clearly considered U-shaped average-cost curves (with increasing marginal cost) and perfect competition compatible (Sraffa 1925, 309).

The question whether the class of industries that employ the whole of one factor and are thus subject to diminishing returns is indeed "minute" (and thus not worthy of analysis) is clearly debatable. It motivates the second part of the article by making the turn toward increasing returns to scale inevitable. Stolper and Samuelson, and (as mentioned in Samuelson 1987, 458) Heckscher and Ohlin clearly do not subscribe to this view, and there are good reasons for not doing so—for instance, the existence of supply shortages of specialized factors. Sraffa's position might be debated, but to call him wrong, implying a logical fault, is too quick a rehabilitation of decreasing-returns industries so dear not only to trade theory but to traditional neoclassical economics as a whole.

The case of increasing returns to scale is less controversial. Here Sraffa proceeds on logical grounds, and does so flawlessly. According to Marshall, external economies had to be internal to the industry and external to the firm in order to yield a competitive supply curve with increasing returns to scale. On the one hand, effects resulting from general technical and organizational progress had to be excluded; on the other, economies internal to the firm would also have to be excluded, as they would lead in the case of the production of a homogeneous good to an immediate monopoly—at least in the world of comparative statics implicitly assumed by Sraffa. Concerning intermediate cases, he states that "it is just in the middle that nothing, or almost nothing, is to be found" (Sraffa 1926, 540). His reasoning holds despite a technical error later pointed out by Pigou (which I will address below). By successive exclusion he arrives in both articles at the same fundamental result. In the English version, this reads: "In normal cases the cost of production of commodities produced competitively—as we are not entitled to take into consideration the causes which make it rise or fall—must be regarded as constant in respect of small variations in the quantity produced" (ibid., 541).

Once having derived this identical result, the two articles differ greatly in their implications. The Italian original ends at this point with a cautious plea for a continued, if sober, use of partial-equilibrium-cum-perfect-competition analysis: "From this point of view, which constitutes just a first approximation to reality, we have therefore to concede that commodities, in general, are produced under conditions of constant costs" (Sraffa 1925, 328).

In order to save orthodoxy, Sraffa is still inclined to assume "approximately" a reality that fits the needs of hitherto standard theory. He places himself once more in a Marshallian tradition in which perfect competition is to be saved at almost any cost. Empirically observable facts are discarded in favor of approximations to support traditional theory. In sharp contrast to this apologetic stance, the English article blazes forth with the well-known words "It is necessary, therefore, to abandon the path of free competition and turn in the opposite direction, namely, towards monopoly" (Sraffa 1926, 542). One year later, Sraffa was willing to push his reasoning to its logical conclusion. This step is usually regarded as the beginning of the theory of monopolistic competition as an independent and self-conscious area of research. The theory of perfect competition was finally rejected as incompatible with the empirically verified fact of increasing returns to scale internal to the firm.

This shift in attitude and the consequent vigorous proclamation, in flowing and forceful English, has given rise to the speculation that perhaps Sraffa did not write the whole 1926 article himself, or that perhaps he wrote it at the suggestion or under the influence of somebody else. Andrea Maneschi, for instance, writes: "Possibly under

Keynes's influence, Sraffa introduced the demand side in the form of downward-sloping demand curves at the firm level, and unwittingly gave birth in 1926 to the theory of monopolistic competition" (Maneschi 1986, 10–11). Nicholas Kaldor, who knew him quite well, writes in his obituary of Piero Sraffa: "It was Gramsci's influence which led him away from his early concentration on problems of money and banking to an interest in the issues raised by the classical theory of value in the version developed by Ricardo, and to discover new methods for overcoming the problems which Ricardo himself left unresolved" (Kaldor 1984, 3). It is tempting to place either the inventor of modern macroeconomic management (and the then editor of the *Economic Journal*) or the leader of the Italian Communist party behind the invention of monopolistic competition theory, especially if one sees those two concepts as linked in their opposition to a theory of self-adjusting, competitive markets. Yet there is no hard evidence in favor of either of these views.

Keynes was and remained an eclectic Marshallian, even at the price of a loss of coherence in his own theoretical constructions (see chapter 16). Furthermore, he had received notice of Sraffa's 1925 article only through Francis Edgeworth, who, until his death the same year, had been his coeditor at the *Economic Journal*. Edgeworth, who wrote and read Italian fluently, was well acquainted with Italian economic theory, as demonstrated, for instance, by his 1922 discussion of Amoroso's oligopoly theory, "The Mathematical Economics of Professor Amoroso." Antonio Gramsci, on the other hand, lacked both interest and an analytical background in theoretical economics. (At least there is no evidence to the contrary in his *Lettere dal carcere*, his *Quaderni dal carcere*, or in his articles in the period 1923–36.) It is unclear on what Kaldor bases his statement, but even granted the possibility of indirect influences it must be assumed that Sraffa really wrote all of his article by himself. In addition, Alessandro Roncaglia quotes from a letter of Sraffa to Keynes during the preparation of the second article for publication: "This conclusion [of the first article] has been misunderstood and taken to imply that in actual life constant returns prevail: although I believe that Ricardo's assumption is the best available for a simple theory of competition (viz. a first approximation), of course in reality the connection between cost and quantity produced is obvious. It simply cannot be considered by means of the system of particular equilibria for single commodities in a regime of competition devised by Marshall" (Roncaglia 1978, 12). The step from a critique of Marshall to an independent vision of monopolistic competition has to be attributed, according to all available evidence, to Sraffa's own originality. Later in the same letter, Sraffa gives in a few sentences the sketch of a theory of monopolistic competition; his letter concludes: "Summing up, I do not know whether there is anything on these lines which might be usefully developed for the *Economic Journal*" (ibid., 13).

This does not leave much room for speculation. Piero Sraffa knew what he was doing. The second article was written to clarify and continue the results achieved in the first. But what was it that Sraffa actually wrote that continues to intrigue researchers even today? He simply wrote the obvious: "Everyday experience shows that a very large number of undertakings—and the majority of those which produce manufactured consumers' goods—work under conditions of individual diminishing costs" (Sraffa 1926, 543). Following that, Sraffa describes the main elements of monopolistic competition. Firms exercise a certain amount of control over their prices by adjusting output optimally to downward-sloping demand curves. Output is restricted only and exclusively by market demand. Different firms compete, using goods of varying degrees of substitutability. Advertising and marketing are introduced as means of extending the respective markets. Due to product differentiation, these firms do not have to fear a total erosion of their market power by new entrants. This, in connection with the step from a theory of the industry to a theory of the firm in a general-equilibrium setting, made the 1926 article a fundamental contribution to economic thought.

Arriving at the right moment in the history of economic thought, arriving with the right arguments addressed to questions of general concern, presenting them carefully and with due respect for tradition, Sraffa initiated monopolistic competition theory and thus opened up a whole new vein of research for theoretical economics. The first article and the second do not contradict each other; there is merely a shift in emphasis. The second part of the second article provides an alternative vision to that of Marshall. Perhaps in 1925 Sraffa had not yet realized the full implications of his critical approach. His criticisms had originally been motivated by a need for logical correctness, not by a desire to topple the existing theoretical structure. Once he realized what those criticisms implied, however, he decided to push them to the limit.

Sraffa had chosen a way out of Marshall's ambiguities by looking exclusively at the necessary conditions for a static equilibrium, rejecting the possibility of the coexistence of returns to scale other than constant ones (especially excluding increasing returns) and competition. The alternative approach—no less brilliant—was pursued by

Allyn Young. It was characterized by a rejection of precisely such reasoning, which tried to apply economic analysis to models in which only one parameter (e.g., output) was variable, all others being held constant. Maintaining Marshall's vision of a situation in which increasing returns and competition would be compatible, he stressed the dynamic side of the increasing-returns phenomenon. His 1928 article could be seen as an elaboration of Marshall's irreversible supply curve, except that in this case, in the course of his general-equilibrium analysis, the terms *industry* and even *the firm*, as usually understood, become meaningless.

Young denies that increasing returns to scale would lead automatically to monopoly. Rather, he sees increasing returns to scale as part of the process of increasing capital intensity and the division of labor ("roundaboutness"), thus linking them intrinsically to technical and organizational improvements. This dynamic growth process is limited only by the size of potential output, or "by the extent of the market," to vary the famous dictum of Adam Smith (Young 1928, 532). Now Marshall's often and emphatically invoked falling supply curve comes into its own; increases in output really do lead to increasing returns, and this without sacrificing competition, albeit under (explicitly stated) temporal irreversibility.

Yet the concept of industry and even that of the firm become useless for economic analysis as firms assume more and more specialized economic functions during this process of increased roundaboutness. Young's careful distinction between increases in total output ("large production") and increases in the size of the single establishment ("large-scale production") carries over to his emphasis on industrial differentiation (ibid., 531). His vision of industrial organization of increasingly differentiated small firms operating under increasing returns to scale, subject to competitive pressures and unable to monopolize further market share, is a dynamic version of the monopolistic competitor as described later by his student Edward Chamberlin. By developing a coherent concept out of the dynamic side of Marshall's sketchy arguments, he completes, together with Sraffa, the work of putting economic science beyond Marshall's ambiguities.

Young's and Sraffa's articles assume similar positions in the history of economic thought. Through skillful employment of general-equilibrium reasoning, both show how to cope with the central problem of increasing returns and competition. Both also show that the concept of a static competitive industry could not cope any longer with the most pressing questions. The differences are equally strong.

While Sraffa basically laid the foundations of monopolistic competition theory, Young's article remained a respected but largely isolated contribution. Undoubtedly, this is largely because Sraffa's comparative-statics reasoning was more in tune with the trend of economic science, and much easier to implement analytically. Naturally, both approaches invited as many new questions as they had answered old ones.

CHAPTER 9

Consequences

The years following Sraffa's and Young's articles brought a burst of activity. In 1927, Pigou tried in "The Laws of Diminishing and Increasing Cost" to give an authoritative response to Sraffa's article. He agrees broadly with the original approach of Sraffa, but disagrees on the crucial point of the compatibility of decreasing costs and competition in the case of effects external to the firm, which Sraffa had disregarded as "not likely to be called forth by small increases in production" (Sraffa 1926, 540). Undoubtedly Pigou is correct when he asserts that a second-order increase in output, provoking a second-order reduction in production costs due to economies external to the firm, can indeed lead to first-order changes in the shape of the supply schedule of a competitive industry (compare Newman 1960; Newman and Vassilakis 1988). Yet Pigou's theory displays the same inconsistencies as Marshall's does when it comes to a specification of these external effects. Subscribing generally to a comparative-statics framework, he calls them "inventions, improved technique, increased specialization" (Pigou 1927, 195). Clearly, this could not invalidate Sraffa's conclusions.

The same can be said about Pigou's second attempt to save the concept of competitive industry one year later, in "An Analysis of Supply." He admirably develops and sharpens the notion of the representative firm, now called the "equilibrium firm," as a construct that, once more, grows only as much as the industry grows, remaining in a not-further-specified equilibrium (Pigou 1928, 239). Like the representative firm, the equilibrium firm is more an intuitive than an analytical concept and does not save him from a renewed muddle between comparative statics and dynamics. Uncharitably, one could say that Pigou simply formulated Marshall's contradictions more clearly than Marshall ever did. But this would disregard the vital role he played in bringing about the establishment of monopolistic competition theory as the dominant approach to microeconomics, precisely through his insistence on the crucial points. Pigou's defense of orthodoxy set the analytical standard to which the monopolistic competition theorists had to conform if their arguments were to carry conviction.

Monopolistic competition theory received a boost the same year with Theodore O. Yntema's reestablishment of the precise concept of marginal revenue. Differentiating and optimizing a monopolist's profit function, Yntema arrives almost nonchalantly at the result that marginal gross revenue equals marginal cost, which was to become one of the fundamental analytical tools of monopolistic competition theory (Yntema 1928, 687). It was to provide the crucial optimality conditions in all cases where a profit-maximizing firm faced a finitely elastic demand curve. Despite Edward Chamberlin's later attacks on the concept of marginal revenue as only a minor analytical tool, he himself could do no more than state the same equilibrium conditions by the equivalent but unwieldy procedure of fitting ever-smaller total-revenue rectangles under the demand curve.

Edward Chamberlin also pointed out, as late as 1961, in "The Origin and Early Development of Monopolistic Competition Theory," that Marshall had already used the concept of marginal revenue in note 13 of the mathematical appendix to his *Principles of Economics*. This is formally correct, as Marshall does take into account that a monopolist's revenue falls when prices fall due to an increase in supply. Yet he does not link the concept in any way to profit maximization, nor does he even bother to find a name for it. The concept of marginal revenue as an analytical tool did not begin with Marshall. Also, Roy Harrod independently (re)discovered the marginal-revenue curve two years later. Nevertheless, there is no doubt that after Cournot's forgotten formulation from 1838, Theodore Yntema was the proper "reinventor," supplying an important theoretical tool for on-going research.

Edward Chamberlin entered the academic discussion for the first time with "Duopoly: Value Where Sellers Are Few," a chapter of his dissertation, in 1929. It contains an overview of duopoly theory with a careful examination of the assumptions made by the various writers. His own solution is summarized thus: "If sellers have regard to their total influence upon price, neglecting no phase of it, the price will be the monopoly one, unless their number is very large" (Chamberlin

1929, 93). Curiously, he distinguishes this behavior explicitly from "tacit agreement" (ibid., 83). This does not prevent him from being the first to introduce the concept of tacit collusion or tacit agreement into the literature. In the context of monopolistic competition theory proper it is important to realize the strong rationality assumption, which Edward Chamberlin implicitly assumes throughout his work. For Chamberlin, firms are usually long-run profit maximizers with perfect knowledge of past and future.

A. J. Nichols, in his 1934 article "Professor Chamberlin's Theory of Limited Competition," pointed out that the tacit-collusion result was due to specific assumptions concerning cost functions, specifically the slope of the marginal-cost curve. He showed that with falling marginal cost, the price under duopoly might be higher than the price under monopoly, because increasing returns to scale are only insufficiently realized as marginal cost is equated to the marginal revenue corresponding to half the demand. Although it is an interesting extension, Nichols's result holds only under the implausible assumption that with such strongly increasing returns (e.g., in the case of falling marginal cost) there would be no overt collusion or (preceding this collusion) cutthroat competition.

In the late 1920s and early 1930s, most of the analytical elements needed in order to form a theoretical synthesis of the work on monopolistic competition were assembled. Although some contributions were only tenuously connected to the others, each article during this period added a building block to the final edifice to be erected by Joan Robinson and Edward Chamberlin. An important step forward—and one much in the spirit of Sraffa—was an article by Harold Hotelling, "Stability in Competition," published in 1929. It contains the first specified model and a quantitative solution for an example of monopolistic competition. Product differentiation is made quantifiable by differences in location along a straight line. Hotelling's solutions for profits, prices, and quantities of the two profit-maximizing competitors imply a trade-off between price and location differences for the individual consumers.

Hotelling's model is one of price competition with transport costs. Transport costs as an expression for quantified differences in commodity characteristics are also a measure of a firm's monopoly power. Hence, it is in a firm's interest to increase these transport costs in order to monopolize market share by increasing differentiation. As was shown fifty years later in the discussion by d'Aspremont, Gabszewicz, and Thisse (1979), nonstrategic Cournot behavior that yields a well-defined equilibrium in prices is only sustainable if firms are not too close to each other. As soon as firms are too close, it becomes profitable to attract the rival's output by quoting a price slightly lower than the sum of his price and the difference in transport costs. The result is the one postulated by Bertrand: that prices equal marginal cost. Thus it is in the firms' interest not to locate too close to each other. This "principle of maximum differentiation" foreshadows the link between product differentiation and monopoly power as developed by later theorists of monopolistic competition.

Hotelling had postulated the "principle of minimum differentiation" in his article, implying that firms would try to monopolize as much of the market as possible (Hotelling 1929, 56). It holds only as long as demand is fixed and the products of the two competitors are not close substitutes—that is, in the absence of price competition of the kind described above. The rationale for this result is that as a firm moves toward the center of the market, its average transport costs are reduced, which implies more potential customers (at the cost of the firm's competitor) and higher profits. This movement toward the center of the market will have to stop at a certain point if firms want to avoid profitless Bertrand competition. Also, in the case of more than two competing firms, no simple equilibrium will be reached. Although Hotelling did overlook the possibility of Bertrand competition for close competitors, his paper remains the first and classic analytical exposition of monopolistic competition. While it succeeded in capturing analytically only parts of the verbal outline given by Sraffa, it continues to be at the basis of many articles on modern game theory. It thus stood at the beginning of an important branch of economic theory growing out of monopolistic competition theory proper that became increasingly significant and developed into a field of research in its own right.

Richard Kahn's 1929 fellowship dissertation, *The Economics of the Short Period*, was another important work concerning monopolistic competition theory. Although first published in Italian translation in 1983 (no English-language edition appeared until 1989), the dissertation was known to Edward Chamberlin and to economists at Cambridge. Kahn links excess capacity under monopolistic competition to a fall in aggregate demand. Monopolistic competition is thus due to firms trying to protect themselves against a fall in prices and profits by restricting output and relying on their nearest and most faithful customers: "Imperfection of the market is now playing the role for which it was cast. It provides an explanation of the apparent paradox that firms work short-time [under excess capacity] although they are making a prime profit [price greater than marginal cost]. And any degree of imperfection, no matter how small, is sufficient to account for any degree of short-time working" (Kahn 1989, 123).

Andrea Maneschi calls the book, on the basis of this result, a "significant stage" in the development of the theory of value (Maneschi 1988, 168) and shows that Kahn independently devised a condition for profit maximization, which is equivalent to the equalization of marginal cost and marginal revenue. That is true, but it should be mentioned that Kahn's complicated trigonometric construction holds only under the rather severe (implicit) assumptions of linear demand curves and constant marginal cost (Kahn 1989, 120–21). Whether this achievement warrants being considered a "significant stage" or whether it should be called "clumsy and unsatisfactory" (Newman 1986, 116) is hard to decide. The whole book is rather loosely fashioned, and only three out of thirteen chapters cover genuinely new ground. Kahn's contribution was not a decisive step forward for monopolistic competition theory proper, as an alternative long-run theory of value in opposition to perfect competition. Later contributions of his, such as the discovery of the tangency solution (see J. Robinson 1932), were in this respect superior.

Kahn's major achievement was to focus, at a surprisingly young age, on monopolistic competition as a short-run phenomenon due to fixed capacity in times of depressed demand. This was a significant achievement, and it led directly to the far-reaching question of the microfoundations for Keynesian macroeconomics. Robin Marris finds in Kahn's dissertation "a missing link in the history of economic thought" (Marris 1992, 1235) and judges it a "significant contribution" (ibid., 1238). Marris considers Keynes's insistence on a rising supply price in the *General Theory of Employment, Interest, and Money* a direct consequence of the ⌐-shaped supply schedule of the single firm postulated by his student. Yet Keynes saw the rising supply schedule as linked to inelasticities in the labor market and to intertemporal profit cost (user cost) and not as a result of the cost structure intrinsic to the firm. Kahn, on the other hand, makes no allusion to labor-market conditions. The link is one of common questions, not of common answers. Kahn's innovative foray stood at the beginning of a continuing, albeit vague, discussion of links between the degree of monopolistic competition and the state of aggregate demand in the works of British economists. His work initiated a train of thought that runs from Harrod to Keynes to Kalecki and Steindl. Unfortunately, these various considerations were never comprehensively formulated in an analytically sound framework (see chapter 17).

The year 1930 is a crucial one on the way to the dominance of monopolistic competition theory. A number of contributions appeared, difficult to subsume under a common heading but all concerned with the discussion about increasing returns and monopolistic competition. Frederik Zeuthen published the collection of articles *Problems of Monopoly and Economic Warfare*, in which he gave an overview of old and new work on oligopoly theory (see also chapter 11). He made an important, though inadequately motivated, distinction between the ability of a firm to attract demand from its closest competitor and its ability to attract demand from the rest of the market, thus increasing the combined demand for the two duopolists. He did not solve the puzzle, which essentially was that of Hotelling's competitors, of optimizing by trying to keep both substitutability and attachment high. But his book—and in particular its preface by Joseph Schumpeter—were proof that economic science was in ferment regarding the search for answers to the problems posed by monopolistic competition.

Luigi Amoroso's article "The Static Supply Curve" is representative not only of his personal contradictions, but also of the state of economic science. It exemplifies the split between the acknowledgment of the market power of a single firm and the preservation of the concept of an industry supply curve. Not surprisingly, today his article is best remembered for linking for the first time in a precise manner monopoly power and the elasticity of demand. The latter part of the article, the construction of a competitive-industry supply curve that employs this formula, showed a curious contradiction and rightly fell into oblivion. By letting the elasticity of demand tend to infinity, he uses his famous formula for the measurement of monopoly power in order to justify the existence of a competitive industry, thus completely defeating its original intent.

In the same year, Keynes, as editor of the *Economic Journal*, saw the whole subject as sufficiently mature for a symposium, "Increasing Returns and the Representative Firm," in which D. H. Robertson, Gerald Shove, and Piero Sraffa participated. Robertson engaged in a last heroic attempt to save Marshall's concept by illustrating the idea of a "macroscopic equilibrium" with a variety of different allegories, alluding to organic concepts of biological equilibrium. With this endeavor he ran counter to the trend of an increasing formalization of economics. It was not the last attempt to reconcile internal increasing returns to scale and perfect competition, but it was the last to do so without being based on a static framework. His position was weakened by an error concerning declining utility, which was promptly pointed out by Sraffa. In evidence again is the opposition between a descriptive approach, concerned with intertemporal developments of single entities in combination with developments in technology or external effects that determine the state of industry, and a comparative-statics approach, concerned only with the structure of industry under given circumstances.

Gerald Shove's article "Increasing Returns and the Representative Firm" is doubtless, by length and quality of argument, the most important contribution to the symposium. Loosely speaking, he fails to make history by his reluctance to tie together the results scattered throughout the article and to advertise them as the final break with the old Marshallian approach and the start of a new one. Shove, in a different context, would talk of himself as a "rebel veteran"; this can only be classified as overcompensation (Shove 1933b, 657). Meticulously he disassembles the concept of the representative firm as a useful instrument in the analysis of increasing-return industries. The principle of product differentiation as a check on unlimited growth of single establishments is clearly recognized. It is in this context that he makes his famous remark about the economic world: "To me, at any rate, the economic problem presented by the real world seems to be much more a question of sorting out and fitting each into its appropriate niche a vast number of heterogeneous individuals and activities than of regulating and directing into the proper channels large homogeneous streams of standardized productive agents: a jig-saw puzzle rather than a problem in hydrodynamics" (Shove 1930, 99).

Shove also straightforwardly accepts Sraffa's conclusion concerning the incompatibility of increasing returns and competition in a well-defined industry (ibid., 108). Yet despite all this, his article has come to be regarded as a last bastion of Marshallian analysis before the advent of monopolistic competition theory. This is due to Shove's own unwillingness ever to criticize a Marshallian concept directly. For example, Marshall himself, with his emphasis on exceptions, is quoted in order to dismantle the concept of the representative firm. Shove seems to be most Marshallian at the very moment when he is moving away from Marshall's own concepts. His sometimes petty insistence on the obstacles to a realization of internal economies, such as the lack of intelligence in entrepreneurs, does not help the impression of a "rebel veteran" at work (ibid., 99). Ultimately Shove does indeed commit himself once more, albeit with a twist, to the orthodox view of the compatibility of increasing returns to scale and competition: "If a firm could enlarge its output to any required size (and consume the additional equipment) *instantaneously*, then indeed the predominance of internal economies would, on our present hypothesis, be incompatible with competitive equilibrium; but since it cannot, the two conditions [increasing returns and competitive equilibrium] can be reconciled" (ibid., 110; emphasis in original). Shove's well-meaning and well-informed but finally unconvincing attempt to absorb increasing returns to scale at the firm level into the concept of competitive industry was the last barrier to the establishment of monopolistic competition theory as the relevant theoretical approach of its day.

Shortly thereafter, Jacob Viner unequivocally clarified the results obtaining for different laws of returns, in a stripped-down comparative-statics framework. In his 1931 article, "Cost Curves and Supply Curves," Viner puts himself explicitly in the Marshallian tradition; rightly so, as far as the partial-equilibrium framework and the concept of industry are concerned. For increasing costs (due to the fixed supply of one factor) and constant costs he deduces the usual competitive supply curves. Yet under the heading "net internal economies of large-scale production"—increasing returns—he dryly dismisses Marshall's concept of competitive industry in the case of long-run declining marginal cost: "Provided that no change in its output will affect market price, it will pay this concern to enlarge its plant whatever the price may be, and whatever its existing scale of plant may be. If thereby it grows so large that its operations exert a significant influence on price, we pass out of the realm of atomistic competition and approach that of partial monopoly" (Viner 1952a, 215). He asserts his position by defending the "reversibility" of the downward-sloping cost curve against Marshall's criticisms noted above: "To negatively-inclined long-run cost curves . . . Marshall has denied the characteristic of 'reversibility' . . . This reasoning appears to involve a confusion between static and dynamic cost curves. The reductions in costs as output is increased . . . are purely functions of size of output when scale is adjusted to output and not of lapse of actual time during which improved processes may happen to be discovered" (ibid., 216).

Viner is right and can only be thanked for a clarity that is not common among authors in the same period. Nevertheless, he does not take into account the different impetus that drove Marshall (and in his wake Shove) to his statements. Marshall was compelled by the desire to combine empirically observed increasing returns of single firms with the concept of a competitive-industry supply curve. It is the falling industry supply curve, not the single firm's cost curve, that is irreversible. Yet at this point Viner already has abandoned the concept of competitive industry and has no sympathy for Marshall's attempts to save it. His paper remains justly acclaimed for its clarity of exposition and analytical depth, despite a now-famous error concerning the graphic representation of short-run average-cost curves in relation to a long-run average-cost curve.

Unfortunately for the increasingly intense discussion in the *Economic Journal* that took place in the years 1930–33 regarding the same problems, Viner's article, published in the *Zeitschrift für Nationalökonomie*, passed—like many other publications—unnoticed in Cambridge. "Cost Curves and Supply Curves" contains two other significant results. First, the case of increasing costs due to internal diseconomies is dismissed on the grounds of the possibilities of replication. Second, the equating of marginal cost with marginal revenue as the profit-maximizing procedure for a producer with monopoly power seems to have been firmly established—in contrast to Harrod's wrestling with the "increment of aggregate demand curve" in his 1930 "Notes on Supply."

The discussion in 1930 involved Roy Harrod, Richard Kahn, Gerald Shove, Joan Robinson, and R. G. D. Allen. It will be shown below that Robinson's *Economics of Imperfect Competition* was a result of this discussion, in parts even falling behind it. Furthermore, some of the topics were discussed in a framework that came much closer to Chamberlin's conception than to Robinson's book. The discussions were influenced by the desire—stemming from Marshall—to combine decreasing returns and competitive equilibrium. This led to some interesting attempts at explanation, but these were of only minor importance in comparison with the main theoretical results concerning monopolistic competition, which were genuine advances.

"Notes on Supply" should have appeared two years earlier, but it was rejected by Keynes, the editor of the *Economic Journal*, because of negative comments by the reviewer Frank Ramsay. Apparently, a full year passed before Harrod managed to point out that the criticisms were due to a misunderstanding; after the misunderstanding was cleared up, the article was finally published (Brown 1980, 11). This certainly heightens the originality of Harrod's contribution, but it also hints at his tendency not to state his results clearly, mixing them either with complicated conceptual constructions or with considerations of a more general nature, and creating new terminology along the way. Neither tendency was helpful in enabling the reader to focus on the crucial contributions his articles made.

Besides giving the apparently new profit-maximizing condition for the monopolist—albeit in rather complicated form—in "Notes on Supply," Roy Harrod states for the first time the connection between excess capacity and decreasing costs. The whole discussion was conducted while speaking about costs, not about returns, as had been done by Sraffa. Usually the expressions are used interchangeably, as it was understood implicitly that the issue at stake was changes in marginal costs with respect to output changes. Yet the use of "returns" might have been preferable, as it refers more precisely to the purely physical phenomenon of internal economies or diseconomies in a single firm.

In all of Harrod's contributions to monopolistic competition theory the phenomenon of excess capacity remained of major concern to him; it seemed to him to violate the principle that a profit-maximizing entrepreneur would choose capacity so as to produce at the most efficient point (see, e.g., Harrod 1934a). Not surprisingly, therefore, production under decreasing costs constitutes for Harrod a phenomenon of depression. As in Kahn's fellowship dissertation, monopolistic competition becomes the state of perfectly competitive firms with ultimately increasing costs in a state of longtime depressed demand.

The condition of decreasing costs is represented by a series of upward-sloping marginal-cost curves, each one lying lower the higher the demand, as long as the firm produces with excess capacity; Harrod starts off by describing the reverse effect for a drop in demand: "If a shrinkage of demand supervenes upon the equilibrium, the marginal product of the long-period prime [variable] factors falls below their price. They will consequently not be renewed in the long period . . . The long-period effect of the fall in demand will be to raise the short-period supply schedules of all sources affected in this way" (Harrod 1930, 236). Thus decreasing costs are just the effect of shifts of several upward-sloping supply schedules due to shifts in demand. This explains Harrod's otherwise ambiguous formulation: "We are still within the domain of the law of *increasing* costs; the kind of response analysed here might be called the law of *increasing* cost conditions" (ibid., 237; emphasis in original). This link between a permanent drop in demand and excess capacity is ensured by his additional assumption that fixed capital can be increased, but not decreased. "Long-period equilibrium is consequently compatible with there being too many sources, that is, too many centers with a core of permanent equipment, and every one or many of these centers working below their optimum capacity" (ibid, 238).

In this interpretation, the existence of monopolistic competition can only refer to an "imperfect" state of nature. So long as the existence of indivisibilities and the potential benefits of product differentiation are not introduced, the existence of two firms producing identical products in the same industry under excess capacity does constitute a waste of resources. In his 1931 article "The Law of Decreasing Costs," Harrod provides another explanation for the vexing puzzle of excess capacity: the desire of individual entrepreneurs to maintain their independence, or in his own florid words: "By presence of individualism is meant that the pertinacious desire of firms to retain their individual identity prevails over the tendency to rush into injudicious amalgamations" (Harrod 1931, 574).

"The Law of Decreasing Costs" centers on the attempt to make decreasing costs compatible with competitive equilibrium, which caused a series of spin-offs on the pages of the *Economic Journal*. The term *competitive equilibrium* is employed rather loosely, encompassing only the two conditions that firms maximize profits and that they make neither losses nor excess profits. The central argument employed by Harrod in order to give a rationale for the general results of his first paper and to find a way around Cournot's dilemma is the existence of marketing costs.

Marketing costs are supposed to rise for each single firm with its market share and therefore block the tendency toward the expansion of the single firm under excess capacity in the short run. Furthermore, declining marketing costs for demand increases on an industry level yield for each firm a series of total marginal-cost curves, each of them sloping upward (for individual-output increases at the cost of its competitors), but each subsequent one lying below its predecessor (for increases in its share of total industry output). This concept has several drawbacks, pointed out one by one in a later contribution by R. F. Kahn.

Harrod failed to make history with "The Law of Decreasing Costs" for another reason: a simple mistake. In his search for the fulfillment of the conditions for competitive equilibrium, he devised a tangency solution without a tangency. The error was quickly found, and it was admitted by Harrod, who later wrote: "Indeed, in the 1931 paper I drew the average cost and demand curves as intersecting at a point at which they should have been tangent, because the marginal revenue and marginal cost curves cut each other vertically below this point" (Harrod 1967, 67).

The decisive contribution of the article consists in a single remark that nonchalantly introduces the concept of product differentiation—which had not been explicitly mentioned before—as another possibility of competitive equilibrium. Harrod was one of the major contributors to monopolistic competition theory, one who perhaps more than either Joan Robinson or Edward Chamberlin helped clarify the topics under consideration. Yet he failed to be recognized as such, probably because he was not interested in advancing a genuinely new field of research but was instead concerned with the old problem of reconciling increasing returns to scale and competitive equilibrium. It is typical of Harrod's 1931 and 1967 articles that important results and concepts are introduced almost in passing, while seemingly arcane constructions of cost curves and rising-supply price curves are given ample space. "The intention of the foregoing analysis has been to demonstrate the possibility of the law of decreasing costs co-existing with competitive equilibrium. To do this it had to be assumed either that there were competitive marketing costs, or that the market failed to be completely unified, so that a falling demand for the products of an individual firm was possible, or both" (Harrod 1931, 572).

In "Decreasing Costs: A Mathematical Note," R. G. D. Allen tries to formalize some of Harrod's concepts, such as the concept of perfect competition, and thus makes them more vulnerable to criticism. His condition for profit maximization is unconvincing, since he assumes the derivative of the cost function to be negative, but the derivative of prices to be zero (both with respect to output), which would lead in perfect competition and marginal-cost pricing to losses (as average costs are greater than price) or to expansion and monopolization. Again, possible excess profits are checked by marketing costs, which rise with the market share.

In "Decreasing Costs: An Addendum," Harrod basically consents to the construction and for the first time states clearly the conditions underlying the hitherto rather vague discussion: "competitive equilibrium is consistent with the Law of Decreasing Costs, when individual firms are held in equilibrium in a given state of demand by being subject to marketing costs that increase, so long as that state prevails, at no less a rate than productive costs increase" (Harrod 1932, 492).

It was left to Richard Kahn in "Decreasing Costs: A Note on the Contributions of Mr. Harrod and Mr. Allen" to cut through some of the incongruities of this discussion. First, he confronts Harrod with a quotation from his own article, in which Harrod seems to admit that all he is treating is the case of increasing total costs—an effect achieved by cleverly omitting contrasting remarks (Kahn 1932, 657). Second, Kahn points out that there is no compelling reason to distinguish advertising and nonadvertising costs at the firm level. Third, and most important, he makes it clear that a reduction of total advertising outlay due to increases in industry demand (which are responsible for the downward shifts of the supply curves) constitutes a "most beautiful" example of an externality. Indeed, the externality is internal to the industry and external to the firm—exactly what Marshall had in mind when he discussed the compatibility of increasing returns and competitive equilibrium. Finally, Kahn points out that in perfect competition there should be no marketing costs and that Harrod does not address full equilibrium, since the number of firms stays fixed throughout.

This group of articles constitutes a paradigmatic case for the difficulties with which economists were grappling in trying to synthesize monopolistic competition theory. These difficulties arose mainly from the desire of the Cambridge economists to maintain the links to the original Marshallian ideas. Harrod's contributions stand halfway between Marshall's attempts to overcome Cournot's dilemma and Keynes's and Kalecki's considerations, which linked the degree of monopoly of the single firm not exclusively to cost conditions, but also to fluctuations in demand. Science proceeds from greater to smaller errors, and Harrod's first attempts enabled Joan Robinson to write perhaps her most mature contribution to monopolistic competition theory, "Imperfect Competition and Falling Supply Price," published in 1932. With regard to the theory itself, it can be judged superior to her famous book *The Economics of Imperfect Competition* of the following year. It remains puzzling that this excellent article is not included in her *Collected Economic Papers* (J. Robinson 1980). It is also odd that her work is seemingly unconnected to that of her husband, Austin Robinson, who proceeds along completely conventional lines in his 1931 book *The Structure of Competitive Industry*.

"Imperfect Competition and Falling Supply Price" maintains the concept of frictions responsible for the imperfections of competition. But by choosing differential transport costs instead of marketing costs, Joan Robinson explicitly introduces product differentiation as the major reason for excess capacity and imperfect competition. Thus she explicitly closes the gap between the British research and the research pursued contemporaneously by Edward Chamberlin in the United States (whose results were not published until 1933). Continuing in Harrod's vein, she restates the double condition for equilibrium, thus establishing the correct tangency solution in 1932: "The equilibrium of the industry thus requires a double condition. Marginal revenue must be equal to marginal cost, and price must be equal to average cost. This double condition of equilibrium can be fulfilled only when the individual demand curve of the firm is tangent to its average cost curve" (J. Robinson 1932, 547). She continues in a note: "I am indebted for this proposition to Mr. R. F. Kahn, who in turn derived it by pursuing Mr. Sraffa's argument to its logical conclusion" (ibid., 547n). Richard Kahn's role in the progress of monopolistic competition theory has not been sufficiently acknowledged by historians of economic thought. Yet any discussion of the conditions for entry into the industry, and any discussion of the concept of industry under product differentiation itself, are still missing. Joan Robinson's definition of "normal" profits as that profit level where no entry takes place reduces the tangency solution merely to an illustration of equilibrium conditions and robs it of independent analytic power.

The conditions for entry of new firms are also not sufficiently addressed in connection with the question of the extent to which falling average costs do indeed result in lower prices when demand expands. Robinson points out, correctly, that this depends on the extent to which existing firms expand the production of their homogeneous products (falling supply price) or whether competitors with slightly differentiated products occupy market niches between existing products (constant supply price): "But the increase in total demand has called into existence firms which exactly meet their [the consumers'] various requirements. The indifferent fringe of the old markets now disappears, and the new firms are each provided with a group of buyers whose preference for their wares is strong" (ibid., 553). The discussion seems to point clearly toward Chamberlin's monopolistic competition, especially if one looks at the subsequent contributions of Gerald Shove and Roy Harrod. It remains mysterious why Joan Robinson took a step backward in *The Economics of Imperfect Competition* by restricting her analysis mainly to the problem of industries with a single monopolist.

In "The Imperfection of the Market: A Further Note," his 1933 "elucidation" of Robinson's article, Gerald Shove enriches the discussion by making two important contributions. First, he generalizes the notion of product differentiation (Shove 1933a, 115); second, he sharpens Robinson's equilibrium concept. He links the existence of normal profits to the absence of barriers to entry and states that there exists no natural tendency toward such a normal profit equilibrium; that is, he retains the possibility of excess profits in equilibrium, here defined as absence of entry or exit. It is no surprise that Robinson fully consented to this point in her short comment (J. Robinson 1948, 124–25).

"A Further Note on Decreasing Costs" by Roy Harrod is a continuing variation on his theme of excess capacity as a result of depressed demand. "It seems to follow from this that after a period of prolonged depression when firms are tending to reach a long-period equilibrium at a low level of output, prices and profits, long-period decreasing costs are more than usually likely to be present in firms that are in imperfect competition" (Harrod 1933a, 340). Correctly pointing out that free entry is an intrinsic condition of perfect competition, he deduces the possible existence of excess profits under excess capacity. Hence, like Shove, he doubts the existence of the tangency solution under all circumstances. His concept of normal profit as the going rate of return on capital (the rate of interest) is undoubtedly more precise. But the paradox of a higher likelihood of excess profits in a depression remains. It is due to a series of assumptions that are implicit, or stated elsewhere: the number of firms remains fixed, capital cannot be dismantled, and capital originally (under normal demand conditions) is perfectly malleable, which excludes the existence of excess profits under those circumstances.

Joan Robinson's defense of her concept of normal profits as an upper limit, "Decreasing Costs: A Reply to Mr. Harrod," adds little of interest, and she already refers to her forthcoming book (J. Robinson 1933, 532). The stage is definitely set for a comprehensive treatment of the various issues connected with the idea that single firms face a less than completely elastic demand. Sraffa's original contribution involved a series of questions that were discussed by people who were all part of a distinctive Marshallian tradition, which sometimes enriched their contributions and sometimes precluded a more energetic grasp of the essentials. Chapter 10 will explore the extent to which Joan Robinson, Edward Chamberlin, and Heinrich von Stackelberg succeeded in integrating and advancing these questions.

· CHAPTER 10

A First Synthesis

A first synthesis of monopolistic competition theory was established by the works of Edward Chamberlin (*The Theory of Monopolistic Competition*), Joan Robinson (*The Economics of Imperfect Competition*), and Heinrich von Stackelberg (*Marktform und Gleichgewicht*). Despite obvious differences, the two Anglo-Saxon economists have more in common with each other than they do with their German counterpart. Their works contain the equilibrium-tangency solution of a single monopolistic competitor—that is, the condition that average-cost curves and average-revenue curves (demand curves) are tangent as long as free entry is assumed. This combines the profit-maximizing condition of marginal cost equals marginal revenue and the no-excess-profit condition of average cost equals average revenue. The two conditions can only be fulfilled together under excess capacity. Their models are essentially equilibrium models. In contrast, the model presented by Stackelberg is essentially a disequilibrium model due to the achievement of modeling the strategic interdependence of oligopolistic competitors in homogeneous markets without product differentiation.

Yet the main difference between these models lies not in product differentiation versus homogeneous goods but in conflicting assumptions concerning rationality. Chamberlin's assumption of "perfect knowledge" would lead in the Stackelberg setting to immediate collusion. This assumption also lacks a sound foundation in Chamberlin's world, where it is a mere ex post facto construct to avoid the complications of potentially ruinous competition for additional markets (see also his work on duopoly, discussed in chapter 9). Further points of comparison are the question of entry and the relationship between static and dynamic considerations. All three authors handle these questions rather imprecisely, and relate them neither to the cost functions they assume nor to the extent of the market. Yet these issues are crucial in the determination of the no-profit tangency solution and the continuing oligopoly profits of Stackelberg.

Chamberlin's work is unsurpassed in its descriptive rendering of the actual behavior of firms in the marketplace. He introduced and described extensively the phenomena of product differentiation and selling costs. Both are characteristic of the monopolistic competitor producing goods under increasing returns to scale (which motivates the use of advertising to increase demand) and facing a downward-sloping demand curve due to the monopoly elements inherent in a differentiated product. The acknowledgment that the existence of these monopoly elements could be due to trademarks and brand names, in addition to patents and technical control over the supply of a commodity, introduced further realism. This increase in realism was sometimes paid for by a loss in expositional clarity when the two-dimensional representation of the relationships among quantity, prices, and selling costs proved inadequate.

Chamberlin denies any connection between his concept of monopolistic competition and the phenomenon of increasing returns to scale, although he also subscribes to the tangency solution under excess capacity (Chamberlin 1962, 193). His restriction of the monopoly phenomenon to the demand side seems a case of excessive product differentiation itself, made in order to distance himself from the British literature. His insistence that "increasing returns in the vicinity of equilibrium for the firm are the result of monopolistic competition and no part in the definition of it" seems pedantic at best (ibid., 194).

The Theory of Monopolistic Competition contains no significant advances in analytical technique over the corpus of knowledge at the time. Chamberlin always insisted that his work was independent of the ongoing discussion elsewhere, and that most of his work was already contained in his doctoral thesis of 1927. Nevertheless, at its publication in 1933, his book was an integrated combination of existing results rather than a genuine advance. Even the vision of a new theory of value strongly resembles the one conceived by Sraffa, though Chamberlin's was much more extensively described.

The only new concept introduced, that of the "large group," turned out to be a hybrid of Marshall's competitive industry and monopolistic competition proper. Consequently, it was later discarded by Chamberlin himself and by his pupil Robert Triffin. Furthermore, it had led, through the introduction of "subjective demand curves," to a postulated behavior of the firm based on a debatable concept of rationality. Chamberlin's conjecture that firms would not engage in ruinous price competition, assuming that their competitors in the large group would not follow them, is untenable. Since everyone has the same motivation, competitors will match any price cut, and this will lead to temporary pricing below average cost. This clashes not only with his earlier assumption of full rationality in the case of duopoly (see Chamberlin 1929) but also with the important role assigned to "business ethics" in avoiding excessive price competition (Chamberlin 1962, 105).

Despite these criticisms, Chamberlin's book rightly became the best-known theoretical work on the subject. It contained all the important elements and indeed managed to integrate many hitherto dispersed elements into a powerful alternative to the model of perfect competition. This conclusion is not invalidated by Chamberlin's attempt to stress the independence of his creation. A distinction must be drawn, however, between the personal originality of the author, which is not in dispute, and the originality of the concepts in respect to the ongoing theoretical debate. Chamberlin's work certainly represented the state of the art and managed to draw attention to the subject of monopolistic competition. But he did not push the frontiers of research concerning the analytical formulation of the problems at hand beyond the results reached by Joan Robinson and her collaborators in the preceding years. The general debate immediately assimilated *The Theory of Monopolistic Competition* together with Joan Robinson's *Economics of Imperfect Competition* as the basis for all future discussion.

From today's perspective, the merit of Robinson's book lies mainly in its advancement of single issues only loosely related to monopolistic competition theory as such, and in its insistence on the inadequacy of perfect competition as the exclusive working assumption for economic theory. Its primary objective is to write a new theory of value in terms of monopoly. Monopolistic competition as such is present throughout the book; all its elements, including product differentiation and selling costs, are presented at one point or another (J. Robinson 1948, 89–90). But they are not assembled into a coherent vision. Despite its title, the book focuses on a comparison of monopoly with competitive industry. In this context it is significant that its working title, at least until 1932, was *Monopoly* (Feiwel 1989a, 187). Robinson's remark that the marginal-revenue curve contains "the heart of the whole matter" (J. Robinson 1948, 6) should be interpreted in the context of monopoly.

Sraffa's (and Chamberlin's) vision of a world of competing monopolists checking each other's demand by offering products with differing elasticities of substitution is referred to on several occasions, but not further explored (e.g., ibid., 5). It has often been said that Robinson's weakest point was her treatment of the demand curve; she noted this herself when without further elaboration she described her work as a "fudge with the demand curve" (J. Robinson 1953, 584). The view that her work is rendered less useful by the cursory treatment of the demand curve has also been supported by comments in the text: "Once the demand curve for the firm has been drawn, the technique of analysis can be brought into play, whatever the assumptions on which the demand curve was drawn up" (J. Robinson 1948, 21). The treatment of the demand curve under the entry of new monopolistic competitors is adequate in the text and does not fall behind Chamberlin's analysis on this account. Even her rough-and-ready definition of "normal" profits as "that level of profit at which there is no tendency for new firms to enter the trade, or for old firms to disappear out of it" can under certain assumptions be made compatible with the concept of an economywide normal level of profits. This could for instance be accomplished by redefining higher profits as the result of rent earnings for specialized factors in inelastic supply (that is, monopoly). Chamberlin's severe criticism of these matters is badly focused (Chamberlin 1937, 561).

The most serious criticisms of *The Economics of Imperfect Competition* arise from a discussion of Joan Robinson's radical comparative-statics approach and her reluctance to discard such Marshallian concepts as "competitive industry," "commodity," "representative firm," and "the economies of large-scale industry" (the effects internal to the industry and external to the firm). Concerning the first point, she often analyzes economic constellations under contradictory assumptions. For instance, assuming homogeneous goods in the case of monopolistic competitors producing under increasing returns to scale would lead not to the tangency solution but to immediate collusion. Furthermore, this is the result of a priori defined equilibrium conditions and not of economic forces.

A discussion of the relationship between cost and demand curves is usually omitted and at one place even explicitly excluded (J. Robinson 1948, 90n). The case of increasing returns in competitive industries is vigorously sidestepped by focusing on falling factor-supply prices, which affect the single firm externally. The catch is that they are very likely caused by internal economies in another industry. Robinson's unwillingness to consider her concepts in a wider context is due to her distrust of her own tools of economic analysis. It seems that her insistence on the abstract character of the analysis relieves her of any responsibility for the realism, as distinct from the purely logical feasibility, of her constructions.

Regarding the remnants of Marshallian partial-equilibrium analysis left in her book, only the concept of the industry is important to its basic structure. Unfortunately, its role is such that it prevents a more coherent formulation of the imperfections that lead from perfect competition in a homogeneous industry to monopolistic competition between different firms. The elements of monopolistic competition that are mentioned are not connected to the general flow of reasoning. In a certain sense, Robinson's book falls behind the results she had already published.

Despite such criticisms, the book has rightly become a classic. Her discovery of the kinked demand curve (ibid., 81) and the elasticity of substitution (ibid., 256, 330), her introduction to the treatment of averages and marginals, and her discussion of monopoly and monopolistic price discrimination are unsurpassed in precision and clarity of exposition. The concept of marginal revenue was not invented by Joan Robinson, but after *The Economics of Imperfect Competition* it will never have to be reinvented. Finally, Robinson makes a first inquiry into the welfare implications of monopolistic and monopsonistic exploitation of labor. Welfare considerations distinguished the works of Joan Robinson from those of Edward Chamberlin. While Chamberlin insisted (without further elaboration) on the welfare-enhancing effects of product differentiation, Robinson never completely shed her distrust of a form of industrial organization she had connected with the word "imperfect."

The simultaneous publication of these two classics of economic theory at a certain point in the scientific debate entitled them to define the synthesis of monopolistic competition, and the definition holds even today. The merits of the two books do not lie in any single technical advance but in their overview of achieved results, which brought the problem of monopoly to the center of economic attention. Perhaps the lack of actual technical differences between them led to the debate over monopolistic versus imperfect competition, which seems so superfluous today.

It seems superfluous because with hindsight one cannot disagree with the generous assessment Robinson herself gave of this debate, which was pushed much more energetically by her American counterpart: "It appears to me when we dealt with the same question, in our respective books, and made the same assumptions we reached the same results ... When we dealt with different questions we naturally made different assumptions. In many respects Professor Chamberlin's assumptions were more interesting than mine, in particular in connection with oligopoly and with product differentiation as a dynamic process" (J. Robinson 1953, 579n). Although it is erroneous to limit the term *imperfect competition theory* exclusively to the results of *The Economics of Imperfect Competition*, Robinson is correct in noting that, when discussing the same issues, the books are characterized by similarities, not by differences. This position is also supported by the introductory review of theories of monopolistic competition in Robert Triffin's *Monopolistic Competition and General Equilibrium Theory*. By no means neglecting the differences, he writes: "The indictment brought forward against traditional concepts, the phenomena pointed out as calling for theoretical recognition by economic science, are in both expositions strikingly identical" (Triffin 1941, 37). Concerning equilibrium under monopolistic competition, which is often cited as a major weakness of Robinson's work, especially in connection with her nonchalant handling of profits and of the demand curve, Triffin writes that "there is revealed a close similarity between Mrs. Robinson's and Professor Chamberlin's conditions of equilibrium. When terminological differences are swept away, there remain only the very dissimilar handling of oligopolistic situations and the increasing qualifications and doubts with which Professor Chamberlin surrounds the concept of entry" (ibid., 49).

Despite Chamberlin's insistence on the difference between monopolistic and imperfect competition, the difference was one of the degree of emphasis, not of analysis. To be sure, the British writers usually preferred to· connect with market "imperfections" frictions such as transport costs (i.e., differences in location). Roy Harrod would at one point characterize imperfection of competition as "due to habit, inertia, and lack of knowledge" (Harrod 1936a, 86). This, in connection with the resulting excess capacity and the supposed wastes of advertising, might have encouraged a predisposition to focus on the negative welfare implications of monopolistic competition. The normative ideal of the Marshallian competitive industry probably gave a negative ring to the term *imperfect competition*. Along with it went a tendency to see firms as substantially "equal," producing potentially homogeneous commodities differentiated by, for instance, location.

Contrary to this attitude was Chamberlin's emphasis on the positive welfare effects of product differentiation, although he qualifies his results quite strongly (Chamberlin 1962, 184–85). Yet in his work the emphasis is undoubtedly on the differences between individual firms. However, at least since Hotelling's 1929 article, it should have been understood that for an analysis of the behavior of monopolistic competitors it is irrelevant whether the monopoly power is created by superior design or by differences in location, by consumer inertia or by clever advertising. All that exists is a group of consumers who prefer, at equal prices, one product to another.

Chamberlin had originally written of "imperfections which are in the nature of monopoly elements" (Chamberlin 1929, 63); this remark is omitted in later versions of the same article in different editions of *The Theory of Monopolistic Competition*. Furthermore, he writes in the preface to the first edition that his advisor Allyn Young had suggested *The Theory of Imperfect Competition* as a title for the forthcoming book. The choice of "monopolistic" over "imperfect" seems to have been a fortunate one, as it emphasizes the blending of the two elements of monopoly and competition. The only blemish is Chamberlin's continued insistence on the singularity and independence from contemporary research of his own creation. The debate as he pictured it also appears distorted from a historical perspective, because Chamberlin chose what was perhaps not the strongest of the British contributions to the subject—Joan Robinson's *Economics of Imperfect Competition*. For all its merits, her book simply does not fully reflect the level of the Cambridge-Oxford-London discussions of imperfect competition, including her own contributions. Once this is taken into account, any actual dispute between "imperfect" and "monopolistic" competition becomes artificial. With some effort Chamberlin might have succeeded in drawing a line between his own and Robinson's book; his more far-reaching attempts at differentiation border on distortion.

In keeping with this attitude, in "The Origin and Early Development of Monopolistic Competition Theory" (Chamberlin 1961) he emphatically denies any links to "the erosion of Marshall's theory of value" as described in Newman's article of that title. According to Chamberlin, there are no links between his new vision of value theory and the debate over increasing returns to scale. Indeed, judging from his misinterpretation of Sraffa, whom he sees linking his version of monopolistic competition to a constant cost curve, he seems free from any reproach of having copied him (Chamberlin 1962, 310). But nobody had made this suggestion. Chamberlin's attempt to link monopolistic competition theory to the secondary debate between Frank William Taussig and Pigou on the divergence of freight rates is only half convincing. Even if the concept of product differentiation had been brought up originally by Allyn Young, who was certainly well aware of the unsolved problem of increasing returns (ibid., 302, and Young 1928), this does not relegate The Theory of Monopolistic Competition to a lower rank.

Chamberlin's vigorous defense of his position, the stature of The Theory of Monopolistic Competition, and the coincidence of The Economics of Imperfect Competition, a book of similar stature, sharing the attention, have prompted questions about the real merit of Chamberlin's contribution to theoretical economics. Historians of economic thought have often echoed Chamberlin's own view of his role in the development of economic theory. Robert Kuenne, for instance, writes on behalf of The Theory of Monopolistic Competition: "With this work he fathered modern industrial organization analysis by giving a theoretical core to what was previously institutional and anecdotal" (Kuenne 1987, 399). And Mark Blaug, comparing Chamberlin's and Robinson's books, writes: "Despite superficial similarities between the two books, it is now perfectly obvious that Chamberlin was the true revolutionary" (Blaug 1968, 399). Both statements must be qualified. While it is true that Chamberlin synthesized the state of the debate on the monopoly power of competitors producing under increasing returns, it involves a considerable stretch of the imagination to classify the work by Cournot, Sraffa, Yntema, Robinson, Kahn, and Young as "institutional and anecdotal." In fact, Chamberlin himself intersperses his work with anecdotal and institutional detail, and it is not the least of his merits that he convincingly manages to integrate these elements of realism into the theoretical framework. At the same time, Chamberlin was no revolutionary. Piero Sraffa had in 1926 taken the decisive step away from Marshall's "imposing edifice" and given the wheel of theoretical progress another turn.

Joseph Schumpeter gives a definitive statement on the merits of Chamberlin's contribution when he writes in his History of Economic Analysis that the success of Chamberlin's theory "was as much due to the force and brilliance of his exposition as it was to the maturity of the scientific situation." He concludes: "Three elements of scientific achievement are particularly obvious in this case: the maturity of the scientific situation, the ability to grasp an important idea with force and enthusiasm and the ability to stay with it and to shut oneself off from the disturbing effects of other scientific ideas or aspects" (Schumpeter 1954, 1151). Schumpeter's statement is not without irony with regard to the defining features of Chamberlin's achievement. Chamberlin was a great economist and monopolistic competition theory was his field; however, his insistence on not wanting to share this field with other great economists added a tragi-comic dimension to an otherwise illustrious career.

Chamberlin's book appeared when most of its technical achievements were no longer new and at a time when it fit into an ongoing debate over the tenability of the concept of perfect competition. With Joan Robinson's *Economics of Imperfect Competition*, it gave final form to a theory in the making. The research had reached a level of maturity that warranted a comprehensive synthesis. In the end, the book must be judged by what it was and by what it became, not by where it came from or what it was intended to be.

The first synthesis of monopolistic competition theory was completed by the contribution of Heinrich von Stackelberg. His *Markt-form und Gleichgewicht* of 1934 integrated the Italian and German debates on the instability of liberal capitalism with the existence of enterprises exhibiting increasing returns to scale and an analytical apparatus constructed on neoclassical building blocks into a form that was comprehensible to Anglo-Saxon readers. In his policy recommendations, which he formulated on the basis of his theoretical results, he provided a benchmark for other policy proposals. In addition, his return to the original duopoly problem of Cournot and his work on conjectural variation proved in the long run a necessary complement to the work on monopolistic competition.

Stackelberg's decisive step forward in regard to the oligopoly problem of Cournot is that in his approach each firm integrates its knowledge of the reaction function of its competitor into its own decision on the quantity of output. This leads in Stackelberg's analysis usually to the Bowley duopoly, a case of instability, in which each of the competitors tries to sell that amount of output which maximizes its profits given the other's reaction curve:

> Each of the two duopolists tries to achieve domination of the market . . . The first duopolist will, for instance, try to convince the second duopolist that the latter will have to regard the output of the former as an independent parameter . . . That is the quantity that the first duopolist would offer if he already dominated the market and the second duopolist were his follower. We call this quantity the "independent quantity" of the first duopolist.
>
> The second duopolist will behave in exactly the same way, because there is no reason to cede right away to the first duopolist. (Stackelberg 1934, 19)

Thus, disequilibrium of markets is inevitable except in the few cases where it is more advantageous for the second duopolist to stay on his or her reaction curve, due to a vastly different cost function. The criticism by modern neoclassical economists such as Jean Tirole and James Friedman that Stackelberg did not adequately model sequential behavior of "leaders" and "followers" in a dynamic context is unfounded; it is due to a common misperception of Stackelberg's work as containing an equilibrium model. For Stackelberg, instability due to the desire of both firms to establish themselves as leaders was by far the most likely result. In modern interpretations, the exceptional case in which two firms establish a harmonious leader-follower equilibrium is seen as the relevant case; only concerning this exceptional case can their criticisms can be justified. James Friedman, for instance, writes: "It is true that leadership is meaningless if decisions are simultaneous. So a discussion of leadership is meaningful only within a dynamic model" (J. W. Friedman 1983, 109). True enough; however, Stackelberg never actually talks about leadership in a definite way, but only about simultaneous attempts of the two competitors to behave as if they were leaders, which results in a struggle for market share that has to be resolved by political means. He envisages that his political solution would encompass a cartelization of the industry under state supervision, an idea that gave rise to much criticism.

It is the implicit bias of modern economists toward equilibrium models that gives rise to a misperception of Stackelberg's contribution. It is not even necessary to emphasize the aspect of commitment in the quantity offered (e.g., by choosing a certain plant size), as Tirole does (Tirole 1989, 316). In order to obtain "Stackelberg warfare," it is enough that both competitors continue to act as pure instantaneous profit maximizers, who assume that their rivals react according to their reaction curves.

There are, however, other, more valid criticisms of Stackelberg's procedure, such as his lack of treatment of questions of exit and entry. In multiperiod models, strong rationality assumptions would have to be made in order to maintain the instability result. Probably his greatest omission is in regard to the concept of product differentiation. He failed to elaborate on this concept, and this failure, combined with the problem of his writing in a language understood by only a few of the English-speaking economists, contributed decisively to an almost complete exclusion of his work from the further development of monopolistic competition theory, although its general importance was immediately recognized. This is all the more deplorable because without product differentiation the alternative of collusion would always remain viable. This was, for instance, recognized by J. R.

Hicks in his review of the work (Hicks 1935b, 335). On the other hand, it could be argued that cartelization in effect amounts simply to organized collusion under state supervision. The concept of product differentiation was subsequently integrated into Stackelberg's later shift away from his early radical-instability results under the heading "Qualitätsvariation."

Maintaining his basic line of reasoning, he introduced in later works elements of inertia and friction into the markets of his models, which would counter the relentless pursuit of maximum profits in perfect markets that leads to the Bowley duopoly. Although he focuses on imperfections in the firms' pricing mechanisms, he mentions the abandonment of price competition in favor of advertising and service competition. Even at this point, product differentiation is mentioned only in passing, under the heading "quality competition," and it does not lead to a general rethinking of his analysis, which in its structure remains tied to oligopolists competing in homogeneous markets (Stackelberg 1938, 137). His short comment on Chamberlin in this context reveals that he (wrongly) views monopolistic competition as a subform of competition under conventionally fixed prices: "As soon as these inertial elements are noticeable, then the special form of imperfect competition developed by Chamberlin becomes pertinent, yet with the restriction that the existing prices are historically determined and cannot be deduced from the [economic] forces existing in each particular case" (ibid., 135).

At this point it is only fair to present briefly Bowley's own version of the Bowley duopoly, which was a fundamental concept for Stackelberg. Arthur L. Bowley's original formulation in his *Mathematical Groundwork of Economics* is richer in potential implications, less precise, and more ambiguous. In effect, he introduces the notion of "conjectural variation" (later so termed by Ragnar Frisch) without following up any particular case:

> To solve these [the two equations for maximizing profits] we should need to know x_2 as a function of x_1, and this depends on what each producer thinks the other is likely to do. There is then likely to be oscillation in the neighbourhood of the price given by the equation,
>
> marginal price for each = selling price,
>
> unless they combine and arrange what each shall produce so as to maximize their combined profit. (Bowley 1924, 38)

Bowley rather loosely combines in this formulation the ideas of Edgeworth (oscillation) and Bertrand (marginal cost equals price) as the unmotivated result of two profit functions, in which each competitor takes account of an unspecified reaction of his or her rival. In Bowley's formulation there is room for conjectural variations other than the one postulated by Stackelberg: A behaves optimally on the assumption that B behaves according to his or her Cournot reaction curve. A critical attitude toward Bowley's research regarding the problem of oligopolistic interaction finds support in Knut Wicksell's generally positive review of Bowley's work. Wicksell considers his views "rather vague" (Wicksell 1958, 216), and writes: "Bowley can hardly be said to have contributed in any essential respect to the classification of the problems just mentioned [the behavior of firms under oligopoly]. In the matter of several monopolists dealing in the same sort of goods, he seems to take up Edgeworth's standpoint, although his reasons for doing so are not at all clear" (ibid., 221). Stackelberg's attribution of the Bowley duopoly to the author of *Mathematical Groundwork* documents an act of generosity, rather than one of genuine intellectual indebtedness.

CHAPTER 11

Discussion and Refinement

The importance of the publication of *The Theory of Monopolistic Competition* by Chamberlin, *The Economics of Imperfect Competition* by Joan Robinson, and *Marktform und Gleichgewicht* by Stackelberg was immediately recognized, and it opened the way for an intense and broad debate on the different features of imperfect or monopolistic competition. Usually, the first two books were reviewed together, which makes it difficult to determine exactly their respective positions in the run of the theoretical argument. Yet it was clear that with these publications, especially those by the two English-speaking authors, the synthesis of monopolistic competition theory had been accomplished. For Corwin D. Edwards, the reviewer for the *American Economic Review*, the two books mark "the maturity of a new approach to value theory"; this view became the general perception (Edwards 1934, 683).

The debate began with the review by Gerald F. Shove of *The Economics of Imperfect Competition* and the review by Roy Harrod of *The Theory of Monopolistic Competition*, both in the *Economic Journal*. Shove complains that Robinson's book is too conservative and that it does not make a clear enough break with the past ideas of partial equilibrium in a competitive industry: "For a product of youth it is surprisingly—to a rebel veteran, disappointingly—conservative" (Shove 1933b, 657). He calls it "a definite contribution, in the classical manner, to the theory of monopoly" (ibid., 659), and deplores its lack of any treatment of imperfect competition as promised in the title. In the light of the subsequent development of monopolistic competition theory, one must agree; nevertheless, his remarks do strike the reader as slightly ironic, for one can see from footnotes in Robinson's work that it was partly Shove's own influence that kept her from advancing further in the direction outlined by Sraffa (e.g., J. Robinson 1948, 116).

In his 1934 review, "Mrs. Robinson's *Economics of Imperfect Competition*," Nicholas Kaldor echoes Shove's interpretation. Regarding its lack of monopolistic competition theory proper, he writes: "In fact, one almost has the feeling that Mrs. Robinson could have written much the same book if Mr. Sraffa's path-breaking article (to which she acknowledges so much debt) had never been written; and if the problem of 'highly substitute but not identical' commodities had never presented itself in the course of the discussion on increasing returns" (Kaldor 1934b, 336). Elaborating his stand in more detail than Shove, he mentions as the book's biggest flaws the clinging to the concept of industry and the treatment of the demand curve.

Harrod's review of Chamberlin's book is generally sympathetic. It points out three rather obvious flaws: the lack of a unifying underlying principle that would give a structure to the different phenomena described in the book; the somewhat arbitrary distinction between large groups and small groups; and the all-too-easy assumption of free entry, designed to prevent the existence of excess profits and thus a discussion of obvious welfare problems.

The reviewers of Stackelberg's *Marktform und Gleichgewicht* (Nicholas Kaldor, J. R. Hicks, and Wassily Leontieff) generally reviewed it positively as an important contribution to the theory of nonperfect markets. For Kaldor it was "much the most comprehensive work that has yet appeared on imperfect markets" (Kaldor 1936, 227), while Leontieff praised it for its "skill and elegance" (Leontieff 1936, 554). Both warmly advocated a translation into English, which has never taken place. Stackelberg's sympathies for a corporatist order were ridiculed by Hicks as a "pæan to the Corporate state" (Hicks 1935b, 336), drawing an indignant rejoinder from the author, whose admiration for the work of Hicks is well documented (Eucken 1948a, 133–34).

Despite this success for a non-English writer on economic theory, these three reviews also marked the beginning of a series of misunderstandings concerning Stackelberg's duopoly theory. Kaldor, for instance, sees differences in conjectural variations as responsible for the different outcomes, not differences in cost functions, which would have been correct. Hicks halfheartedly defends Harrod's ill-fated approach; finally, Leontieff, who has by far the best understanding of the work, comes up with an equilibrium solution of his own. This solution, which amounts to joint-profit maximization, has its merits but runs counter to Stackelberg's assumption that both competitors try simultaneously to maximize their instantaneous profits by forcing their adversary into the less advantageous position. Leontieff's solution would probably be the outcome in a long-run version of Stackelberg's model.

The debate developed mainly along two major lines of research. The first concerned oligopoly and duopoly theory. Here, strategic interaction between producers of very close or complete substitutes became the most important issue. The more vigorous branch concerned itself with monopolistic competition per se, attempting to define conditions that would be valid for all firms in an economywide setting. Monopolistic competition distinguishes itself from perfect competition through product differentiation, while direct interaction between competitors is kept to a minimum. The main concerns are the establishment of equilibrium and welfare considerations in their broadest form.

The first line of reasoning, stemming from Cournot and his treatment of duopoly, leads to the game-theory literature of today. It comprised various contributions, some of them only loosely connected to monopolistic competition theory. Spanning the gap between the classic contributions on oligopoly and game theory, Frederik Zeuthen's 1930 *Problems of Monopoly and Economic Warfare* had contained several important new concepts that deserved greater attention than they actually received. It was ahead of the field in that it already toward new directions of research, when economists were still looking for a synthesis. Zeuthen's book belongs in character and emphasis among the works that tried to extend and refine the state of knowledge of monopolistic competition theory. In addition to providing an overview of the fields of monopolistic and oligopolistic competition, it discussed under the heading of "economic warfare" the notions of threat, possible bargains, and expectations, in particular a crude form of expected utilities and disutilities in labor conflicts. These concepts are rather loosely formed, yet by introducing them in connection with wage bargaining between management and labor, the book pointed in the direction of an economic theory of conflicts of interest.

Another significant addition to the first line of research was made by Ragnar Frisch, who in his 1933 article "Monopole-Polypole: La notion de force dans l'economie" greatly contributed to a sharpening of the discussion by defining different "types stratégiques." Concerned as much with bargaining under bilateral monopoly as with oligopolistic competition, Frisch's analysis foreshadows game-theory analysis in its definitions of parameters of action, sequential timing of action, and conjectural variations (a term coined by Frisch). A by-product of his research is the introduction of the "courbe d'offre forcée," the all-or-nothing supply curve in the case of a producer facing a monopsonist with superior bargaining power.

Frisch's most important contribution was the classification and analysis of different conjectural variations—in today's jargon, the determination of the players' information sets about their adversaries' objective functions. "L'action autonome" characterizes Cournot behavior, taking the rival's strategic parameters to be fixed. "L'action conjecturale" is "the case where each oligopolist acts as if the possible change in the other parameters was going to be a continuous function of the change in his own parameters, or more precisely, a function which has a derivative" (Frisch 1951, 31). These derivatives are then called "coefficients conjecturaux," and they need not correspond with reality. "L'action autonome" is then just a special case of conjectural action where the conjectural coefficient is zero. Finally, "action superieure" is the case where the conjecture applies correctly and the rival does not make any conjectures—that is, the rival takes the parameters as given. This corresponds to the familiar Stackelberg equilibrium, in which a leader optimizes, taking into account his or her rival's reaction function, whereas the rival, the follower, restricts himself or herself to behavior on the reaction function. The discussion in both Stackelberg's and Frisch's cases is loaded with the vocabulary of the Darwinist world-view characteristic of the times. This case of superior knowledge can then be extended to higher and higher levels.

It can be maintained that Frisch's treatment of conjectural variation is not only more comprehensive but also more explicit than Stackelberg's treatment of the same problem. But Stackelberg has a huge advantage in the way in which he applies his results to concrete situations of duopoly. Frisch's own applications fall curiously short of the analytic power of his definitions. His example for equilibrium under duopoly is just a more complicated version of Cournot equilibrium, and his introduction of conjectural variation as a shift in the reaction curves seems at best inadequate.

The importance of Frisch's contribution was underscored, however, by the false results reached by Roy Harrod in "The Equilibrium of Duopoly," published in 1934, due to his nonchalance about conjectural output variation. He attempts to describe equilibrium output for two competitors who choose quantity as their strategic variable. One competitor assumes Cournot behavior of its rival and maximizes its output accordingly, which should lead, in principle, to a leader-follower equilibrium. Harrod's mistake lies in assuming the *same* procedure for the second rival. This would lead to Stackelberg warfare (or Bowley duopoly), as each optimizes under the assumption that the other stays on the reaction curve, whereas in fact neither of them does. Certainly this does not result in a well-defined equilibrium.

As was pointed out by Stackelberg himself in "Probleme der unvollkommenen Konkurrenz," this leads to a contradiction. It is assumed that each firm has zero conjectural variation (when deriving its competitor's output) and at the same time a positive conjectural variation according to its rival's reaction function (when deriving its own output). To put this another way: it is impossible for a firm to be a leader and a follower at the same time. Harrod's solution, although elegant, and as such accepted by Kaldor and Hicks, suffers from an internal contradiction (Stackelberg 1938, 115).

Harrod's 1934 article "Doctrines of Imperfect Competition" had a major impact. After giving a helpful overview of the state of the discussion, Harrod analyzes the implications of monopolistic competition for welfare and the trade cycle—that is, shifts in aggregate demand. Concerning the first point, he reveals himself as a cautious advocate of wage fixing in order to avoid monopolistic exploitation of workers who get paid less than their marginal physical product. Moreover, he advocates compulsory rationalization to overcome the problem of excess capacity; this would, as long as the elasticity of demand stays the same, result in higher profits that could be taxed away. These findings had direct relevance to the policy discussions taking place in Great Britain at the time. Concerning the second point, he argues, along the lines of Kahn, that monopolistic competition is a countermeasure for firms, which reduce quantities and stabilize prices in order to check a fall in aggregate demand.

One of the last articles written on oligopoly theory in pre–game theory terms was "Demand under Conditions of Oligopoly" by Paul M. Sweezy. It foreshadowed the exact analysis of the strategic behavior of individual firms by establishing the kinked oligopoly demand curve as an "imagined demand curve" of the single firm. "From the point of view of any particular producer this means simply that . . . (his demand-curve tends to be elastic going up) . . . [and] . . . (his demand-curve tends to be inelastic going down). In other words, the imagined demand curve has a 'corner' at the current price" (Sweezy 1939, 569). Sweezy was certainly not the first to mention the phenomenon of the kinked demand curve. Richard Kahn had noted in his fellowship dissertation in 1929 the idea of two duopolists remaining at a stable price, "for no other reason than that happens to be so" (Kahn 1989, 103). But he did not insist on the concept, and retained the Bertrand outcome as a distinct possibility. In a discussion of Kahn's book, Andrea Maneschi mentions H. Gordon Hayes as having been the first to publish the concept of a kinked demand curve in 1928 (Maneschi 1988, 161). Joan Robinson had also already introduced the kinked demand curve, complete with discontinuous marginal-revenue curve, in *The Economics of Imperfect Competition* in 1933. In 1939 it had also been established as an empirical reality by R. L. Hall and C. J. Hitch in their study "Price Theory and Economic Behaviour." But Robinson had limited the phenomenon to the case of a monopolist facing potential entry above a certain price level, and this had hindered the appropriate acknowledgment of the important concept (J. Robinson 1948, 81). Sweezy instead linked the kinked demand curve to the profit-maximizing behavior of oligopolistic competitors, and also pointed out a series of important related phenomena: increases in marginal cost will not necessarily lead to a rise in prices, but only to a fall in excess profits; there exists an increasing premium on secret price cuts, the more inelastic the kinked demand curve is; the kink will become less pronounced in times of rising demand, and vice versa.

The result that price stability increases in a depression provides a nice rationale for Kahn's conjecture that competitive firms under similar circumstances become more monopolistic by restricting output than by lowering prices. Finally, Sweezy suggests abandoning the search for the one equilibrium price, and instead studying individual pricing policies under given circumstances. This was as far as Marshallian partial-equilibrium analysis could go in this particular field. New insights would only be gained by focusing on the individual cost and demand conditions and relating them to each other.

In the field of monopolistic competition as such, the last word was not to be had so easily. After all, the analysis of the complete underlying microeconomic structure of a capitalist economy, including its far-reaching implications for welfare, was at stake. In "The Concept of Monopoly and the Measurement of Monopoly Power," A. P. Lerner devised the well-known formula for monopoly power as the percentage excess of price over marginal cost, which is equal to the inverse of the demand elasticity (Lerner 1933–34). Although Lerner most likely devised this formula independently, Amoroso's formulation in "The Static Supply Curve" had come four years earlier and was more comprehensive.

Lerner's article also suffers because quite a few of his concepts, such as product differentiation, had been adequately developed in the meantime. As there is no reason to doubt his intellectual honesty (his generous disclaimer seems proof of this), it supports the hypothesis that there is no such thing as truly independent scientific discovery. Two of his more original results are the tangency solution for an upward-sloping demand curve and the conjecture that monopoly does not lead to losses in general welfare so long as all supplies (including labor) are monopolized to the same degree (ibid., 174–75).

Hicks's "Annual Survey of Economic Theory: The Theory of Monopoly" is an overview of the work in monopoly theory, monopolistic competition theory, and the theory of duopoly. With regard to monopoly theory, he provides a link to future research by pointing out that monopolists suffer only second-order losses from nonmaximizing behavior, and concludes his analysis with these famous words: "The best of all monopoly profits is a quiet life" (Hicks 1935a, 8).

Addressing monopolistic competition theory, Hicks analyzes the question of profits. The inclusion of normal profits in average cost is legitimate only for perfect competition. He emphasizes the monopoly elements in monopolistic competition by regarding the profits that differ from producer to producer as the rents received for a nonhomogeneous fixed factor of production that is linked to the specific firm and its product. His attribution of increasing returns to scale under monopolistic competition to indivisibilities in the production function, as distinct from physical indivisibilities of factors, could have made Chamberlin's subsequent all-out attack on the concept of indivisibilities superfluous, if properly received.

But Hicks's real objective appears to have been to hustle the whole concept of monopolistic competition out the back door, the better to concentrate on general equilibrium under perfect competition (as he did in 1939 in *Value and Capital*). By introducing product differentiation inside the single firm and the possibility of rival firms producing close substitutes, he argues that the demand curve for any given product tends toward perfect elasticity: "this consideration does seem to go a good way to justify the traditional practice of economists in treating the assumption of perfect competition as a satisfactory approximation over a very wide field" (Hicks 1935a, 12). Following his previous discussion, he wants to treat the imperfections due to specialized factors, patents, or technology under the heading of monopoly. The distinction between a certain location and a "specialized factor" is unconvincing. For all its clarity of exposition and argument, Hicks's contribution to monopolistic competition theory is in the last analysis a questioning of its raison d'être.

New topics in monopolistic competition theory were defined in a series of articles by Nicholas Kaldor and Joan Robinson. After making genuine progress in sharpening their analytical tools, the exchange of arguments among the various writers (who included Chamberlin) ended in a reaffirmation of well-known positions. Despite Hicks's counterattack in disguise, monopolistic competition theory was by now a well-established field of research. The tangency solution was, notwithstanding differences in the definition of "normal" profits, a generally accepted result, and research now focused on the elaboration of isolated technicalities.

But the Marshallian past of monopolistic competition theory still made its presence felt from time to time. In his 1934 article "The Equilibrium of the Firm," Kaldor attempts once more to find the conditions for the individual firm that would allow the construction of a static downward-sloping supply curve under competitive equilibrium. Although the article is in its scope not necessarily part of monopolistic competition theory, its line of reasoning and its conclusions earn it a place in the debate about monopolistic competition. Kaldor rejects Marshall's attempt, with the concept of the "representative firm," to embrace the possibility of both industry equilibrium and growth for the individual firm as an ad hoc construction: "The 'representative firm' was . . . meant to be no more than a firm which answers the requirements expected from it by the supply-curve" (Kaldor 1934a, 62).

In his own search for a rationale to counter increasing returns to scale due to indivisibilities, and thus the unlimited expansion of the individual firm, he identifies the coordinating function of entrepreneurship. This supposedly fixed factor would eventually lead to decreasing returns and allow the construction of an industry supply curve. But the following problem leads him to reject the compatibility of perfect competition and static equilibrium: "For the function which lends uniqueness and determinateness to the firm—the ability to adjust, to coordinate—is an essentially dynamic function" (ibid., 70). This results in the rejection of the idea of a static industry supply curve, although Kaldor allows for a not very clearly defined dynamic equilibrium as long as the firms actually do, or at least try to, take advantage of increasing returns. Kaldor's lasting contribution in "The Equilibrium of the Firm" was the introduction of indivisibilities as the main reason for increasing returns to scale and thus ultimately for monopolistic competition. This includes his result of the indeterminateness of the individual firm under perfect competition and perfect divisibility of factors due to constant returns to scale.

Kaldor repeated this assertion in his broad discussion of monopolistic competition theory published the following year, "Market Imperfection and Excess Capacity." It is ironic that at this point Kaldor emphasizes the differences between the results of Chamberlin and Robinson (Kaldor 1935, 34), whereas later he was to oppose strongly any distinction between monopolistic and imperfect competition. After a long analysis of the different assumptions employed, Kaldor introduces welfare considerations as a genuinely new element in the discussion. On excess capacity due to internal product differentiation, he writes: "there will be a 'technical wastage,' since the physical productivity of resources will be less than what it would be if each producer produced a smaller number of products and a large proportion of the total output of each" (ibid., 49). It had been pointed out by Hicks that internal product differentiation might rather lead to a better use of capacity if similar products were produced. Yet Kaldor's point is still valid for external product differentiation, as increased competition by new entrants leads to reductions in technical efficiency instead of reductions in price or increases in output.

Joan Robinson also had elaborated on the function of the entrepreneur under imperfect competition in 1934, in "Euler's Theorem and the Problem of Distribution." For her, the question of the equilibrium of the individual firm does not constitute a problem—it is automatically established, as the tangency solution holds as soon as neither exit nor entry take place. Her concern remains with the distributional justice of remuneration under monopolistic competition. Her assertion of the applicability of Euler's theorem (the exhaustion of total revenue under constant returns to scale if all factors are paid their marginal product for a linearly homogeneous production function) at the point of tangency under imperfect competition is wrong in a narrow sense and tautological in a colloquial sense, even if the question of excess profits is disregarded (J. Robinson 1934, 411–12).

The desire to prove the applicability of Euler's theorem seems to be driven by an underlying normative ideal of distributional justice. Thus, it comes as a surprise when Robinson concludes her article by employing Euler's theorem to show the existence of monopolistic exploitation under monopolistic competition. Under the doubtful proposition of imperfect competition with constant physical returns to scale, she postulates: "the marginal physical product of an entrepreneur is equal to the output of a firm *minus* the amounts of the factors employed by a firm each multiplied by its marginal physical product. But the factors are paid less than the value of their marginal physical products; therefore the earnings of the entrepreneurs are greater than the value of the marginal physical product of entrepreneurship" (ibid., 413). This is correct, but it has nothing to do with Euler's theorem. The income of the entrepreneur as the claimant of the residual is determined by demand conditions. Furthermore, the differentiability of the production function with respect to entrepreneurship seems a strong assumption, since there exists neither a measure of entrepreneurship nor a criterion to distinguish it clearly from the input of other labor.

The question of profits as a price for entrepreneurship is connected with the questions of entry and the degree of competition in Robinson's next article, "What Is Perfect Competition?" Arguing that low profits and easy entry characterize industries where only little entrepreneurship is required, she wants to separate the question of competition from the question of entry (J. Robinson 1935, 106). She acknowledges no link between the elasticity of the demand curve and the possibilities of entry. Again, distributional considerations are viewed solely as cost-determined, whereas the interaction between cost conditions and demand conditions is given short shrift. Her practical definition of "perfect competition" as opposed to "absolutely perfectly perfect competition" blurs the distinction between monopolistic competition and perfect competition as usually understood. Neither article was written in Robinson's finest hour, and each is best interpreted as part of a slow move away from monopolistic competition theory pure and simple and back toward problems of competitive industries. They foreshadow her growing dissatisfaction with the subject, expressed for instance in 1953 in "Imperfect Competition Revisited."

Apart from Richard Kahn's 1935 article "Some Notes on Ideal Output," in which he advocates the shifting of resources from industries with a lesser degree of monopolization to those with a higher degree in order to increase total welfare, the debate came to be exemplified by the dispute between Chamberlin and Kaldor. In his 1937 article "Monopolistic or Imperfect Competition?" Chamberlin's declared aim was to "correct some misconceptions" and to establish his version of monopolistic competition as a new *Weltanschauung*. Regarding these alleged misconceptions of the British economists, he seems to argue from a defensive posture against the more "authoritative" imperfect-competition theorists from Cambridge, who could claim for themselves the tradition of Marshall, Sraffa, Pigou, and Shove. His attack on the marginal-revenue curve as not being "at the heart of the matter" can only be understood from this perspective. Also, his opposition to Kaldor's conjecture that perfect divisibility would lead to perfect competition is understandable only with his own restrictive definition of divisibility in mind.

Other points made by Chamberlin are valid: the tangency solution is indeed the result of heroic assumptions and does not rule out that in reality positive profits would be observed; an increase in the number of firms does not lead automatically to perfect competition, as the grid of product differentiation just grows finer; under monopolistic competition in a strict sense there is freedom of entry only to the extent that substitutes are produced (this actually represented a change from the first edition of *The Theory of Monopolistic Competition*); finally, product differentiation is a necessary and sufficient condition for monopolistic competition. The last point had been debated by Joan Robinson in "What Is Perfect Competition?"—but she did not take into account that "frictions" (e.g., transport costs) constitute product differentiation in exactly the same way as do different brand names.

Chamberlin's willful contrasting of monopolistic with imperfect competition stems not from these technical arguments but from other sources. First, there is his fixation on *The Economics of Imperfect Competition* as the only expression of Cambridge economic thought. If he had truly studied the contributions of Shove and Harrod, or even of Sraffa and pre-1933 Joan Robinson, he would have discovered research much like his own. But to acknowledge this would have cast doubt on the objective originality of his own blend of monopoly and competition. It is true, however, that in *The Economics of Imperfect Competition* monopolistic competition as such is mentioned and then dismissed in favor of a comparative study of monopoly and perfect competition (J. Robinson 1948, 4–5).

Chamberlin's dislike of the word "imperfection" as implying a state of at least potential suboptimality leads to the next fundamental difference: his judgment on welfare matters. Always eager to defend his creation, he opposes the idea of monopolistic exploitation under monopolistic competition with the untenable argument that entrepreneurship is a hired factor like any other (Chamberlin 1937, 579). This says nothing about monopolistic exploitation; it only addresses the ownership rights of possible monopoly profits. Whether the owners of capital run their own firms or hire others to run them changes nothing.

The attack by Chamberlin on imperfect competition was too blunt to remain unanswered. Ironically, the task fell to Kaldor, whose vision had been rather close to that of Chamberlin. In "Professor Chamberlin on Monopolistic and Imperfect Competition," countering Chamberlin step for step, pointing out different assumptions here, mitigating Chamberlin's stand there, he maintains (correctly) that there is no fundamental difference between the two approaches. Unfortunately, he stumbles by introducing the colloquial meaning of "monopoly" as being connected with restrictions of entry, thus seeming to advocate the view that there is a clear-cut distinction between monopoly and competition (Kaldor 1938, 528).

There remain, however, two real points of debate. The first concerns freedom of entry under monopolistic competition as opposed to monopoly, since Kaldor wants to preserve the difference in kind between the grocer at the corner and the Ford Motor Company (ibid., 523). This distinction stems from honorable motives and deserves preservation on different grounds. But the two businesses *are* indistinguishable in the sense that both lack competitors able to produce complete substitutes for their products. If anything, the cross-price elasticities between Ford and General Motors are probably higher than those between two corner stores. In his "Reply," Chamberlin does not fall into this trap; he sharpens his argument by taking definite steps away from the concept of industry, pointing toward Triffin's research in insisting on the impossibility of producing complete substitutes in either case: "The very concepts of a 'market for a product,' its 'limits' and its 'density' . . . *necessarily* become vague and confused when this 'product' is an aggregate of products differentiated from each other" (Chamberlin 1938, 533).

The second point gave rise to a prolonged debate. It concerned indivisibilities as a reason for increasing returns to scale at the point of tangency under monopolistic competition. Again, behind this technical point lurks a possible confrontation on welfare grounds, as the acknowledgment of indivisibilities could invite arguments in favor of exploiting them to a greater degree, for example by influencing industrial organization through directive measures. The necessary dual to this proposition is that complete divisibility of factors will lead automatically to perfect competition, as maintained by Kaldor: "The important point is that unless economies of large scale, or rather the diseconomies of small scale production, set a limit to the inflow of competitors; . . . there can be no equilibrium until producers equate price with marginal costs; and equality of price with marginal cost *is* perfect competition" (Kaldor 1938, 521). Chamberlin's favorite brainchild—product differentiation—had to account in the "Reply" once more for a downward-sloping demand curve as long as product differentiation rises faster than divisibility (Chamberlin 1938, 535), even though Kaldor had already mentioned the obvious, that this increase in close substitutes raises the elasticities of substitution (Kaldor 1938, 517). There is no theoretical argument in which Chamberlin would not have the last word and stick completely to his previous positions, no matter how personal his attack and no matter how abstruse his reasoning. He permitted no outside comment on his theory to remain unanswered. This time Chamberlin deferred the argument to a "forthcoming article" (Chamberlin 1938, 535).

That article, "Proportionality, Divisibility, and Economies of Scale," appeared ten years later, at a time when discussion of monopolistic competition had already lost most of its appeal. Included in the later editions of *The Theory of Monopolistic Competition*, this article sparked a small debate of its own; it is a typical example of the inward-looking reasoning to which monopolistic competition theory reduced itself, attempting neither to formalize its results nor to extend them to policy matters. Chamberlin's thesis is that the U-shape of the long-run average-cost curve, as the envelope of short-run average-cost curves, is determined by different efficiencies due to different absolute amounts of factors combined in optimal proportions. Hence, he is saying that the size of the firm matters. His main object of attack is the thesis that complete divisibility of factors will lead to an indeterminate size of the firm and to perfect competition: "To assume that factors are 'perfectly divisible' carries with it no implication whatever as to how their efficiency will be affected in the process" (Chamberlin 1948, 238).

As reasons for the downward-sloping long-run average-cost curve, he mentions increased specialization and qualitatively and technologically more efficient units of factors. The first point "verges on the high theme of economic progress," to employ Marshall's critical assessment of his own efforts in that direction, and must be treated with extreme circumspection in a comparative-statics framework such as that of Chamberlin. The second point hinges completely on the definition of what is understood by a factor of production and by its divisibility. If divisibility of a factor is understood to mean just its physical divisibility, then there is no point in debating Chamberlin, who can claim the obvious observation that certain gains in efficiency can only be obtained at certain minimum sizes as proof of his position.

Yet if the "divisibility of method" (Lerner's term) or "divisibility of the production function" (Hicks 1935a, 10) is included in the definition of perfect divisibility such that the effects of specialization are displayed at each and every factor size, then the size of the firm is indeed indeterminate, constant returns to scale hold, and the results of perfect competition will be achieved by an indeterminate number of firms, each of which is of indeterminate size and behaves as a perfect competitor so long as there are no barriers to entry. As long as factors display increasing returns to scale at different sizes, the downward-sloping part of the long-run average-cost curve is explained.

The question is whether the gains of specialization (accruing only after a certain total size of output is reached) are to be regarded themselves as an indivisibility necessary for efficient production, thus constituting a reason for sufficiently large plants and increasing returns to scale. In 1949, A. N. McLeod and Frank Hahn pointed out, again in the pages of the *Quarterly Journal of Economics*, that this cleavage between definitions could easily be overcome. McLeod states: "The difference between Professor Chamberlin and those whom he criticizes comes to no more than this: they are concerned with the fact that in certain circumstances it is impossible to apply certain factors of production with equal efficiency, except in discrete units, whereas he is concerned with the fact that in these same circumstances any attempt to apply these same factors other than in discrete units . . . involves some loss of efficiency" (McLeod 1949, 130). Frank Hahn concurs: "Perfect divisibility leaves no room for increased specialization with increased size" (Hahn 1949, 134). Chamberlin, never accepting compromise, in his reply (Chamberlin 1949) picks out some ambiguous formulations and a mistake by Hahn concerning the definition of constant returns to scale and sticks staunchly to his position as the defender of economic realism. So much for increasing returns to scale.

The rest of Chamberlin's 1948 article is devoted—without any attribution—to a discussion of two ideas developed years earlier by Nicholas Kaldor and Joan Robinson. Difficulties in coordination explain the upward-sloping part of the long-run average-cost curve. "The plant curves which compose the [long-run] average cost curve have, after a certain point, successively higher minima, and hence define an upward course for the average cost curve because of the greater complexity of the producing unit as it grows in size, leading to increased difficulties in coördination and management" (Chamberlin 1948, 249). Entrepreneurship as a fixed factor had been excluded earlier, yet without it there can be no other reason for decreasing returns, once it can be combined freely with all other factors.

Chamberlin's "proof" that Euler's theorem holds at the point of tangency for a monopolistic competitor is a repetition (with graph) of Joan Robinson's earlier version, and it is of equally dubious value in asserting any implications of distributional justice. Paul Samuelson had already cleared the matter up in 1947 in his *Foundations of Economic Analysis* (Samuelson 1976, 81ff.). Even though linearly homogeneous functions do not display ∪-shaped cost curves, it is true that at the point of tangency the sum of the several marginal-revenue products times the quantities of inputs equals total revenue. But this is a priori true because of the tangency solution itself and because excess profits have been assumed away. It does not constitute in any way a proof of Euler's theorem in the sense of an identity along the whole ray of production of a constant-returns technology with constant marginal productivities and costs. The normative implications of Euler's theorem can thus not be employed for monopolistic competition per se. These implications would have had to be analyzed in each single case by categories such as freedom of entry, or the relationship of indivisibilities (or, for that matter, economies of scale) to market size, or the relationship between gains from product differentiation and economies of scale. Only with these categories could a meaningful discussion of monopolistic competition have begun. Chamberlin's article was written when the profession had already moved on to other areas of interest; the discussion had lost the chance to cope with the problems of the day.

But the lack of vigor in mainstream monopolistic competition theory did not preclude the development of its various features. The shift in emphasis from an analysis of the industry to an analysis of the monopolistically competitive firm had brought with it an interest in the "nature of the firm." Ronald Coase's 1937 article of that title was the earliest, yet it is still the most lucid, expression of interest in the hierarchical organizational entity known as the firm. He set out to identify the forces that determine the number of economic transactions completed inside a firm (independent of market forces), as opposed to the number of transactions completed in the market. Strictly applying the principle of substitution at the margin, he deduces that the profit-maximizing firm "will tend to expand until the costs of organising an extra transaction within the firm become equal to the costs of carrying out the same transaction by means of an exchange on the open market or the costs of organising in another firm" (Coase 1952, 341). In other words, positive marketing costs are the rationale for the existence of the firm, and decreasing returns to scale for organizing capacity (Kaldor's fixed-factor "entrepreneurship"), and a rising supply price for individuals who value their independence, limit this process. Uncertainty and labor's aversion to risk were mentioned as additional rationales.

This approach led to a significant extension as late as 1972 in the article by A. Alchian and H. Demsetz titled "Production, Information Costs, and Economic Organization." According to its authors, the main advantages of a firm are the cheap supervision and the "metering" of group efforts, which yield higher results than the sum of individual efforts, yet provide incentives to shirk as the assessment of individual marginal productivities becomes increasingly difficult. This effect might even supersede the effects of transaction costs. The entrepreneur as claimant of the residual has an interest in optimal supervision and is able to offer higher wages due to the superiority of the group effort. In this framework the entrepreneur becomes a central common party devising simple bilateral contracts, facilitating complicated multiparty bargaining (Alchian and Demsetz 1972, 84).

The discussion about the size of the firm concluded with sociological determinants assuming the function of physical indivisibilities in motivating its existence and determining its size. The capacity to lower information and communication costs inside a hierarchical firm became the fixed factor defining its size. The fixed factor, and thus the size of the firm, are entirely determined by frictions in the factor markets—an ironic change of perspective from the usual concern of monopolistic competition theory with frictions in the product markets. Despite Coase's promising new insights, the profession had at this point lost interest in engaging in the necessary subtleties to link this debate to the theoretical work on monopolistic competition theory. The discussion of indivisibilities remained incomplete.

CHAPTER 12

A Loss in Vigor

Four important theorists—Stackelberg, Amoroso, Robinson, and Chamberlin—continued to develop their ideas after monopolistic competition had first caught the attention of the scientific community. Each of them proceeded in a different way, none entirely convincing; their works prepared the ground for the subsequent methodological attack of the Chicago school. The eventual move away from monopolistic competition theory was the result of these mutually reinforcing lines of inquiry.

The further theoretical developments by Heinrich von Stackelberg are characterized by an increasing emphasis on elements in his arguments that had first been presented in *Marktform und Gleichgewicht*. Together with his original instability result for oligopoly he had mentioned three possibilities for overcoming disequilibria:

Elimination of market forms without equilibria
Elimination of the free formation of prices
Elimination of profit maximization

(Stackelberg 1934, 98). At the time, the elimination of market forms without equilibria as part of a corporatist restructuring of the economy had been the most frequently debated possibility. Yet all three possibilities would, once enacted, have abolished monopolistic competition as it is usually understood: the profit-maximizing behavior of privately owned firms facing downward-sloping demand curves in contestable markets. During his scientific career, Stackelberg emphasized each of these possibilities at different times in order to overcome what were, in his view, the negative results of untrammeled oligopolistic or monopolistic competition.

In *Marktform und Gleichgewicht*, he favors a corporatist restructuring of the economy, in the form of bilateral monopolies under state supervision. Under this form of compulsory cartelization, it would be possible to achieve "conventional equilibria," preferably close to the optimal outcome of "natural equilibria" under perfect competition. This elimination of market forms without equilibria has far-reaching political and social consequences. Perhaps for this reason he later modified his original, extreme, position. In subsequent articles he mentions a series of factors that might mitigate the instability result obtained for monopolistic competition, and thus make introduction of a corporatist alternative unnecessary.

"Probleme der unvollkommenen Konkurrenz," published in 1938, is a revised statement of his oligopoly theory. In this essay he gives ample room to considerations that question and contradict the premise of rational, profit-maximizing agents. "Therefore, we have to abandon, for all its beauty, the idea of a closed and general theory of value, like the one envisioned by classical and neoclassical economics" (Stackelberg 1938, 127). Stackelberg introduces two groups of empirical factors, inertial factors and institutional factors, that make monopolistic competition less of a problem. His inertial factors include near-rationality in market analysis, cost calculation, and price setting (e.g., considerations of menu costs and business ethics). His institutional factors include price control and the supervision of market forms. The emphasis is on the inertial factors, which guarantee smooth operation of the economy, even if pure theory, assuming profit maximization, would predict chaos.

Still later he elaborated his final vision of how to overcome the problem of oligopoly in a competitive order guaranteed by a liberal state. In "Geistige Möglichkeiten und Grenzen der Wirtschaftslenkung," published in 1949, he favors free competitive markets combined with adequate redistribution as the best means to achieve the highest possible community indifference curve. Stackelberg became less interested in monopolistic competition theory as such, which in his works remained basically unaltered from its first formulation in 1934, and more concerned with finding extratheoretical solutions for a real-world problem. On a theoretical level he regarded the problem as solved.

Despite this theoretical coherence, Stackelberg's shift in emphasis from necessary instability to inertial factors implied a radical change in the theory's political implications. Parallel to the shift in his theoretical work is his gradual shift from convinced National Socialist with corporatist tendencies to antifascist neoliberal with a personal vision of the social market economy. The role of the state is confined to social welfare and income redistribution; actual decisions about prices and quantities of commodities are to be made by the competitive market system rather than some corporatist authority.

Luigi Amoroso also lost interest in questions of oligopoly, monopolistic competition, and potentially suboptimal market forms. Originally, Amoroso had been the official voice of the fascist regime on economic policy. At the same time he was a mathematical economist steeped in the tradition of the School of Lausanne. It does not matter in this context that his belief in the optimality of free competition of profit-maximizing agents sometimes openly contradicted his eulogies for the fascist state overcoming "l'idolatria di mammona" (Amoroso and de' Stefani 1933, 411). To a large extent these contradictions reflected the contradictions of fascist ideology and practice—as opposed to more coherent corporatist approaches, as for instance in the work of Ugo Spirito.

Yet at the moment of the demise of the fascist system Amorosoo simply abandoned the theory of monopolistic markets completely. After the 1938 publication of *Principi di economia corporativa*, in which he had restated the results of "The Static Supply Curve," the subject never again appeared in his writings. With the reformulation of his political preferences came a complete reversal of his economic writings. His 1949 *Economia di mercato* contains no entry on monopolistic or imperfect competition. Instead, he emphasizes the benefits of competition and laissez faire, thus returning to his intellectual roots.

For Amoroso the theory of monopolistic markets was always linked to his engagement with the fascist state and the corporatist restructuring of the Italian economy. With the change in his political preferences (which he admittedly did not base on considerations of economic theory), he also changed his emphasis on the advantages and disadvantages of free markets. His attitude exemplifies the idea that the theory of monopolistic competition has to be viewed against the changing social and political background of the time; otherwise neither its prominence nor its sudden decline can be completely understood. This holds for economists in corporatist countries as well as for those in countries with essentially free markets.

The case of Joan Robinson, however, is quite different. In her case too the interest in monopolistic markets bore evidence of motivations stemming from social and political concerns. Her personal conviction of the need for a drastic reformation of liberal capitalism grew, if anything, stronger over time. Yet she had always been interested in a variety of topics other than monopolistic competition theory: monetary theory, macroeconomics, capital theory, and growth theory. After the publication of Keynes's *Treatise on Money* in 1930, she had become an active member of the study group known as the Cambridge Circus together with her husband (Austin Robinson), Richard Kahn, Piero Sraffa, and James Meade. The purpose of this informal group was the discussion and critique of Keynes's new work, out of which arose the collective effort, under Keynes's leadership, to formulate some of the concepts contained in the *General Theory*. Thus during the early 1930s she was already far from focusing entirely on monopolistic competition theory. After the publication of *The Economics of Imperfect Competition* she participated in the debate only once—in "What Is Perfect Competition?" Yet in Nicholas Kaldor she had an able defender of her position.

With hindsight, Joan Robinson came to view her own work increasingly critically, admitting especially that she had followed Pigou too closely and had not made a clear enough break with the concept of industry (J. Robinson 1980, 1:viii). Later articles abound with quotations such as "the exploration of imperfect and monopolistic competition . . . proved to be a blind alley" (ibid., 5:1) and "*The Economics of Imperfect Competition*, on which I was working with R. F. Kahn in 1932, was pre-Keynesian and it is based on a fudge— confusing comparisons of possible alternative equilibrium positions with the analysis of a process taking place through time. I postulated that every manufacturing firm is faced by a demand curve for its own product, showing how much could be sold at various prices, and that the firm finds out its position and shape by trial and error" (ibid., 5:112). True, her book does not take into account the strategic interdependence of competitors, either through time or otherwise. Yet it is not clear whether a return to purely Marshallian concepts (as she proposed in 1953, in "Imperfect Competition Revisited") such as "fear of spoiling the market" and the irreversibility of the supply curve, implying a "fudge" of a different kind between static and dynamic considerations, is a viable solution. In the same article Robinson puts strong emphasis on Chamberlinian concepts such as product differentiation, advertising, and sales ability, and on Stackelberg's concept of price leadership. But these references are made in an ad hoc fashion, in order to increase the realism of the description and not in order to be part of a new, integrated framework.

Joan Robinson lost interest in monopolistic competition theory partly because she considered the work of Keynes and Kalecki as more relevant to the problems of "latter-day capitalism," and partly because of her disappointment that monopolistic competition theory (including her own contribution) had been unable to deal adequately with the problem of time. The contribution made by Keynes's and Kalecki's work to the sudden and not easily understandable turn away from monopolistic competition theory by Joan Robinson and others is discussed below. Her dissatisfaction with that theory was due partly to an overcritical attitude toward her own work after the ungenerous attacks of Chamberlin, and partly to her inability or unwillingness to let go completely of her Marshallian heritage, especially the concept of industry, despite her clear perceptions of the limitations of her initial approach.

Robinson may have come to doubt the usefulness of the approaches pursued in the early 1930s, but not so the other pillar of the monopolistic competition "establishment," Edward Chamberlin. He was the only major economist to occupy himself during his lifetime exclusively with monopolistic competition theory—the only exceptions being his short piece called "Purchasing Power" and his 1958 essay "The Economic Analysis of Labor Union Power." He never directly recanted a single element of his 1933 publication, and he spent the rest of his academic career defending, justifying, and explaining it. In his 1957 collection of essays *Towards a More General Theory of Value*, virtually all the entries deal with *The Theory of Monopolistic Competition*. Of sixteen entries, four deal critically with other people's publications, eight elaborate on special aspects of his original book, three address monopolistic competition in special circumstances (e.g., labor markets) and only one, "Proportionality, Divisibility, and Economies of Scale," covers somewhat new ground.

All through the collection, and in short pieces not contained therein, there is a defensive attitude toward possible or actual criticisms or deviations from the original formulation. The only extension of his concept that he accepted was the work by Robert Triffin and his consequent dismissal of the ill-conceived group concept (Chamberlin 1957, 78). One man alone could not carry on monopolistic competition theory, but this man's attitude did not invite others to join in answering the still numerous open questions. A critical assessment of Chamberlin's role in the direction taken by monopolistic competition theory could hardly blame him for having abandoned it through lack of attention! His attitude precluded productive connections with other strands of economic theory, especially because of his zeal to stress the original purity of monopolistic competition theory and his personal role in that conception. A telling example of this attitude is his deliberate decision to exclude the whole literature on increasing returns from his supposedly comprehensive bibliography on the subject.

Despite their diversity, these four authors exhibit a tendency to shy away from further inquiry into the imperfections of markets due to monopolistic elements. Chamberlin's view on welfare questions had always emphasized the welfare benefits due to product differentiation, and downplayed the possible welfare losses due to elements of monopoly. Thus, his work was most easily compatible with a swing of the public mood from a critical to a positive attitude toward free markets after World War II. This change in mood is part of the background against which the dominance of one theoretical approach was followed by that of another. It made the resurrection of perfect competition as the general assumption of microeconomic behavior possible through the double impact of the Keynesian revolution and the positivist critique of the Chicago school.

The attack on monopolistic competition theory on methodological grounds by the theorists of the Chicago school—most importantly Milton Friedman and George Stigler—basically declared monopolistic competition theory unscientific and hence not worthy of further inquiry. Methodological discussions are never free from the question of desired results. Especially in economics, the methodology chosen in conjunction with corresponding concepts of optimality implies certain assumptions about the economy, and produces certain statements about desirable policies. The success of the positivist critique presented in the following chapter depended largely on its implications being accepted by the public and by the economics profession itself. The case studies of the four protagonists of monopolistic competition theory explain to some degree why the defense of alternative methodological precepts was not put forward more forcefully.

CHAPTER 13

Ending without Conclusion

Following the efforts described in the previous chapter by the original
protagonists of the debate on monopolistic competition, mainstream
research on monopolistic competition theory was synthesized for the
last time by Robert Triffin in *Monopolistic Competition and General
Equilibrium Theory*. The book was written as a dissertation under
Chamberlin's supervision; it had to build on the Chamberlinian
framework. Yet it manages to take quite an independent stand. The
book's merits do not lie in the explicitly announced extension of the
theory of monopolistic competition to general-equilibrium theory
(Triffin 1941, 4), for Triffin's notion of "Walrasian equilibrium" is
much too vague; neither the conditions nor the results of that theory
are ever defined. Triffin's achievement lies in giving the most coherent vision of monopolistic competition theory. He achieves this by
developing the ideas of Chamberlin and Robinson in a framework
free from the elements of compromise with the obsolete concept of
competitive industry.

Triffin leaves behind the remnants of the Marshallian industry
and the concepts of large group and small group, and opens the idea
of monopolistic competition to the whole economy. He describes a
system of monopolists checking each other by means of the different
elasticities of substitution for their respective commodities. This
"theory of external interdependence," formulated for the supply side
as well as the demand side, sees mutual influences between firms
as a matter of degree and not as the by-product of certain a priori
definitions of terms such as *industry*, *small group*, or *large group*:
"It is held that a concept of group or industry has no place in the
... theory of value; strictly speaking, it is even incompatible with

monopolistic competition, and its survival from the wreckage of purely competitive assumptions serves only to provide a simplified, but purely conventional, solution for the now dominant problem of inter-firm competition" (ibid., 13–14). In particular, this implies the abandonment of the artificial assumption of negligible influences among the members of a large group. Naturally, the notion of commodity also loses its conventional meaning, being reduced to denoting only the output of one particular firm.

Triffin's fundamental building block is the "cross-price elasticity of substitution," the percentage change in the quantity of output of firm "i" in response to a percentage change of the price of firm "j." Based on this elasticity of substitution, he derives a whole new set of definitions for different market forms (ibid., 125ff.). Triffin's vision of the economy under monopolistic competition as a heterogeneous continuum of single firms, without any attempt to define general equilibrium, let alone give any stability conditions, was also implicitly accepted by Chamberlin. The latter moved subsequently further and further away from his original concept of large-group equilibrium, emphasizing its existence due to "heroic assumptions" in revisions of his 1933 work (Chamberlin 1962, 314), and denying the existence—contrary to his original editions—of group demand curves (ibid., 302). His article on the origins of monopolistic competition theory spells the end of the group concept as an analytical tool: "I can see no escape . . . from the conclusion that the ubiquitous forces of oligopoly and of nonprice competition . . . must be responsible for many loose ends, multiple optima and indeterminateness in one sense or another in 'groups' and in the system, which must be expected either to assert themselves or to achieve a de facto stability thanks to inertia or similar forces" (ibid., 315). In addition to being a continuation of the initial concepts of product differentiation and the market power of the individual firm, Triffin's version is also close to Sraffa's article of 1926. Monopolistic competition is brought full circle in the sense that the original conjecture is now supported by the analytical framework around the tangency solution and a host of conceptual results clarifying and illustrating the process of interfirm competition.

Triffin's purified version of monopolistic competition theory could have been an excellent starting point for a more rigorous formulation of actual pricing mechanism in the sense of Smithies' article "Equilibrium in Monopolistic Competition," published in 1940–41, in which he researches conditions for the stability of price formation with two (later n; see Smithies 1942) competitors. Yet Triffin's is the high-water mark of research in monopolistic competition theory rather than a new beginning; after 1941 there are only scattered articles to be found. Triffin himself went into international economics, and William Fellner's *Competition among the Few: Oligopoly and Similar Market Structures*, first published in 1949, already written from a historical point of view, regarding the theoretical work of the prewar years.

The rapid decline of monopolistic competition theory after 1940 is a complex phenomenon in which theoretical and extratheoretical factors reinforce each other. Two clusters of arguments can be discerned in this loss of interest. One revolves around the immense popularity of Keynes's new approach to economic analysis after the publication of *The General Theory of Employment, Interest, and Money*. Most of the economists in Cambridge, Oxford, and London who had occupied themselves with monopolistic competition theory as an alternative to the apparent failure of self-regulating neoclassical models became quickly absorbed into macroeconomics as a field of research that combined realistic analysis with potentially powerful policy prescriptions. Unfortunately, Keynes's ambiguous stand on microeconomics helped prevent a fruitful combination of the two approaches.

The other cluster, of at least equal importance, is concerned with the scientific content of monopolistic competition theory, in particular with its alleged inability to furnish valid predictions and its failure to provide an equilibrium model susceptible to comparative-statics analysis. The two arguments are closely linked but not identical, as the predictive power of monopolistic competition models is not necessarily compatible with the restrictive definitions of equilibrium (containing, for instance, a no-profits condition) employed in perfect-competition theory. This discussion took place mainly in the United States and arose from the criticisms of the Chicago school. During the late 1940s and early 1950s, several scholars connected in one way or another with the University of Chicago (the most important of whom were Milton Friedman and George Stigler) formulated serious criticisms of monopolistic competition theory. Without presenting any conclusive theoretical or empirical evidence for their allegations, they managed to undermine the scientific credibility of the work undertaken in monopolistic competition theory. At all times this methodological debate was connected with strong a priori preferences concerning industrial organization, namely the adoption of a policy of laissez faire and an unquestioned belief in the optimality of free markets.

The debate originated with the publication of Stigler's *Theory of Price* in 1946, which discussed under the heading "imperfect competition" cost and demand conditions under monopoly. Monopolistic competition proper, focusing on product differentiation and advertising, is given scant space and reduced to an uninteresting, not very important phenomenon due to consumer ignorance. Even this was a concession, considering that an earlier version in 1942 called *The Theory of Competitive Price* had not mentioned it at all. Chamberlin's review set the tone for subsequent contributions: "Our criticisms have passed from matters of pure organization to a questioning of how far the author has really digested his new subject" (Chamberlin 1947, 415). In a third edition of Stigler's book, published in 1966, the chapters on imperfect competition are again omitted in favor of a lengthier treatment of oligopoly. The Chicago school's critique was based largely on the conjecture—indeed, the assertion— that perfect competition and monopoly are usually sufficient to capture all the essential phenomena of economic life. One criticism in connection with the later formulation of monopolistic competition theory by Triffin was offered by Milton Friedman in his essay "The Methodology of Positive Economics": "The theory of monopolistic competition offers no tools for the analysis of an industry and so no stopping place between the firm at one extreme and general equilibrium at the other. It is therefore incompetent to contribute to the analysis of a host of important problems: the one extreme is too narrow to be of great interest; the other too broad to permit meaningful generalizations" (M. Friedman 1953, 38). This condemnation, echoed by George Stigler, seems not entirely fair. The theory of the firm is not usually considered "to be too narrow to be of great interest," and it seems circular reasoning to reprimand monopolistic competition theory for not contributing to the theory of the industry when one of its main achievements had been the establishment of intraindustry product differentiation and thus the dissolution of the concept of the Marshallian competitive industry. A fairer judgment would have included an evaluation of analytical gains and losses by this change of theoretical approaches; a simple rejection a priori is a matter of belief, not of proof.

Curiously circular reasoning was employed by Alfred Sherard. His advocacy of rejection was based on the incompatibility of monopolistic competition theory with the "philosophical framework of economics" (Sherard 1951, 140). It is not at all obvious why product differentiation and advertising should be incompatible with the general problem of satisfying different wants with scarce means. By asserting that economic science was incompatible with monopolistic competition, Sherard defined away its attack on traditional theory. Although Sherard came from American University, Chamberlin nevertheless placed him among the Chicago scholars in his reply "The Chicago School" (Chamberlin 1957). This reply basically confined itself to an attack on the model of perfect competition as the basis for the criticisms.

The most important criticism was of the claim of monopolistic competition theory to be a more realistic model of the actual economy. Monopolistic competition proceeded from initial assumptions that were far closer to reality, such as the downward-sloping demand curve for a single firm even in industries with some degree of competition. This was countered with the argument that the value of a theory does not lie in the realism of its assumptions, but in the realism of its predictions. In Milton Friedman's words, "the relevant question to ask about the 'assumptions' of a theory is not whether they are descriptively 'realistic,' for they never are, but whether they are sufficiently good approximations for the purpose in hand. And this question can be answered only by seeing whether the theory works, which means whether it yields sufficiently accurate predictions ... The theory of monopolistic and imperfect competition is one example of the neglect in economic theory of these propositions" (M. Friedman 1953, 13). George Stigler strikes the same chord: "One can but show that a theory is unrealistic by demonstrating that its predictions are wrong" (Stigler 1949, 23). The two scholars are correct in their statements as long as the natural sciences are chosen to provide the relevant methodological model, yet the implicit assertion that monopolistic competition theory is incapable of delivering correct predictions is never made openly, much less proved. This gives their attacks a certain air of the same kind of ad hoc reasoning that they so despise in connection with monopolistic competition. On the other hand, their implicit conjecture points in the right direction. The end of monopolistic competition as the dominant form of scientific research is at least partly attributable to its failure to develop a testable comparative-statics model.

With Triffin's formulation the last word on the subject, the quest for a comparative-statics model had become more difficult, precisely because with the dissolution of the large-group concept, a generally acceptable definition of equilibrium, going beyond the absence of exit and entry under profit maximization, was no longer available. That is why some writers still continued to deal with the large-group concept even after it had become untenable on conceptual grounds.

The impossibility of performing "qualitative calculus" with the existing formulations of monopolistic competition was the topic of
G. C. Archibald's 1961 article "Chamberlin versus Chicago." George
Stigler, in "Monopolistic Competition in Retrospect," had already
noted in 1949, "It will be observed that the theory of monopolistic
competition now contains no conditions of equilibrium, only a definition of equilibrium" (Stigler 1949, 18). Basically, there are two
solutions to this problem: the abandonment of comparative-statics-
equilibrium reasoning when dealing with increasing returns to scale
(which is the approach taken by Allyn Young), and a more intensive
search for a formulation appropriate for comparative statics. (One
could also take an approach that would give inherent reasons for the
impossibility of doing either.)

If the abandonment of comparative statics is not an acceptable
alternative, then the problem poses itself in the way succinctly formulated by Frank Hahn: "The literature on this subject is quite large. It
appears to suffer from two deficiencies: it has not produced a simple
diagrammatic technique to represent the decisions in question and
it does not contain an adequate statement of the second-order conditions of a maximum . . . Without these, however, the theory cannot
be applied to an examination of such questions as the effects of excise
taxes and/or sales-cost taxes on the decisions of the firm, nor can the
theory be said to be complete" (Hahn 1959, 293).

After Roy Harrod's incomplete attempt in 1936 to analyze different
states of monopolistic competition caused by shifts in the business
cycle (see chapter 17), the first serious attempt to construct an equilibrium model containing the necessary first-and second-order conditions was undertaken by Arthur Smithies in "Equilibrium in Monopolistic Competition" and "The Stability of Competitive Equilibrium."
Explicitly he is concerned with "definite solutions," which in his
particular case means the conditions for the stability of first two, and
later n, monopolistic competitors. His second article especially is of
great merit in developing techniques similar to those being used
contemporaneously by Samuelson for the determination of conditions of competitive equilibria in multiple markets. Yet neither of
them included the essential phenomena of monopolistic competition
such as questions of entry and exit, product choice, or advertising
expenditure.

Despite his claims, Smithies competitors are essentially Cournot
competitors who take price as their strategic variable—that is, they
take their competitors' prices as fixed. This holds even though each
competitor does not regard actual prices as fixed, but instead forms

"expected prices" as a linear combination of actual prices and its own actual price. No matter how this reaction curve is derived, however, it is supposed to remain stable during the profit-maximization process. Not surprisingly, this unnecessary complication was omitted in the second article and replaced by straightforward Cournot behavior. The reason why competitors, taking price as the strategic variable, do not fall into the trap of the Bertrand paradox seems to be product differentiation, although that is nowhere explicitly mentioned. In other words, as long as products are not differentiated it would be optimal for each firm that proceeds under the assumption that its competitor does not change prices to lower its own price slightly and to capture total market demand. The other firm would do likewise, and consecutive price cutting would ensue. This process would under the stipulated information assumptions lead to an instantaneous equating of price with marginal cost. For Smithies it seems sufficient that both competitors face a downward-sloping demand curve.

The question of collusion can be avoided only by assuming product differentiation, yet in the discussion of potential cutthroat competition it almost seems that Smithies has homogeneous markets in mind. Excess capacity is a possibility but by no means a necessity; thus excess profits are likely to arise. All in all, Smithies analyzes how the Cournot reaction functions have to behave in order to yield equilibria. Under his behavioral assumptions the following result, which coincides with Cournot's, comes naturally: "the attainment of stability . . . involves the virtual elimination of competition, and, for a given number of competitors, the benefits to the economy which are held to accrue from competition are derived through ignorance rather than through knowledge" (Smithies 1942, 274). Smithies' papers, important for their stability results, could not achieve the desired analytic formulation of monopolistic competition theory.

Neither Hahn nor Archibald succeeded in developing a convincing model capable of performing comparative statics. But they left unresolved whether this was due to a logical weakness in monopolistic competition theory or to the complexity of the problem and the lack of adequate mathematical tools. The matter is, for instance, complicated by the attempted integration of advertising expenditure, which affects demand and cost conditions alike. Archibald involved himself on the pages of the *Review of Economic Studies* in a heated exchange of argument and insult with the two eminent proponents of the Chicago school, George Stigler, and Milton Friedman. His argument that their previous criticisms lacked analytical rigor was correct, yet his own failed attempt to construct an empirically testable model of monopolistic competition theory placed him in the ranks of those who denied its practical applicability. Stigler gleefully points out Archibald's failure and sees it as a vindication of his own position. Friedman, along the same line, accuses Archibald of excessive product differentiation (M. Friedman 1963, 65).

The difficulty in designing a convincing analytical model of monopolistic competition was a major reason for its rapid loss in popularity. But lacking any conclusive theoretical evidence for doing so, the abandonment of monopolistic competition theory seems in the American case due more to the growing popularity of the views of the Chicago school than to its specific criticisms. It is surprising that George Stigler, a distinguished historian of economic thought, was unable or unwilling to connect the coming into existence of monopolistic competition theory with Marshall's difficulties over Cournot's dilemma. His writings sound as if the conception of Joan Robinson's and Edward Chamberlin's ideas had been immaculate. Stigler pays no regard to the "necessity to turn towards monopoly," as deduced by Sraffa. The reestablishment of Marshall's competitive industry, against the concept of monopolistic competition, seems superficially a choice between two equally acceptable theoretical approaches. Yet it is paid for by logical inconsistency, unless the empirical fact of internal increasing returns is flatly denied. The position of Stigler and Friedman can only be sustained by excluding the phenomenon of increasing returns to scale, also and particularly in a comparative-statics framework. It is this unmentioned by-product that sometimes gives their attacks the air more of a crusade than of an honest attempt to further economic science.

The supporters of monopolistic competition theory, particularly Chamberlin, saw themselves as theorists, concerned with the scientific construction of a new theory of value. Triffin, for instance, does not tire of pointing out the "ethical neutrality" of his research (Triffin 1941, 189). This position holds even if we consider that the debate on the "great corporation" reflected popular concern about the increased market power of single firms, to which Triffin refers in passing (ibid., 184–85). The work of Chamberlin had become part of a theoretical approach that had been started elsewhere, but the demise of that approach was mainly an American phenomenon, linked to theoretical considerations and the influence of the Chicago school. The developments in continental Europe and in Great Britain show a different pattern, although American economic thought gained increasing importance there also.

In Europe the theory of monopolistic competition had been linked to a discussion about the merits and demerits of the existing liberal order. The debate about corporatism as an alternative way of organizing economics had originated with the same doubts concerning the validity of the assumption of perfect competition as had the theory of monopolistic or imperfect competition. The "discovery" that market power in the hands of single establishments was not only a matter of some well-defined monopolies but a pervasive phenomenon had deeply troubling implications. This link between theoretical advances in economic science and an ongoing debate about the viability of laissez faire was strong in the cases of Heinrich von Stackelberg and Luigi Amoroso. In their work, scientific results had led directly to policy proposals; sometimes the results themselves were motivated by a priori sympathies for certain policies. This should not lead to an a priori rejection; as Schumpeter once said: "advocacy does not imply lying."

In the cases of Italy and Germany, monopolistic competition theory proper came to an end with the collapse of the socioeconomic order that had furthered an increased criticism of laissez faire. Yet its most valid elements became part of a new economic order, the social market economy, formulated in the immediate postwar period. It essentially embraced the idea of free enterprise, but mitigated it by assigning explicitly to the state the responsibility for the enforcement of the competitive order, including extended social services (see chapter 18).

The case of Great Britain, which assumes the middle ground between the two extremes, is the most intricate and complex. Here, the debate over increasing returns had been started by Sraffa's article, which had given the initial spark for British theoreticians to come to terms with Marshall's ambiguities. This development definitely established monopolistic competition as a thoroughly theoretical phenomenon. Yet the theory remained linked to a polemic attitude toward perfect competition, which was held to be incapable of explaining important real-world phenomena, such as the absence of price cuts in depressions and the market power of single firms. Welfare considerations, as an expression of the concern for the well-being of all economic agents, had become an important part of monopolistic competition theory. Its pursuit had also been part of an attempt to understand the world better, in order to make it a better place. The many personal links between academic economists (especially those in Cambridge) and the political world confirm this attitude.

Only by taking account of this motivation for much of the work undertaken in Great Britain between 1926 and 1940 is one able to understand why, together with monopolistic competition theory, microeconomic theory at large lost its appeal for many British economists. Piero Sraffa, Joan Robinson, Roy Harrod, Richard Kahn, Gerald Shove, Nicholas Kaldor, Dennis Robertson, and even A. C. Pigou, who had constituted the core of British research on monopolistic competition, abandoned it rather quickly and remorselessly. Piero Sraffa stands a little apart from this group, since he was, in addition to his editorial work on Ricardo, pushing his own agendas, such as the maintenance of his contact with Gramsci and his work on linear production models. But all the others became quickly involved in macroeconomics after the publication of the *General Theory* in 1936. Most of them had at one point or another occupied themselves with questions of monetary policy. Keynes's work was familiar to them and many had been part of the Cambridge Circus discussing Keynes's *Treatise on Money.* Yet only after 1936 did macroeconomics command the attention of virtually all British economists interested in economic policy, including all of those named above.

Keynes's work combined what many economists had been explicitly or implicitly looking for in monopolistic competition theory—a convincing analysis of the contemporary dismal state of the economy and an equally convincing, and easily implementable, set of policy prescriptions. Moreover, these policy prescriptions were in line with the gradual, reformist Fabian stance that was at the basis of much of the social engagement of Britain's academic circles. The reason why the sudden embrace of Keynesianism spelled the end of monopolistic competition theory in Great Britain is explored in part 3. The possibility of a fruitful combination of the two approaches was prevented by a number of different factors, paramount among them perhaps Keynes's own ambiguous stand on microeconomics.

PART IV

The Synthesis That Never Was: Keynesianism and Monopolistic Competition Theory

CHAPTER 14

Issues

The most intriguing factor responsible for the sudden end of monopolistic competition as the primary approach for microeconomic problems was the almost complete domination of the interest of British economists by Keynes's work after the publication of *The General Theory of Employment, Interest, and Money* in 1936. During this founding period of modern macroeconomics, microeconomics of a kind incompatible with monopolistic competition theory was implicitly reestablished. Keynes's extraordinary influence thus not only had a direct impact in turning attention away from monopolistic competition toward macroproblems, but also an indirect impact that led to a renewed acceptance of concepts already given up as untenable in microeconomics.

Keynes did not pursue a purely Marshallian/Pigovian vision of competitive industry when he spoke about microeconomic problems. In fact his very eclecticism, loosely combining elements of perfect competition with traits of firms facing downward-sloping demand curves, managed to create confusion concerning the microfoundations of Keynesianism, and does so to this day. This prevented an integration of monopolistic competition theory into modern mainstream economics more effectively than any explicit reestablishment of a theory of perfect competition, which had only recently been discarded.

The preceding chapter hinted at the reasons for the rapid acceptance of most of Keynes's results and policy prescriptions by the British academic community. Keynes could only exert such influence because his work satisfied the hopes, connected hitherto with monopolistic competition theory, for an economic science that would not only be analytically correct but also formulate policies that satisfied widely agreed-upon normative principles. The willingness to abandon former research projects in order to follow the new macroeconomic way out of depression, and the dissatisfaction with neoclassical equilibrium postulates, can only be understood by taking account of the conviction of many contemporaries that they were witnesses to, if not participants in, a scientific revolution of the first order. One example is Keynes's former student and collaborator, D. M. Bensussan-Butt, who writes: "The mystery of contemporary iniquity had been unveiled by a masterpiece of sustained intellectual effort. All the other tangled turgid stuff which lesser men were producing to rationalize the mess around us simply faded away. Now we all knew why" (Keynes 1989, 4). In the face of such dramatic scientific developments, other theories became less interesting.

A further element in the sudden loss of interest in monopolistic competition theory, at least in Great Britain, was the publication of studies by R. L. Hall and C. J. Hitch on pricing behavior under oligopoly and monopolistic competition. The discovery that most businesspeople never even bothered to equate short-run marginal cost with marginal revenue, but usually pursued some kind of average cost plus mark-up pricing, shook the confidence of the British researchers in the effectiveness of one of their most beloved instruments—the concept of marginal revenue. In hindsight it seems strange that this should have so bothered theoretical economists, as the rationality assumptions underlying profit-maximizing entrepreneurs had never been specified, and their decision-making processes had usually been treated as black-box phenomena. Why should economists worry about businesspeople's actual trains of thought, especially as average cost plus mark-up pricing is not incompatible with profit maximization? But at the time the published results further shook confidence in any kind of closed theory of value.

From today's perspective the sudden loss of interest in monopolistic competition theory comes as a surprise, as Keynesian macroeconomics certainly do not exclude monopolistic competition. Indeed, the behavior of the firm under monopolistic competition can provide rationales for many of the assumptions of Keynesian models, including Keynes's own model presented in the General Theory. Explorations in these directions were, at the time, confined to some isolated attempts. Aside from Kahn and Harrod, only Michael Kalecki and Josef Steindl linked the market power of individual firms to the idea that economies do not automatically come to rest in full employment equilibria. However, neither of these approaches ever fully materialized as part of a wider research project.

Despite the enormous potential of a fruitful combination of monopolistic competition theory and the new Keynesian macroeconomics, Keynes's writings diminished rather than enhanced the attractiveness of monopolistic competition theory. The reasons for this paradox are subtle and manifold, and shed a revealing light on the workings of the community of British economists.

· CHAPTER 15

Modern Perspectives

Despite the failure or unwillingness of Keynes's contemporaries to grasp the opportunity to provide his new macroeconomics with convincing microeconomic rationales, several approaches have been developed since then that accomplish just that. New theoretical insights, advancements of existing theories, and empirical studies all continue to prove the existence of an intrinsic link between the effects of aggregate-demand shifts for the real economy and the limited monopoly power of the single firm.

By combining two highly original approaches undertaken separately in the early 1960s by Kenneth J. Arrow and Robert W. Clower, one can show that, given the existence of Keynesian unemployment equilibrium, policies designed to elevate the economy to a full-employment equilibrium would automatically involve the existence of monopolistic competition between firms. Clower explicitly developed his "dual-decision hypothesis" as an underlying microeconomic rationale for Keynes's model of an economy in underemployment equilibrium in his 1963 article "The Keynesian Counterrevolution." Emphasizing the discrepancy between the notional or ideal quantities of demanders and suppliers, he develops the concept of an economy that lacks proper incentives to move to an optimizing state, even though Walras's law is not fulfilled.

The dual-decision hypothesis maintains that the idea that agents can always trade up to the point where marginal rate of substitution equals marginal rate of transformation is counteracted by the principle that agents have to meet their budget constraints. The underlying rationale is a quantity restriction, usually imagined as a demand restriction in the labor market, which constrains agents to nonoptimal choices. This implies a distinction between the concepts of "notional" and "real" quantities, where notional means the quantity demanded or supplied under full optimization and real the quantity actually affordable given the budget constraints.

Despite suboptimality, an equilibrium, in the sense that effective demand equals effective supply, is obtained. But Walras's law does not hold. Given the effective demand on the goods market, planned or notional supply equals zero, while in the labor market planned demand is smaller than planned supply. The working of Walras's law is interrupted, since effective demand for goods is crucially dependent on real income and not on planned income (equal to planned labor supply), and thus the theorized link between the supply side of labor and the demand side of goods is destroyed. This corresponds to the exogenously given real income in the Keynesian consumption function. This dependence of consumption on given income alone prohibits a readjustment in the neoclassical sense, by which unconstrained agents would develop excess demand in the goods market, anticipating the satisfaction of their planned labor supply. This in return would raise prices, output, and employment, and thus soak up the excess supply in the labor market—strictly satisfying Walras's law. But since constrained demand and supply are consistent, there is no incentive for agents to trade at different prices. Moreover, no agent has an incentive to trade different quantities, as he or she could not afford to do so. Clower emphasized that, contrary to Walras's law, Say's principle instead is reconfirmed; the demand for goods is defined by the labor-market constraint, which in turn is defined by the supply of goods (Clower 1984, 51).

Clower's analysis has great implications for an economic policy concentrating on demand management, since a temporary increase in effective demand would after a while become self-sustaining as the quantity restriction on the labor market was removed and the economy was moved out of the unemployment equilibrium. The increase in effective demand would have to be stopped at the point of the equation of marginal values—which is exactly the point of coincidence of real and planned quantities. This is also the point at which Walras's law holds again. For all its beauty and intuitive appeal, Clower's dual-decision hypothesis does hinge on a crucial but implicit assumption: that there is no possibility of signaling the notional quantities between traders. Market prices are considered fixed, since the existence of a Walrasian auctioneer is not involved.

If, on the other hand, notional quantities could be effectively communicated, price changes would follow until notional supply and demand matched. Although there are no Walrasian auctioneers in the real economy, utility-maximizing agents should have an interest in communicating information regarding notional demands. Therefore, it is likely to happen as soon as the number of agents is sufficiently small and information gathering is easy. Yet, on the macroeconomic level for which Clower's theory was designed, the situation might well be different. This would leave room for an exogenous, aggregate-demand management policy.

The point at which monopolistic competition comes into this basic Keynesian picture is the transition from a constrained underemployment equilibrium to a situation of full employment. Relaxing the assumption of strongly imperfect information, and allowing rational profit-maximizing agents to give price signals in order to overcome quantity rationing and to realize their notional supplies or demands, does not lead to instantaneous adjustment to the notional quantities envisaged by neoclassical theory. As Kenneth Arrow shows in his 1959 article "Toward a Theory of Price Adjustment," the pricing process during the gradual achievement of economic equilibrium is necessarily incompatible with perfect competition and involves monopolistic price setting. In other words, as soon as the economy adjusts itself to notional quantities, monopolistic competition becomes the relevant form of industrial organization. Only at the end point of this process, when notional supply matches notional demand, does an assumption of price-taking perfect competitors again become possible.

Arrow developed his theory for any kind of price adjustment, whether caused by Keynesian policies or otherwise. Clower showed that Keynesian underemployment equilibria involve trading at "false" (i.e., suboptimal) prices. Combining the two approaches makes it clear that Keynesian policies moving the economy to an equilibrium of notional quantities involve monopolistic price setting.

In "Toward a Theory of Price Adjustment," Arrow elaborates the idea that the Walrasian *tâtonnement* involves by definition monopolistic price setting. He shows that a unique price at any one time will exist only in equilibrium. "Indeed, suppose we have a situation . . . in which the aggregate supply forthcoming at the 'market' price exceeds the demand at that price. Then . . . the individual firms are in the position of monopolists as far as the imperfect elasticity of demand for their products is concerned" (Arrow 1959, 46). Under conditions of disequilibrium, no single market-clearing price is defined. This is due to the underdetermination of three variables—quantity supplied, quantity demanded, and price—when only the laws of supply and demand are given. Only at the point of equality between demand and supply is the system well defined. In times of price adjustment, firms have to move prices, which they will only do if they consider it profitable; this implies that they dispose of some degree of monopoly power.

In this context, Arrow's discussion of the uncertainty surrounding the monopolist's pricing process until equilibrium is reached (precisely because the monopolist lacks information about the correct market price) is less important than his description of the actual form of this process. When supply exceeds demand, then the firm faces a demand curve that is less than infinitely elastic; by lowering its price slightly, it could not sell indefinite amounts of goods. In the case of excess demand, as long as supply is not infinitely elastic, a firm will quantity-ration demanders by raising its price, thus again acting as a monopolist facing a downward-sloping demand curve.

The move from one equilibrium to another (for instance the exit from a Keynesian underemployment equilibrium) thus involves monopolistic competition. In fact, an economy would only fail to involve monopolistic competition in two cases: either long-run full employment (a case certainly not typically Keynesian), or a situation in which all agents resign themselves to their quantity restrictions, not trying to exploit profit opportunities. The latter case would in any event (arguing in the vein of Kahn's dissertation) likely involve some kind of monopolistic quantity restriction by firms. This leads to the conclusion that only full employment would be compatible with perfect competition. In principle, this result should imply that a microeconomics based on monopolistic competition theory is the appropriate foundation for Keynesian macroeconomics, which is so concerned with moving economies back to their capacity outputs.

The kind of monopolistic competition invoked by Kenneth Arrow is a dynamic version of the static model previously analyzed (because it was by far the dominant model under discussion). The problem of product differentiation is not addressed by Arrow, as the slope of the demand curve is determined by limitation either of the market or of productive capacity. However, there is no fundamental difference between the pricing mechanism outlined by Arrow and that usually found in monopolistic competition theory.

Modern macroeconomists in search of microeconomic rationales for Keynesian macroeconomics have concentrated on the original static model of monopolistic competition. N. Gregory Mankiw, George A. Akerlof, Janet L. Yellen, and Oliver Hart all put their main emphasis on finding a reason for the empirically observed "stickiness" of prices and wages (Akerlof and Yellen 1985, 825). The downward-sloping demand curve is the reason agents can afford not to adjust prices or wages in response to shocks in aggregate demand. It does not matter whether this is due to adjustment costs, near-rationality, or specific functional forms of the demand functions; the result is the same—the effectiveness of aggregate demand increases is assured.

In "Small Menu Costs and Large Business Cycles: A Macroeconomic Model of Monopoly," Mankiw postulates the existence of small-menu costs (costs incurred by a producer when it changes prices, such as the "printing of new catalogs and informing salesmen of the new price" [Mankiw 1985, 529]) that make it costly for the agents to change prices. Assuming downward-sloping demand, perfectly rational agents will not adjust their prices to a demand shock so long as the gains from adjustment are lower than the menu costs. This leaves considerable room for nonadjustment, since the losses from nonoptimization are of second-order magnitude compared to first-order changes in demand. This is so because with a downward-sloping demand curve, relative price increases are offset by decreases in the quantity demanded, and vice versa. The likelihood of adjustment increases with the size of the shock and the elasticity of the demand curve.

In a discussion of welfare effects of pricing behavior, Mankiw shows that society gains in consumer surplus from nonadjustment under aggregate demand increases, whereas in a demand contraction society loses if prices are not adjusted. Thus for pricing behavior determined by private profit maximization, he can state for monopolistic competitors: "In this sense, prices are downwardly rigid but not upwardly rigid" (ibid., 536). In other words, downward rigidity should concern the policymaker, whereas upward rigidity is of no concern, or is even beneficial. This asymmetry is solely due to the nature of the welfare effects of the adjustment process and not to the nature of the pricing procedure. The policy implications are necessarily Keynesian: "An economy of this sort does not recommend passive monetary policy. As long as new information about exogenous demand factors (e.g., velocity) is made available to the monetary authority after private agents set their prices, systematic feedback rules can stabilize output. These exogenous demand shocks cause substantial and inefficient fluctuations in output and employment if the monetary authority does not react" (ibid., 537).

A similar model was developed by George A. Akerlof and Janet L. Yellen in "A Near-Rational Model of the Business Cycle, with

Wage and Price Inertia." Again, monopolistic competitors facing downward-sloping demand curves are assumed to be the basis of a macroeconomy. This time the underlying rationale for price and wage rigidity is "near-rationality," suboptimal behavior that is not very costly for the individual firm: "Firms that behave suboptimally, adjusting prices and wages slowly [to a shock in aggregate demand], may suffer losses from failure to optimize, but those losses may be very small . . . Technically, very small is defined as being second-order in terms of the policy shocks that create a disturbance from a long-run, fully maximizing equilibrium" (Akerlof and Yellen 1985, 825).

A necessary requirement for second-order smallness of losses from failing to optimize is the differentiability of a firm's profit function in its own prices and wages. Differentiability in terms of wages is given by a labor-market model of efficiency wages, in which firms minimize wages not per worker but per efficiency unit. This implies gains in efficiency if wages should be too high in a recession, and losses offsetting the benefits from too low a wage (nominal and real) in a boom. Both effects are due to the increased (or decreased) worker's effort due to his or her increased (or decreased) fear of being caught shirking and laid off in times when the worker's wage exceeds (or approaches) his or her marginal opportunity cost. Differentiability in terms of output prices is given by the downward-sloping demand curve of monopolistic competitors. This is the same reasoning, albeit with different wording, employed in the paper by Mankiw. It is assumed that each firm's price is unaffected by its competitors' decisions. If some near-rational firms do not adjust their prices to shocks in aggregate demand, there will be sticky prices and real effects of the first order in output and employment.

The third model in this vein is presented by Oliver Hart in "A Model of Imperfect Competition with Keynesian Features." He sees himself explicitly in the tradition begun by Clower, but tries to integrate some degree of price flexibility: "We shall show that the equilibrium of an economy in which prices are fully flexible, but where agents are imperfectly competitive, exhibits a number of non-Walrasian or Keynesian features" (Hart 1982a, 110). His fully developed general-equilibrium model (which sets his paper apart from the other two) displays the following Keynesian features:

Too low an equilibrium level of activity
A multiplier greater than one for exogenous demand shocks
Quantity adjustment instead of price adjustment
Possibility of increasing employment by government policy

Except for the first result, all the others depend on the idea that prices do not change in response to a shock in aggregate demand.

In Hart's approach, prices do not change because the increase in aggregate demand is defined to affect the demand for each firm's good in such a way that it is optimal to continue to charge the same price as before. This relies on the idea that the elasticity of demand remains the same for each price after the increase. Although Hart's paper contains other significant points, this remains his central assumption concerning monopolistic competition as a microeconomic foundation for Keynesian results. The introduction of price rigidity with the device of a specific mathematical formulation makes it less apt for my purpose, which is to show that a general compatibility between monopolistic competition theory and Keynesian economics is not only possible but logically inevitable. But since Hart's emphasis is on general equilibrium, this does not constitute a criticism of his research.

Even thought these papers focused scientific attention on new and important features of the economy and are thus significant contributions, they are not flawless. All three papers display the assumption of monopolistic competition in an ad hoc manner, without giving the subject adequate analytical treatment. Each of them is written from a macroeconomist's point of view, searching for rationales behind empirically observed facts. They all display peculiarities that would have been avoided if the monopolistic competition literature of the 1930s had been adequately integrated. None of the papers actually specifies the downward-sloping demand curves. Their demand functions are related neither to the cost function of the firms nor to the market structure. Without further assumptions, the firms as presented in all these papers will not be monopolistic competitors, but firms working in perfectly competitive markets.

Mankiw assumes that the firms in his paper display constant returns to scale. As Paul Samuelson emphasizes in his essay "The Monopolistic Competition Revolution," this is incompatible with monopolistic price setting. No firm that works under constant returns to scale is able to sustain a price higher than the competitive one: "even if a firm has 99 or 100% of the output it has under stipulated returns conditions [constant returns to scale] it has zero long-run monopoly power . . . leaving it with a horizontal long-run personal demand curve" (Samuelson 1967, 114). But Mankiw postulates exactly that: his firms leave their prices unchanged after a contraction in demand and thus quote prices higher than the competitive one. This is only possible if there are barriers to entry into the industry, such as patents or protected trademarks. This would imply large monopoly profits. Neither corollary of monopolistic competitors producing under constant returns to scale is mentioned in the text. If restrictions to entry are not assumed to exist, a monopolistic price setter would have to produce under increasing returns to scale.

Similar reasoning applies to the articles by Akerlof and Yellen and by Hart. Both works assume decreasing returns to scale for their firms, without further specifications. To take these assertions literally, in the sense that decreasing returns apply over the whole range of production, would lead to an absurdity. Everyone could produce goods at home more cheaply than buying them from outside firms, competition would be perfect, and Hart's Keynesian economy would collapse into a completely Walrasian one. Assuming that the authors in fact meant that firms produce at locally convex points, the matter becomes complicated.

A standard equilibrium of monopolistic competition equilibrium would require that firms produce at excess capacity—that is, under increasing returns to scale. In order to achieve local convexity under monopolistic competition, the authors would have to assume that at least some of their firms made excess profits, which would imply that they are not monopolistic competitors, but "real" monopolists, whose markets would be protected by external barriers to entry. The assumption of decreasing returns to scale fails to fulfill any other important function in the mechanics of the model of Akerlof and Yellen; in the paper by Oliver Hart, the assumption of decreasing returns is needed for the proof of existence of general equilibrium (see chapter 19).

It seems that none of these authors deemed the issues at stake sufficiently important to warrant a more consistent treatment. Nevertheless, these questions must be addressed, or monopolistic competition theory will be reduced to an arbitrarily formulated downward-sloping demand curve. Even if these authors are not concerned with the resurrection of monopolistic competition theory for its own sake, features of monopolistic competition will have to be formulated in a more logically consistent way in order to yield the desired microeconomic rationales for Keynesian macroeconomics.

Robert E. Hall proceeds in a substantially more consistent way in his 1986 paper with the weighty title "Market Structure and Macroeconomic Fluctuations." Aware of the previous attempts, he searches for empirical verification of the assumption of monopolistic competition in the United States economy used to motivate the effectiveness of increases in the money supply to stimulate demand. His starting point is the empirical observation of procyclical productivity shifts in United States industry. His procedure is as simple as it is effective: by analyzing first the ratio of price to marginal cost, he finds that firms in most industries display ratios of around 1.5, and in some cases of up to 3, a clear sign that firms have at least some monopoly power. Second, he analyzes the average profit level and finds that it is not substantially above the rate of interest. Together, the results imply that firms must be producing under increasing returns to scale. This would also explain the procyclical productivity gains due to falling average costs in times of expansion of aggregate demand. Higher levels of profit would have to be expected under the assumption of constant returns to scale, assuming that firms have some kind of natural monopoly.

This implies production under excess capacity, which Hall explains as being due to indivisibilities, possibly in selling costs and product establishment. In the light of the aforementioned results, the following statement should come as no surprise: "The results developed here have implications for several important issues in macroeconomics. They add to our understanding why measured productivity varies cyclically; they demonstrate that economic supply or capacity can be highly elastic; and they explain why market forces provide no strong tendency to move the economy to high-employment levels of operation" (Hall 1986, 311). The last statement is due to near-rationality, as firms fail to optimize out of an underemployment equilibrium. Near-rationality thus provides a rationale for the failure of Clower's agents to communicate their notional quantities, and at the same time Mankiw's conclusion that downward rigidity of prices presents a problem is confirmed.

Hall's paper is an important complement to the contributions by Mankiw, Akerlof, and Yellen. It frees them from the suspicion of being mere intellectual exercises of a priori supporters of Keynesian economics; it adds to them a relevance far beyond their possible academic and theoretical attractiveness. In combination, the theoretical and the empirical results make a powerful statement of the need to reemploy monopolistic competition as the relevant form of industrial organization for theoretical study as well as for the practical implementation of economic policy in general and Keynesian demand management in particular.

In contrast to these conclusions stand the hesitant attempts of Keynes and several of his followers to provide the theory of aggregate demand with convincing microeconomic foundations. Their failure to combine the two theories is all the more astonishing because the analytical elements employed in the recent synthesis were readily available and well understood at the time, when Keynes's *General Theory* was discussed at Cambridge. Keynes's ambiguous attitude toward monopolistic competition provided an additional reason, beyond the shift in mood and the shifts in methodological emphasis and ideological preference, to deflect the attention of British economists away from monopolistic competition theory. That theory would have added considerable conviction to the work that soon would define their future research interest—*The General Theory of Employment, Interest, and Money.*

CHAPTER 16

The Riddle of
Keynes's Microeconomics

The reasons for the failure of contemporary attempts to pursue research along the lines described in the preceding chapter have already been mentioned: Keynes's own disproportionate influence and his ambiguous assembly of microeconomic elements used in the *General Theory*, the sobering influence of the study by Hall and Hitch, and the failure of business-cycle theorists such as Kalecki and Steindl to integrate their views on monopolistic competition either with other contemporary work or with stringent analytical criteria. The most important factor of these three is undoubtedly Keynes's position on microeconomics.

It has often been maintained that John Maynard Keynes, as far as the theory of value is concerned, remained a true Marshallian at heart. In this view the Marshallian vision is equated with the assumption of perfect competition in homogeneous industries. Comments such as "it is clear that Keynes assumed perfect competition" abound (Thomas K. Rymes in Keynes 1989, 11), and for once James Tobin follows the conventional wisdom:

> Greater stress might be placed on Keynes's uncritical acceptance of the neoclassical competitive model. By assuming that firms are price takers in auction markets rather than price setters in monopolistic competition or oligopoly, he made it harder to sustain his vision of disequilibrium, with failures of coordination, communication, and adjustment. Imperfect competition was the other revolution in economics in the 1930s; one of its sites was Keynes's Cambridge, and two of its agents, Joan Robinson

and Piero Sraffa, were in his group. Yet, for some mysterious reason the two revolutions were never meshed. (Tobin 1981, 207)

The matter is in fact more complicated. It can be greatly elucidated by following up on some of the challenges to the picture of Keynes as an advocate of perfect competition pure and simple. The idea of competitive industry had been badly battered and was not a very appealing concept anymore in the mid- and late 1930s, due to the deconstructive work of Sraffa, Robinson, Shove, and their colleagues. The Chicago school had not yet started its counterreformation, and any work explicitly reestablishing the assumption of perfect competition for all forms of returns would have definitely sparked a response, even taking into account the great willingness to follow the new macroeconomic path. On at least two occasions Keynes speaks critically of the "classical school" for assuming "free competition" (Keynes 1973, 11 and 26). And "imperfect" competition is certainly a possibility for him (ibid., 379).

A different attempt to commit Keynes firmly to a precise microeconomic framework is undertaken by the authors of "Keynes's Neglected Heritage: The Classical Microfoundations of *The General Theory*," Evelyn L. Forget and Sharam Manouchehri. They argue that the dynamic models of competition used by the classical economists John Stuart and John Elliot Cairnes were communicated to Keynes through Marshall, who supposedly contained their insights regarding the behavior of firms in the more descriptive parts of the *Principles of Economics*. They contend that a resulting "fix-price assumption" of a medium-run price-setting mode, based on expectations and capacity, survives implicitly in the *General Theory* (Forget and Manouchehri 1988, 408). At first sight this is not unappealing, especially in the light of the results discussed in chapter 15. But despite this appeal, their argument is a pure ex post facto construction. There is no evidence in any of Keynes's work for it, although it could explain some of the features of that work; but the fix-price assumption shares this property with monopolistic competition theory. It is not surprising, then, that the two authors fail completely to cite any direct reference in favor of their thesis.

Superficially convincing, yet not very illuminating, is the contention that Keynes simply did not bother about microeconomics. In this view, microeconomics was not regarded by Keynes as essential to the main questions dealt with in the *General Theory*. Keynes would thus have stood at the beginning of the popular dichotomy between microeconomics and macroeconomics, continuing without any further thought the traditional dichotomy between value theory and monetary theory. This is a position maintained, for instance, by Joan Robinson with her usual poignancy: "Keynes himself was not interested in the theory of relative prices. Gerald Shove used to say that Maynard had never spent the twenty minutes necessary to understand the theory of value. On these topics he was content to leave orthodoxy alone. He carried a good deal of Marshallian luggage with him and never thoroughly unpacked it to throw out the clothes he could not wear" (Robinson 1962, 79). The picture contains a deeper truth than its ironic tone might suggest. Although not a Marshallian in the pure sense, and without ever actually committing himself firmly to it, Keynes did not approve of any attempts that directly challenged the received view of value theory. Keynes's position is characterized by an eclecticism that combined elements according to their usefulness to his main scheme, quite like a bag filled with clothes thrown in indiscriminately.

The view that Keynes lacked interest in an elaborate microeconomic framework is corroborated by his own statements, such as the following in a letter to Gerald Shove in April 1936: "What you say about the classical analysis as applied to the individual industry and firm is probably right. I have been concentrating on the other problem, and have not, like you, thought very much about the elements of the system" (Keynes 1971–83, 14:2). Yet if we consider that Shove in the preceding letter to Keynes had chided him for having been "too kind to the classical analysis as applied to the individual industry" and had characterized it as "wrong or completely jejune unless very artificial assumptions are made" (ibid., 14:1), we are getting closer to a Keynes whose intuition was ahead of his willingness to take on the neoclassical theory of value as energetically as neoclassical monetary theory.

This contradictory stance toward microeconomics is reflected nicely in Keynes's long obituary of Alfred Marshall in 1924. The deference shown to the work of the revered master does not preclude Keynes from expressing his personal doubts about results that, one paragraph before, he had asserted to be the last word on the subject. It heightens one's interest that these comments are made with respect to the problem of increasing returns: "there are further distinctions, which we now reckon essential to clear thinking, which are first explicit in Marshall—particularly those between 'external' and 'internal' economies and between 'prime' and 'supplementary' costs." The note reads: "The vital importance of this distinction to a correct theory of Equilibrium under conditions of increasing returns is, of course, now obvious. But it was not so before the *Principles*" (Keynes 1924, 351n). It is rather surprising, then, that Keynes says on behalf of these "obvious" truths: "All these are path-breaking ideas which no one who wants to think clearly can do without. Nevertheless this is the quarter in which, to my opinion, the Marshall analysis is least complete and satisfactory, and where there remains most to do" (ibid., 351). Unfortunately, and (in connection with this issue) characteristically, he does not elaborate.

In the meantime, others had done quite a lot of the remaining work. Nevertheless, in his introduction as the editor of the *Economic Journal*, Keynes describes Sraffa's contribution to the "Symposium on the Representative Firm" as "some negative and destructive criticisms" (Keynes 1930, 79). And as late as 1941 Keynes considered himself "still innocent enough to be bewildered" by imperfect-competition theory (Feiwel 1989a, 121). One can discern at this point in Keynes a certain lack of interest in microeconomics, linked with a superficial acceptance of traditional positions and an intuitive tendency toward positions contrary to those needed to do justice to Marshall.

The assertion of Keynes's lack of interest in microeconomics is given some methodological justification by post-Keynesians, who maintain that indeed for Keynes it was not important which kind of industrial organization was to be expected. This is considerably closer to the truth than the quick assertion that Keynes assumed perfectly competitive markets throughout his work, which he certainly did not. Jan Kregel reflects the post-Keynesian point of view: "The discussion about what kind of market Keynes was assuming is thus nugatory—any would do, for Keynes felt it could make no difference to the exposition of effective demand . . . it [market structure] is not crucial to Keynes's own position as long as the degree of competition, whatever it is, can be taken as given" (Kregel 1976, 218n).

For this position there is evidence in the *General Theory* itself—for instance, when Keynes states: "We take as given the existing skill and quantity of available labour, the existing quality and quantity of available equipment, the existing technique, the degree of competition, the tastes and habits of the consumer, the disutility of different intensities of labour" (Keynes 1973, 245). This seems to confirm Kregel's position, even if we consider that Keynes immediately thereafter hedges his bets by asserting that "this does not mean that we assume these factors to be constant; but . . . we are not considering . . . effects and consequences of changes in them" (ibid.). Robin Marris concurs by adding that Keynes wanted his theory to be truly applicable to all forms of competition (Marris 1992, 1241). In *Reconstructing Keynesian Economics with Imperfect Competition*, Marris advances the most idiosyncratic theory to date for Keynes's contradictory statements on microeconomic theory: being convinced that Keynes implicitly leaned toward monopolistic competition as the relevant microeconomic foundation for his *General Theory*, he argues that Keynes nevertheless chose to exclude it from his work for personal reasons, namely his ambiguous attitude toward Joan Robinson and her friendship with Richard Kahn (Marris 1991, 183ff.).

Personal motivations can often be seen from a distance as rationales for the influence of deeper underlying forces. It is true that Richard Kahn in his fellowship dissertation under the advisorship of Keynes had first explored the degree of competition in connection with the level of demand, and that he had substantially contributed to Joan Robinson's work on monopolistic competition before and during the writing of *The Economics of Imperfect Competition*. It is also curious that Keynes, who was the editor of the *Economic Journal*, would not comment more extensively on the important research undertaken by both of them while in close intellectual and geographical proximity to him, while at the same time Keynes had no difficulty integrating Kahn's important concept of the multiplier into his work.

But Keynes had decided to focus his concentration exclusively on the theory of effective demand. He was well aware of the potentially disruptive effect of his contribution on traditional theory. He saw himself as the guardian of the Marshallian legacy, as well as the promoter of a fundamental paradigm shift. This double role led to an attitude of righteous indignation when he saw Marshall "unfairly" attacked on microeconomic grounds, while he himself prepared an equally devastating attack in other areas. His remarks on Sraffa show that he did not approve of an overthrow also of the microeconomic part of Marshall's analysis also, however necessary it seemed from the point of view of logic (and intermittently from the point of view of his own intelligence). Keynes's ambivalent attitude toward the Marshallian heritage is shown in his obituary of Marshall: his respect for the great teacher, and his unwillingness to discard his results without further ado, predate the times of Kahn and Robinson at Cambridge. In this case the personal might have reinforced an attitude of ambiguity about the theory of the firm, yet it cannot be seen as the underlying cause of that attitude.

Despite Keynes's nonchalance toward the question of the degree of competition, which evidences an unwillingness to deal with the subject, one must still inquire about the implicit microeconomic assumptions of the General Theory, for three reasons. First, Keynes continued to return to microeconomic questions without ever attempting to extend the analysis into some kind of coherent framework, however loose. His interest in the question of user cost in relation to excess capacity is the most important example of a much greater implicit interest than his explicit statements would lead one to suspect. Second, the General Theory revolves around the single firm with the entrepreneur as the decisive decision-making unit. Without going into the complex questions of the formation and optimization of expectations under conditions of uncertainty, it is indispensable that one flesh out Keynes's assumptions about industrial organization in order to find at least an intuitive direction for the microfoundations of the General Theory. After all, books advocating cheap-money policies and state-sponsored employment programs were nothing new in the Great Britain of 1936. What distinguishes Keynes's work from all previous attempts is the totality of a vision ultimately linking certain policy effects to the maximizing decisions of individual economic agents following certain psychological laws. Keynes himself finally shows a heightened awareness of the problem of a firm's cost schedule in this connection in his 1939 article "Relative Movements of Real Wages and Output."

Last but not least, the question of the microfoundations of the General Theory is an important element of the answer to the question why research in monopolistic competition theory became so completely supplanted by work in the new theory of Keynesian macroeconomics. Any possible attack on the new book from the monopolistic competition side was deflected by an integration of the most openly empirically observable traits of monopolistic competition, such as price-setting and quantity-setting firms working under excess capacity. By mixing those elements with a tenacious insistence on the notion of a short-run rising marginal cost, and therefore a rising supply price, Keynes conveyed the impression that the problem of a theory of value could be overcome with a mixture of common sense and trust in tradition.

In addition, he did not distinguish clearly between long-run and short-run phenomena, making it possible to maintain competition as a long-run vision and letting firms act as monopolistic competitors in what was for him the all-important short run. The latter point certainly did not further fruitful discussion with such theorists of monopolistic competition as Sraffa, who considered monopolistic competition a long-run phenomenon due to increasing returns to scale and product differentiation. But it should have facilitated discussion with Kahn and Harrod, who had the tendency to link monopolistic competition to excess capacity under a temporary fall in demand. There was clearly considerable room for discussion. Yet Keynes's theoretical inconsistencies were at the time neither pointed out nor discussed; they were hard to find due to Keynes's pronounced aloofness on the subject, which made them seem not of paramount importance. Keynes's eclecticism, which made him careful never to confront the Marshallian orthodoxy in value theory, appears to have been the result of his fear of getting into a discussion about these matters, which would detract from the issue he considered of paramount importance, namely the theory of aggregate demand.

For those who saw in Keynes someone who faithfully carried on the Marshallian vision of perfect competition in a homogeneous industry, the most important argument was certainly his insistence on a rising marginal cost and a rising supply price. This element of Keynes's system has the property, somewhat awkward for his own results, that output and employment increases due to increases in demand and investment are immediately checked by rising prices; nevertheless it is faithfully preserved. Yet for Keynes there is no technological reason for decreasing returns at the plant level. Neither does he make any reference to a law of decreasing returns in the Ricardian sense of the declining marginal productivity of successive units of a homogeneous variable factor applied to a given amount of a fixed factor. Keynes displays an intuitive tendency toward a constant-returns-to-scale production function, and he goes to great trouble to construct rising marginal costs. For him they are monetary phenomena linked primarily to the remuneration of workers on the basis of effort instead of efficiency—that is, the inelastic supply of workers of equal quality.

A typical passage from the *General Theory* concerning the cost structure of an expanding firm reads like this: "To elucidate the ideas involved, let us simplify our assumptions still further, and assume (1) that all unemployed resources are homogeneous and interchangeable in their efficiency to produce what is wanted, and (2) that the factors of production entering into marginal cost are content with the same money-wage so long as there is a surplus of them unemployed. In this case we have constant returns and a rigid wage-unit, so long as there is any unemployment" (Keynes 1973, 295). The Keynesian wage unit is measured on the basis of efficiency units, not on the basis of individual workers. The result of decreasing returns comes only with the following ex post facto qualification:

"Since resources are not homogeneous, there will be diminishing, and not constant, returns as employment gradually increases" (ibid., 296).

This process is later elucidated and generalized for any factors, not just labor:

> the distinction between diminishing and constant returns partly depends on whether workers are remunerated in strict proportion to their efficiency. If so, we shall have constant labour-costs . . . when employment increases . . . Moreover, if equipment is non-homogeneous and some part of it involves a greater prime [variable] cost per unit of output, we shall have increasing marginal prime costs over and above any increase due to increasing labour-costs. Hence, in general, supply price will increase as output from a given equipment is increased. (Ibid., 299–300)

The term "given equipment" should in this context be interpreted neither as the "fixed factor" of the law of diminishing returns, nor as the "indivisibilities" invoked in monopolistic competition theory as a rationale for increasing returns. Rather, it is used in order to emphasize that diminishing returns will prevail due to rising labor costs (in terms of efficiency units) even if equipment is homogeneous. In subsequent pages Keynes clearly links these considerations to the existence of finite supply elasticities, a line of reasoning that leads directly to Joan Robinson's article "Rising Supply Price." It is a remarkable proof of Keynes's influence that Robinson tried to base results of constant returns to scale on this kind of analysis, rather than insisting on her own work in monopolistic competition theory.

Keynes's idiosyncratic approach to the important issue of price formation at the firm level can also be seen on the subject of his favorite brainchild—"user cost." It shows the lengths to which Keynes was willing to go in order to justify a rising supply price even under clearly stipulated conditions of excess capacity. The definition of user cost as the change in asset value during one period due to plant use in the production of goods, as opposed to plant use and goods production in a later period, is perhaps best captured in Paul Davidson's expression "intertemporal profit opportunity cost" (Davidson 1987, 4:766). Keynes's calculation rule is given as follows: "It must be arrived at, therefore, by calculating the discounted value of the additional prospective yield which would be obtained at some later date if it were not used now" (Keynes 1973, 70). With its pronounced dynamic character, it is a concept much more naturally applicable to depletable resources, but Keynes uses it mainly in connection with the problem of wear and tear on plant and equipment. This is certainly admissible, although it could be argued that the fixed-cost character of a given plant and equipment is more relevant in Keynes's short-run analysis of aggregate-demand management.

Keynes's fascination with the concept of user cost becomes more understandable if one takes into account that the concept of user cost is mainly employed to deal with the problem of scrapping of excess capacity. This problem constituted one of the few policy questions actively tackled by the British government during the 1930s. It was thus a topic of considerable public and professional interest. The scrapping of excess capacity in the shipbuilding industry, for instance, was a conscious attempt to substitute a de facto cartelization of the industry for cutthroat competition. Consequently, prices were raised due to monopolistic output restrictions, a policy that was supported by a cautious modernization of plants, which helped lower average cost and thus raise profit margins. In short, this was a case in point for the applicability of monopolistic competition theory to "real-world" scenarios.

For Keynes, the scrapping of excess capacity had the sole effect of sharply increasing marginal user cost, due to the disappearance of redundant capacity. He argues, rather unconvincingly, that the excess capacity had held the loss of future profit opportunities due to the present use of equipment to a minimum, and had thus contributed to low marginal user costs. Its scrapping would in turn raise prices, which in standard fashion are equal to total marginal cost, of which marginal user cost is an important part: "the concept of user cost shows how the scrapping of (say) half the redundant plant may have the effect of raising prices immediately. For by bringing the date of the absorption of the redundancy nearer, this policy raises marginal user cost and consequently increases the current supply price" (ibid., 71). This effect also comes about when the redundancy is only partly scrapped, as businesspeople revise their expectations concerning the end of the slump and the now earlier end of overcapacity.

Keynes makes an important implicit assumption in order to make his conception work: user cost, as the opportunity cost of future profits, will rise only if the redundant equipment has any relevance for future production—that is, if it is assumed that demand will return to levels at which the scrapped equipment could usefully have been employed. This reasoning is only applicable in cases of short-period lapses in demand. Moreover, if the redundant equipment is ever to be used again, such a procedure would also raise the average cost of production by advancing the date of replacement of worn-out plant and equipment—a dubious policy aim. Assuming no implicit cartelization, this behavior would spell havoc for every businessperson who acted accordingly. Profit maximizers, acting individually, would keep their redundant equipment and produce at lower average cost in the future. Keynes's reasoning assumes two contradictory behavioral modes: a collective, organized effort to raise marginal prices and competitive pricing behavior equating marginal cost with prices.

The concept of user cost is useful as long as prices are determined by demand conditions affecting a fixed or quasi-fixed factor—that is, in the determination of rent or quasi-rent. Its present discounted value is the price of capital as determined by its future profit possibilities, not by its cost of production. As soon as the price of production of capital as a renewable factor of production comes into play, then this factor will be employed up to the point where its marginal-revenue product is equal to marginal cost, independent of profit opportunities already exploited. It can clearly be argued (with Marshall) that a plant of a given size has in the short run the characteristics of a nonrenewable resource, but then price determination cannot be purely competitive, since there are barriers to entry in the short run. Furthermore, as soon as the fixed character of equipment is acknowledged, elements of increasing returns to scale due to lower overhead costs are present. User cost is a sensible concept only when changes in demand are assumed to be more frequent than changes in productive capacity—in other words, when adjustment costs are assumed that make capacity adjustments costly.

Returning to the original argument of Keynes's microeconomic framework, the concept of user cost is a nice example of his tendency to mix elements of pure competition and monopoly without proceeding to a synthesis. The principle of rising marginal cost in connection with increases in output is saved, or so it seems, even for cases of excess capacity or redundancy, thanks to the complex construction of user cost. This conveniently avoided any direct confrontation with the orthodox theory of Marshall and Pigou. There are other cases of Keynes's tendency to include elements of monopoly or monopolistic competition in his reasoning. The insistence on rising marginal cost is a handy justification for Keynes's intuitive belief that demand increases would lead to price increases. However, his avoidance of the theory of monopolistic competition precluded him from seeing monopolistic price setting, exploiting demand inelasticities, as a possible reason for this phenomenon.

The rising marginal-cost curve is nowhere used in the *General*

Theory as a motivation for the actions or decisions of firms. Although there can be no doubt that Keynes believed in rising marginal costs, they are not linked to any diseconomies intrinsic to the firm. They are the result of two macroeconomic arguments: the homogeneous remuneration of nonhomogeneous factors, and the rising opportunity cost of future profits due to capacity exhaustion. Decreasing returns seem to be a *conditio sine qua non*, but are not an essential part of an integral microeconomic approach. On the contrary, Keynes postulates results that are not attainable under perfect competition, and that are made compatible with decreasing returns only with great difficulty.

One of these postulates is the assumption that profits are a varying residual after wage payments: "Thus if employment increases, then, in the short period, the reward per unit of labour in terms of wage-goods must, in general, decline and profits increase" (ibid., 17). Profits can only increase if entry is restricted in the short term—if firms have some kind of short-term monopoly power. Similarly: "The entrepreneur's income [defined as the excess of finished output sold over prime cost], that is to say, is taken as being equal to the quantity, depending on his scale of production, which he endeavours to maximize, i.e. to his gross profit in the ordinary sense of this term" (ibid., 53–54). This definition has a lot of commonsense appeal, yet it is incompatible with marginal-cost pricing under increasing returns to scale. It rather implies a fixed profit margin per unit of output, as in average-cost-plus-markup pricing.

Elsewhere, Keynes introduces errors in perception in order to justify output expansions greater than those warranted by production under decreasing returns: "For a time at least, rising prices may delude entrepreneurs into increasing employment beyond the level which maximises their individual profits measured in terms of the product. For they are so accustomed to regard rising sale-proceeds in terms of money as a signal for expanding production, that they may continue to do so when this policy has in fact ceased to be to their best advantage; i.e. they may underestimate their marginal user cost in the new price environment" (ibid., 290). It is an open question how the entrepreneurs could ever get accustomed to that kind of behavior. Real increases in demand under perfect competition would lead rather to the entry of new firms than to output expansion over capacity for old ones. Even if one assumes that Keynes refers only to the Marshallian short run, his argument would presume entrepreneurs usually operating below capacity, under increasing returns.

At a later point Keynes assumes that inelasticities in supply create additional profits that accrue entirely to the entrepreneur in the case of increases in demand—again a case in point for monopolistic competition theory, assuming some barrier to entry (ibid., 283). In the same context, he also assumes that an output elasticity of unity with respect to employment is a distinct possibility. This would necessarily imply a constant-returns-to-scale production function (ibid., 284).

Although it is difficult to pin down a definite form of Keynes's microeconomic vision in the *General Theory*, it should be clear that his eclecticism accumulated elements containing implicitly some form of nondecreasing returns, as becomes clear from his assumptions about the behavior of single firms. Instead, he committed himself explicitly to increasing returns. But this failure to provide a coherent vision made the subject less attractive to scientists interested in Keynesianism.

In order to achieve real output increases through increases in aggregate demand, some form of monopolistic competition has to be assumed, at least in the short run. Keynes's superficial yet unyielding commitment to remnants of a Marshallian vision deflected early research in that direction. But such convictions as he had concerning the theory of the firm were not necessarily part of a coherent, encompassing view of economics; this is documented in the article "Relative Movements of Real Wages and Output." In this article, published three years after the *General Theory*, Keynes questions on empirical grounds his earlier assertion that a rise in the level of output will bring about a decline in the real wage due to decreasing returns to additional labor in the short run. He also emphasizes how inconvenient this earlier assumption had been for his own work. This contains, from today's point of view, quite an ironic twist, considering that this assumption had been instrumental in discouraging research in monopolistic competition as a microeconomic rationale for his *General Theory*. His insistence on diminishing returns was a major reason for the abandonment of monopolistic competition theory. An earlier emphasis on the usefulness of increasing returns might have kept it alive as a research project. Keynes even asks explicitly: "Is it the assumption of increasing marginal real cost in the short period which we ought to suspect?" (Keynes 1973, 405). But old habits die hard: "Even if one concedes that the course of the short-period marginal cost curve is downwards in its early reaches, Mr. Kahn's assumption that it eventually turns upwards is, on general common-sense grounds, surely beyond reasonable question; and that this happens, moreover, on a part of the curve which is highly relevant for practical purposes. Certainly it would require more convincing evidence than yet exists to persuade me to give up this presumption" (ibid.). From these considerations he makes a big jump to empirical observations of average-cost-plus-markup pricing, questioning the identity of price and short-run marginal cost due to the "practical workings of the laws of imperfect competition" (ibid., 406). Evidently Keynes did not notice that this would imply a contradiction, by way of the industry structure, of his earlier statements concerning the slope of the marginal-cost curve. His position is all the more confusing because he now also assumes the possibility of constant marginal real costs. Keynes's position remains ambiguous at best, and he refers to future statistical inquiry.

For Keynes, the question of the microfoundations of his general theory did not arise until it was explicitly posed by statistical evidence. Then, even though he saw which kinds of assumptions would better fit his macroeconomic results, he stuck to tradition. This attitude was certainly discouraging to possible inquiries into the relationship between the two theoretical approaches. Keynes did not approve of a theory that did not include the assumption of rising marginal cost, even if that meant occasional sacrifices in the plausibility of his own work and occasional assumptions against his own intuition.

CHAPTER 17

How the Chance Was Missed: Keynesians after Keynes

The empirical evidence concerning pricing mechanisms proved to be another strong point against a continuation of research in monopolistic competition theory. After the extensive discussion of Keynes, this point may seem minor, but that would underestimate its psychological impact. The empirical discovery that businesspeople do not set their prices by equating them to short-run average cost, but by pricing them according to average variable or "prime" cost plus an "appropriate" markup to account for overhead costs (known as the full-cost principle), had caused confusion in the ranks of British economists.

This result had been established in a project undertaken by the Oxford Economists Research Group, and had been published in a 1939 article by R. L. Hall and C. J. Hitch, "Price Theory and Economic Behaviour." It consisted of a series of interviews with thirty-eight businesspeople (thirty-three of them from manufacturing establishments) regarding their pricing policies and the rationales underlying them. In these interviews almost all of the participants proclaimed their adherence to the full-cost principle. Empirically, a tendency toward price stability was discernible that found its graphical expression in the kinked demand curve.

Roy Harrod vividly described in the foreword to his *Economic Essays* the shock that these findings caused for economists working in monopolistic competition theory. Overnight, the redeveloped tool of marginal revenue lost its sharpness. A theoretical approach that had set out to bring economic theory closer to economic reality saw itself reduced to academic shadowboxing: "What the theory of imperfect competition . . . did was to vary the assumptions, so as to bring them nearer reality in that part of the field in which competition was not perfect . . . What the Oxford interviews suggested was that these new assumptions, on which high hopes had been built, were still deplorably far removed from the reality" (Harrod 1952, viii–ix). That perfect-competition theory was based on equally weak assumptions provided little consolation. Chamberlin's gloating that he had never made extensive use of the marginal-revenue curve is just as ill justified because he derived the same results through an analytically equivalent yet more cumbersome procedure; his denial of having had full profit maximization as an underlying principle in *The Theory of Monopolistic Competition* is unconvincing (Chamberlin 1957, 271).

Harrod himself had been rather disingenuous in this affair, and had overemphasized the importance of the findings. As a member of the Oxford Research Group he had participated in the research and expounded its results in a speech given in 1937 before Section F of the British Association. What is more, he had given a first authoritative interpretation of the results in a "tentative essay in economico-ethical thought," as he called it, in which he implied that the abandonment of the principle of profit maximization was a necessary consequence of the research findings: "It has been impossible not to be struck by the devastating completeness of entrepreneurs' uncertainty about matters usually assumed to be known in the text-books" (Harrod 1939, 5). References to the importance of "fair," "just," "equitable" pricing as the result of moral rules of conduct, and his positive attitude toward it, speak of more than a little remnant of corporatist thinking in Harrod.

It seems that the psychological impact was greater than necessary. As Lorie Tarshis, among others, pointed out, pricing decisions made by the full-cost principle come close to those made by equating marginal revenue to marginal cost (Tarshis 1983, 3:526). Furthermore, underlying rationales such as fear of entry of new competitors, experience, tacit agreements on the basis of "business ethics," an emphasis on stable markets, and "quasi-moral objections to selling below cost," to use Hall and Hitch's terms, are not only not contradictory to, but the very essence of, long-run profit maximization under monopolistic competition.

The relationship between the theoretical principle of profit maximization as postulated by the economic scientist and the actual realization of this principle was not adequately treated by the members of the Oxford Research Group. The surprise of Harrod and his co-workers about the actual pricing behavior of businesspeople reveals the remarkable ignorance of the academic community in Oxford and Cambridge about the "real" economy, which refused to behave as predicted by the textbooks. Moreover, they were surprised that businesspeople did not behave according to principles they themselves had elaborated only a few years earlier. No one at the time posed the question how businesspeople were supposed to have behaved before the reestablishment of the concept of marginal revenue in 1928.

Two essential things could have helped the theorists to overcome their puzzlement on theoretical grounds. First, following the reasoning employed by Coase regarding the size of the firm, a businessperson will equate at the margin the costs of gathering and processing information, plus the costs of acquiring theoretical knowledge, to the gains to be made from complete profit maximization. Second, even taking into account that the businessperson lacks knowledge of the mechanisms involved in profit maximization, market forces will select those businesspeople who by accident or intuition achieve the correct result.

This aspect of Social Darwinism in the working of a liberal system was expounded with admirable clarity by Heinrich von Stackelberg. Although speaking of the correct mix of factor inputs, his reasoning holds analogously for goods pricing: "Even if he [the entrepreneur] is incapable of finding the most efficient combination of factor inputs with the help of rational calculation—his economic fortune depends on the degree to which he actually succeeds in producing as if he had carried out the marginal calculation. The irrational human talents are here in competition and the winner is the one to whom it is given to solve the problem, not theoretically, but actually" (Stackelberg 1949, 196). Although Stackelberg is here talking about perfect competition, while the study by Hall and Hitch found oligopolistic or monopolistically competitive constellations to be the basis of actual business life, the analogy holds. As noted above, the monopolistic competitor suffers only second-order losses from nonadjustment to optimality. But with sufficiently low barriers to entry, the free flow of capital will force entrepreneurs to a position at least close to profit maximization.

These rather obvious remarks disprove the necessity of the abandonment of the principle of marginal revenue as the basis of theoretical work. Not surprisingly, it has been firmly reestablished as the basis of modern research. Monopolistic competition theory had lost its splendor not only with respect to Keynesian macroeconomics, but also as a convincing representation of economic reality; this was more the result of the overreaction of the academic community than the necessary implication of the research findings. The discussion about marginal analysis did not have to spell the end of monopolistic competition theory; it was renewed several years later on the pages of the *American Economic Review*.

Based on research (by interviews with businesspeople, this time by questionnaire) regarding the employment policies of several dozen firms, Richard Lester rejected the marginal analysis in his 1946 article with the programmatic title "Shortcomings of Marginal Analysis for Wage-Employment Problems." He found that employers do not necessarily reduce the number of employees in the case of a wage increase and that labor/capital ratios remain unchanged. This warranted in his view a rejection of marginal analysis.

The next issue of the *American Economic Review* contained an article by George Stigler that offered a similarly naive view of marginal analysis. In "The Economics of Minimum Wage Legislation," Stigler predicted exactly what had just been empirically refuted by Lester: that increases in the rate of minimum wage would necessarily lead to reductions in employment. Stigler remained staunchly committed to marginalism and subsequently ridiculed Lester for his naive view of marginalism, without acknowledging that it was Stigler's own kind of abstract, purely deductive reasoning, insensitive to empirical evidence, that was indeed most vulnerable to Lester's attacks.

Despite a rather lengthy debate in the next two years in which Henry Oliver, Fred Blum, R. A. Gordon, and Lester intervened on the side of the "antimarginalists," the matter had been righted by Fritz Machlup in "Marginal Analysis and Empirical Research." In addition to questioning the methods of the empirical studies done so far (including the Hall and Hitch study), he stated that marginal analysis was the necessary consequence of the subjective decision to maximize profits (Machlup 1946, 519ff.). He pointed out that the terminology of economists who are concerned about what businesspeople *do* is quite different from that of businesspeople who *think* in entirely different terms. Under this point of view certain forms of average-cost pricing (such as choosing different markups at different outputs) are not only compatible with marginal analysis, but its very consequence (ibid., 540). That employment is not directly responsive to wages can be the result of adjustment lags, constant long-term expectations (which disregard cyclical influences), or near-rationality. Today, efficiency-wage theory would provide a perfect rationale for constant employment when wages change only slightly, without in the least endangering marginal analysis.

Antimarginalists such as Gordon and Blum continued to doubt the usefulness of a rigid marginal analysis for empirical research, but their pleas for a reformulation of economic theory (Gordon 1948, 287) sounded hollow because no convincing alternatives were proposed. Gordon correctly pointed out that the old marginal analysis suffered from the restriction of giving regard only to a few parameters, such as output, that could be adjusted in order to satisfy profit maximization. He is correct—but progress would then consist in qualifying too simple a marginal analysis, not rejecting the principle per se.

Only P. W. S. Andrews undertook the task of constructing a new theory useful for empirical analysis. His attempt, "Industrial Analysis in Economics," is a resurrection of the concept of the Marshallian industry enriched by monopolistic competition theory. In his framework, firms produce under increasing returns to scale in both the short and long run, yet the realization of these internal economies is impeded by a host of factors, among them product differentiation, adjustment costs, the need for newcomers to introduce a product and uncertainty, that together lead the businessperson to behave as if he or she were facing constant costs: "It will, therefore, be very reasonable for a business man to take his present costs as a good guide to his probable costs of production for most increases in output that appear likely" (Andrews 1951, 162). His approach is not unlike the one pursued by Gerald Shove and Dennis Robertson twenty years earlier. Internal economies in the firm are realized, but laden with so many caveats that their realization in a static equilibrium is virtually impossible and constitutes no danger to competitive industry (see chapter 9). In the end his rather free reinterpretation of Marshall ("It must be admitted that all this is a *reading* of Marshall, but it does make sense" [ibid., 155]) is an attempt to reconcile the logical consistency of monopolistic competition theory with the descriptive power and handiness for empirical research of competitive industry.

That Andrews himself was not convinced by the theoretical consistency of his new structure becomes clear when he restricts its use to "general analysis" and "teaching purposes" (ibid., 169), leaving monopolistic competition theory for the few strong enough to approach economics without Marshall's guiding hand. Generally, nothing can be said against a plea for the continuing use of the industry concept for empirical and administrative purposes, but the attempt to connect a new value theory with it must fail: "In the process of making the analysis, however, the supply curve concept has dissolved in the same way as we have earlier suggested occurred on a strict interpretation of Marshall's own analysis" (ibid., 170).

Sraffa had not written in vain. All in all, looking exclusively at the debate over the usefulness of marginal analysis, monopolistic competition theory should have been strengthened rather than weakened by the rather weak arguments of its opponents. As in the case of the Hall and Hitch study, the impression prevails that monopolistic competition fell in disgrace for reasons outside pure scientific logic.

But the pervasiveness of the trend away from monopolistic competition was so strong that Joan Robinson explored alternative approaches in search of microeconomic rationales for Keynesian macroeconomics. In "Rising Supply Price," she resorted to general-equilibrium reasoning in the vein of Sraffa and Hicks in order to dispel the notion that any increase in demand for the goods of a particular industry would have to lead automatically to a rise in their prices. Her results would hold even in the case of production under perfect competition with increasing marginal cost.

Robinson argued that stable or dropping prices become more likely in case of an increase in output when the following conditions are fulfilled: the factor supply is flexible, the industry is small, its factor proportions are different from the economy's average, and there are possibilities of substitution. Along the lines of Alfred Marshall, she stated: "For the general run of manufactured commodities . . . in the perfect competitive world postulated by our assumptions, almost constant supply price would be the rule" (J. Robinson 1941, 8). Despite its positive reception, her article failed to make a strong impact. This was because more attention was given to its methodology of analyzing with comparative-statics methods a competitive industry in a general-equilibrium setting than to its surprising and potentially important result (Viner 1952b, 227; Samuelson 1987, 458).

The negative conclusions regarding research into the combination of monopolistic competition microeconomics and movements in aggregate demand must now be qualified. During the 1930s some researchers were concerned with a link between the two. Nevertheless, the peculiar nature of these contributions gave the impression that monopolistic competition theory had exhausted itself. The first was made by Roy Harrod in 1936, in "Imperfect Competition and the Trade Cycle" and The Trade Cycle. The most important was made by the Polish economist Michael Kalecki, who elaborated a constantly revised and rewritten theory of the business cycle with an underlying oligopolistic industry structure which appeared for the first time in

1937; its most complete formulation came in 1954, in *Theory of Economic Dynamics*. Finally, and strongly influenced by Kalecki, was the Austrian Joseph Steindl, who worked on a long-run version of Kalecki's model. He had met Kalecki at Oxford, where Steindl was employed as a lecturer in statistics from 1938 to 1941.

Unfortunately, all three attempts fall seriously short of fulfilling the analytical standards of contemporary monopolistic competition theory. None of these approaches managed to motivate continuing research in the direction to which they pointed. On the contrary, their ad hoc assumptions in order to justify particular a priori postulated results must have strongly contributed to the impression that monopolistic competition theory had grown sterile, unable to proceed from a few clearly formulated assumptions to testable results.

Admittedly, this claim sounds strange in the case of Roy Harrod, who was at the time a leading authority in the field of monopolistic competition theory. His article is published not in one of the major economic journals of the time but in the lesser *Review of Economic Statistics*. "Imperfect Competition and the Trade Cycle" is looking for a rationale for the "well-known phenomena of the trade cycle" (Harrod 1936b, 84) that profits fluctuate more strongly than prices and wages over the business cycle. The article is pre-Keynesian in the sense that it contains no concept of aggregate demand, nor a discussion of the difference between changes in real prices and changes in money prices.

Harrod's article is based on a series of arguments that each isolate certain aspects of the problem but do not relate them. His most idiosyncratic argument relies heavily on the psychologically motivated idea that demand grows more inelastic in a boom and with rising marginal cost. This is particularly strange in an imperfect-competition framework. But combined with the assumption that rising marginal revenue implies greater total profits, it leads to the following result: "If the amplitude of profit fluctuation is greater than the amplitude of fluctuation in the total income of the community, the ratio of price to average prime cost must rise in the boom and fall in the slump. But the ratio of marginal revenue to marginal cost is assumed to be constant. Therefore the ratio of average prime cost to marginal prime cost must fall in the boom and rise in the slump sufficiently to account for the profit fluctuation and/or the ratio of marginal revenue to price must fall in the boom and rise in the slump" (ibid., 87).

That Harrod assumes rising marginal cost (ibid., 85) is unusual, but his reasoning also holds for constant marginal cost. There are other factors that make his article less than satisfactory. With rising marginal cost and increases in demand, the entry of new firms producing close substitutes could be expected. As firms approach their capacity, demand for the single firm would grow not less but more elastic. This would be in keeping with the ideas of previous writers such as Kahn (and Harrod himself in earlier writings), who saw imperfections, then measured in terms of deviations from capacity output, growing in a slump. Harrod's one-sided approach, which sees imperfection of the market as a purely consumer-determined phenomenon, overlooks the imperfections stemming from barriers to entry—setup costs that can be overcome only if total demand is sufficiently large: "Imperfection of competition is due to habit, inertia, and lack of knowledge. Imperfection is greater, the less the elasticity of demand for the product of a particular entrepreneur" (ibid., 86). His arguments hold only in the absence of entry and if consumers are really willing to pay higher prices in a boom, because they care less about comparing prices. That implies a form of windfall profits for a given number of entrepreneurs. Apart from this, it remains a question how Harrod would motivate the existence of serious imperfections in a regime of rising marginal cost. All in all, the article seems to be an intellectual exercise to justify an assertion postulated a priori, rather than a serious advance of economic knowledge.

Harrod's article was apparently a spin-off of his contemporaneously published book *The Trade Cycle*, in which it is called an extension (Harrod 1936b, 43). The theory of imperfect competition is referred to explicitly in the preface, and it does play some role throughout the work, although it is, with few exceptions, based on firms producing under decreasing returns to scale. Downward-sloping demand curves for single firms account for imperfections in the market. The reasoning is much more straightforward than in the article, and contradicts its curious assertion that the degree of imperfection will be reduced in a depression. Harrod follows the argument conceived by Kahn for a situation of depressed demand: "Obeying the principle that marginal cost must be equated to marginal revenue, he [the 'capitalist producer'] restricts activity; by so doing he may reduce marginal cost—and on this, if he is in perfect competition, he must rely—but more commonly the chief consequence of restriction is to raise marginal revenue above the value it would have if he continued to attempt to dispose of his former quantity of output to an impoverished world" (ibid., 32).

This is the usual, and certainly interesting, idea of a short-run theory of monopolistic competition in connection with a fall in demand as it was mentioned in quite a few British publications at the time: Producers seek to stabilize their revenue by reducing output in order to exploit lower elasticities of demand for smaller quantities, thus becoming able to charge higher prices than otherwise, or the same prices as they charged before the depression set in. Unfortunately, with this single conclusion the concept was usually exhausted. No one inquired whether these output restrictions might in themselves contribute to the persistence of the depression. There were two reasons for this: the almost exclusive concern of theorists was still partial equilibrium, and a theory of aggregate demand was only in its earliest stages.

The only time increasing returns to scale are mentioned in *The Trade Cycle* it is with reference to the phenomenon that Keynes also mentioned in his 1939 article, viz., that under increasing returns increases in demand might actually lower prices instead of raising them: "It is not impossible to imagine a state of affairs in which the Law of *Increasing* Returns operated so strongly throughout . . . [that] the natural tendency to get into a vicious circle of expansion or contraction was only checked by a tendency for prices to fall as output expanded and to rise as output contracted" (Harrod 1936a, 47–48; emphasis in original). But two interesting ideas do not make a theory. Although Harrod's contributions are well worth noting, they are put forward in so isolated a form, disconnected from the ongoing argument, that it is no surprise that these ideas were never again taken up.

The situation is quite different in the case of Michael Kalecki, who attempted in the late 1930s the most elaborate combination to date of a theory of aggregate demand with a microeconomic structure based on monopoly. Theoretically, his approach constituted the only workable alternative to the ending of monopolistic competition theory in the face of the overwhelming interest in Keynesian-style macroeconomics. His work was highly regarded by Joan Robinson, not least for its inclusion of monopolistic competition theory. Writings on Kalecki by Joan Robinson and George Feiwel convey the impression that monopolistic competition theory had thus indeed found a coherent representation, fruitful for further research, which unfortunately only lacked the adequate response of the scientific establishment. George Feiwel writes: "he scored a breakthrough by introducing the degree of monopoly into his dynamic model. His pioneering integration of imperfection and macrodynamic strands of analysis is perhaps one of his most original contributions" (Feiwel 1989a, 51).

A closer look at Kalecki's model, in which effective demand is dependent on the distribution of income and thus on the degree of monopoly, shows that his "theory of the firm" cannot be regarded as a proper continuation of monopolistic competition theory—nor was this Kalecki's intent. His work on the monopolistic firm is an ex post facto construct to rationalize a given degree of markup pricing over marginal cost, rather than a model built on clearly specified behavioral and technical assumptions. Kalecki's Marxist view of a conflictual economic world leads him to the dubious procedure of calculating only wages and raw material costs (variable or prime costs) as costs, whereas "salaries" and capital costs that accrue to capitalists play no role in the pricing process. Thus constant variable cost, due to infinitely elastic supplies, makes for constant average cost, an assumption a priori incompatible with the exercise of monopoly power (see chapter 15): "It is assumed that supply is elastic . . . and that the prime costs . . . per unit of output are stable over the relevant range of output. In view of the uncertainties faced in the process of price fixing it will not be assumed that the firm attempts to maximize its profits in any precise sort of manner. Nevertheless, it will be assumed that the actual level of overheads does not directly influence the determination of price since the total[s] of overhead costs remain roughly stable as output varies" (Kalecki 1954, 12).

Kalecki never specifies the role of overhead costs in the cost/ revenue calculation of the firm. Further, he disregards completely the role of the individual demand curve for the firm. His framework of "semi-monopolistic price formation" is not only not a continuation of work in imperfect or monopolistic competition theory, it leads to gross contradictions if contrasted with any reasoning based on profit-maximizing assumptions. There is no link between Kalecki's ad hoc reasoning and mainstream scientific economics. For instance, he postulates: "Elasticity of supply and stability of unit prime costs over the relevant range of output is incompatible with so-called perfect competition. For, if perfect competition were to prevail the excess of the price p over the unit prime costs u would drive the firm to expand its output up to the point where full capacity is reached" (ibid., 13). Not only is perfect competition quite compatible with constant variable cost as long as overheads are negligible, but any excess of price over average cost would lead to a complete loss of customers. There are several other lapses of the same sort. Prices are formed as a linear combination of unit prime cost and the average price of all firms; prices are supposed to be positively correlated to both of them. This is misleading. A high degree of price correlation, as could be suspected from competitors producing similar goods, actually signals a high markup over unit prime costs and thus a high degree of monopoly. The purely ad hoc character of this pricing procedure is no reason for further criticism, as it is an inevitable consequence of the rejection, without substitution, of the profit-max-imization assumption.

Perhaps it is wrong to subject Kalecki to the standards of main-stream economic science. His theory of the firm sees the firm, implic-itly, as a machine of exploitation of one social class by another, as much as a profit-generating entity operating in contested or contesta-ble markets; thus his disregard for questions of entry. The term *degree of monopoly* is more an expression for the "degree of exploitation" of the worker/consumer than one for stringently defined market power. This is shown by his identification of capitalists' profits with the "degree of monopoly," thus equating questions of income distribu-tion under bargaining with those of industrial organization: "The existence of powerful trade unions may tend to reduce profit margins. A high ratio of profits to wages strengthens the bargaining position of trade unions in their demands for wage increases since higher wages are then compatible with 'reasonable profits' at existing price levels . . . Thus, the degree of monopoly will be kept down to some extent by the activity of trade unions, and this the more the stronger the trade unions are" (ibid., 18).

In Kalecki's view the economy is, at least in the short run, a zero-sum game between capitalists and workers, not between different firms. This radical difference in outlook also kept his more important work on the theory of effective demand in the business cycle outside the academic community. The incompatibility at a theoretical level was not overcome by a sometimes impressive display of statistical evidence in support of his claims. The long-term stability of the ratio of prime cost to proceeds (total revenue) at about three to four has never been sufficiently explained by traditional theory. But an ex post facto rationalization of given data is contrary to the procedure in modern economics to test models derived by making coherent theoretical assumptions about past or future data. For those among the Cambridge scholars who accepted Kalecki's work to some degree, his insistence on constant cost as the relevant basis for pricing con-firmed the results found by the Hall and Hitch study.

The incompatibility of Kaleckian microeconomics with main-stream research has been documented. The argument of Josef Steindl is a little different. Steindl attempted research in a direction similar to that of Kalecki. In fact he explicitly put himself in this tradition by describing Kalecki's economics as a "fairly complete system that is only somewhat open at the 'long-term' end" (Steindl 1976, xiii). What for Kalecki was the "degree of monopoly" is for Steindl the "degree of oligopoly." With a rise in the degree of oligopoly, profit margins rise and effective demand falls (due to capitalists' and workers' different propensities to consume). This leads to a lower degree of capital use and to a slowdown in investment and ultimately in the rate of growth—a potentially self-reinforcing process.

The methodological criticisms mentioned in connection with Kalecki hold in part for Steindl. Yet he is much better acquainted with neoclassical theory than Kalecki is, and he avoids its obvious pitfalls. In the 1945 booklet *Small and Big Business*, he had already demonstrated his approach of presenting modified versions of neoclassical theories and confronting them with statistical data in support of his concepts (although in the latter case he was flogging a dead horse by attacking Marshall's concept of the representative firm in a competitive industry).

In *Maturity and Stagnation in American Capitalism*, Steindl uses statistical evidence to discredit the usual theory of the profit-maximizing firm under monopolistic competition. Citing broad evidence for the existence of excess capacity and price rigidities, he challenges standard monopolistic competition theory for having failed to produce convincing rationales for these facts. His own reasons for the usefulness of excess capacity could be readily integrated into standard frameworks: Steindl sees excess capacity either as a production reserve for demand uncertainties, or as a necessary by-product of the gradual expansion over time of a newcomer to the market (Steindl 1976, 9–10).

The case for price rigidities, or kinked demand curves, is made by quoting the empirical evidence of very low demand elasticities (around −0.3). This makes price cuts unprofitable. Price increases are excluded on the ground of the dangers of new entry—again following reasoning not incompatible with standard theory (ibid., 17). Steindl's book, which was published first in German in 1952, contains well-informed studies about advertising and quality competition before offering to his work on effective demand. He usually proceeds from statistical evidence, and subsequently modifies neoclassical reasoning sufficiently to make it fit the data. Often he uses an informal introduction of dynamic arguments. His book is thus more in the tradition of the industry studies of Berle and Means (see chapter 6), although he commands a thoroughly neoclassical technique. Steindl deserved an earlier translation into English and a warmer reception. It seems, though, that his effort was too far removed from the work of English-speaking scientists, and came too late to connect in any meaningful way with the discussions of Keynes's work. Although in style and motivation not a theoretical economist as that term is usually understood, Steindl did manage a possible integration of monopolistic competition theory and macroeconomics.

It should be clear that Kalecki and Steindl are not "wrong" in any objective, normative sense. Rather, they proceeded along lines of research and in mental frameworks at odds with those of modern economics. What makes their work incompatible with standard research in the neoclassical tradition, for instance in the theory of imperfect competition, is not so much their results, unusual as they were at the time, but their methodology. Indirectly, their work reconfirms Keynes's greatness. He arrived at similar results while proceeding along lines given by the existing mainstream theory, taking neoclassical economists—or at least a number of them—along with him. That his microeconomic foundations are less than convincing is, in this context, of secondary importance.

The sudden demise of monopolistic competition theory in Great Britain resulted from the interaction of three different phenomena. First came the extraordinary influence of Keynes's work and his eclectic and ambiguous relationship to microeconomic foundations. Second, the impact of the Hall and Hitch study on pricing behavior took the wind out of the sails of a movement that had set out to bring economic theory closer to the reality of economic life. The times lacked an analytic mind who would have forcefully reclaimed the principle of profit maximization by relegating average-cost-plus-markup pricing to its proper role: an intuitive rule of thumb for businesspeople unversed in theory, but entirely compatible with the theoretical principle of marginal cost equals marginal revenue. Third, the few attempts at integrating a theory of monopolistic or imperfect competition into the new macroeconomics did not adhere to the abstract standards of the new positivist postulates increasingly applied to research in theoretical economics.

It is with the last two points that the experiences of the British and the American scientific communities intersect. The debate about marginalism and pricing procedures on the one hand and the methodological critique of the positivists on the other combined to strip monopolistic competition theory of its practical relevance as well as its theoretical usefulness. Originally, the antimarginalists and the Chicago school had been seen as antagonists, yet they ultimately combined to undermine the legitimacy of research in monopolistic competition. Monopolistic competition theory had lost its relevance and attractiveness in a much more general way than any of the single debates of the time would suggest.

There is no one mysterious reason that monopolistic competition theory and the theory of aggregate demand did not come together. Such a combination not only might have provided sound micro-foundations for Keynesian macroeconomics, but also might have upheld an interest in monopolistic competition theory. A combination of factors in a concrete historical situation derailed the combined research effort at a stage of consolidation and little excitement. Economists in the meantime were working in government offices, allocating scarce goods according to strategic priorities for the war effort or, in the case of consumer goods, according to general-welfare considerations. In any case they were superseding market forces and thus making discussions about industrial organization obsolete. Just as the coming into existence of monopolistic competition theory was motivated by factors outside purely theoretical considerations, so its end came at a time when problems of economic warfare and monopolistic exploitation became less important than actual warfare and national unity.

After World War II the problem, at least in Europe, was not to curb the power of monopolies but to get production going in any way possible. The defeat of fascism also spelled the end of any corporatist ventures inside more democratic political frameworks. Thus any critique of laissez-faire policies on the ground of deviations from perfect competition lost its force. Elements of it were to reappear, however, in theorizing about the social market economy. The development of monopolistic competition theory shows well how science is determined by a variety of factors inside and outside itself. There exists an inner logic to the development of science, particularly in the movement toward increasingly abstract formulation with the intent to adhere to the norms of positivist science. But this logic does not assert itself in a vacuum; it interacts with the political, economic, and ideological determinants of its time. In the case of monopolistic competition theory, both inner and outer determinants coincided to propel the subject to almost complete dominance of its discipline, and then to push it into disregard only fifteen years later.

· PART V

The Legacy

· CHAPTER 18

Political Legacy

After monopolistic competition theory had ceased to exist as a general research project, it nevertheless retained influence in theoretical research as well as in matters of economic policy. Its influence in economic practice has proceeded indirectly but essentially uninterrupted since the end of World War II, while the developments in economic theory show a different pattern. A widespread loss of interest, leading to a hiatus of more than thirty years, has only recently been followed by a resurgence of interest in a variety of fields where the importance of monopolistic competition for a relevant economic theory is being rediscovered. The influence in policy can be divided into direct references to the theoretical research project and more subtle, indirect links between monopolistic competition theory and political projects, building on its questions and results.

Direct Influences

Monopolistic competition theory helped shape the mood of its time, and was shaped by it. In almost all countries, with the exception of Great Britain, microeconomic policy during the 1930s was to a large degree concerned with competition control. It ranged from the comprehensive framework of Italian corporatists to the purely propagandistic use of theory by German National Socialists and the pragmatic ad hoc references by American New Dealers, to the reluctance of British policymakers to try new methods despite an intense intellectual debate. Though the four countries in question varied widely with respect to the degree of competition control, all four witnessed a tendency to increase rather than to decrease state control over a predominantly liberal private-enterprise economy. In all cases "market failure" and inefficiencies in connection with the monopoly power of single firms were cited as rationales. Yet in implementation, the links between economic policy and theory differed widely.

In Germany, with the National Socialists' rise to power in 1933, economic policy was put completely at the service of the party's extraeconomic objectives. These included the creation of a monolithic one-party state and preparation for an expansive and aggressive foreign policy. Only on a purely formal level was reference made to corporatist structures, in the sense of state-regulated conflict of interest. Part of this propagandistic exercise consisted of the creation of the German Labor Front and the adaption of a Magna Carta of German labor. Ultimately, the measures of the National Socialists were designed to introduce the *Führerprinzip* into the labor market, a restructuring in the form of a military-style hierarchy, which could be easily controlled from the center. References to monopolistic competition theory were used in order to emphasize the drawbacks of free-enterprise systems. There were several attempts inside the National Socialist party to enact corporatist structures, most notably in connection with the *Mittelstandspolitik* (politics in favor of small artisans and traders) of Otto Wagener. But his ideas of breaking up huge private economic entities in favor of a guild system based on the single artisan were already defeated in the planning stage.

The importance of the corporatist experience as a reference point for Italian economic theory and practice has been highlighted above. Certainly, the Italian fascists also abused theory in order to justify an economic system that furthered their political ends, yet the relationship between economic theory and practice was more complex. This was demonstrated, for instance, by the examples given in chapter 4, in which many economists spoke out quite openly on economic problems of the day. Genuine solutions for the conflicts arising out of a still predominantly capitalist economy were demanded by, among others, the syndicalist followers of Edmondo Rossoni.

The claim to be able to organize conflicts of interest under state supervision was vital in the legitimation of a regime that had to compromise with different pressure groups to a much higher degree than its forceful rhetoric would lead one to expect. Thus, theoretical work in monopolistic competition, which at that time in Italy was invariably work in corporatist theory, had tangible effects with the final introduction of corporations in 1934. Although their function was by then mainly restricted to consulting and coordination, the introduction of organized and pervasive competition control was a major victory of corporatist theorists over powerful private interests.

Great Britain was one of the centers of monopolistic competition theory, yet the direct influence of theory during the 1930s remained the lowest among the countries in question here. Of all the sessions of the Economic Advisory Council in the 1930s, not one contained any reference to problems of competition. British economic policy restricted itself to commercial and monetary policy. Internal economic policy amounted to a policy of cheap money, with interest rates around 2 percent and occasional subsidies to faltering industries. Great Britain's recovery proceeded at a slow but steady pace through the 1930s. Undoubtedly, this did not contribute to a possible implementation of competition control. On the other hand, the lack of response to the theoretical work did not provide additional stimulus for research in monopolistic competition theory.

Direct state intervention was limited to isolated, though highly publicized, cases. But throughout the 1930s there was a strong tendency toward monopolization, a tendency that received official blessing with the government's own effort to cartelize coal mining and the iron and steel industries (to name only the most important) in order to help these highly labor-intensive industries over their decline in exports. Price fixing, quotas, and compulsory cartelization were part of these efforts, which were hampered by the contradictory nature of the government's objectives. These efforts did not constitute a breakthrough for monopolistic competition theory. In Great Britain the direct links between monopolistic competition theory and political practice were small or nonexistent.

The United States, on the other hand, implemented, for a short period, policies that seem to have been designed by a theorist concerned about the shortcomings of free competition. Ironically, the theoretical response by economists, as opposed to that of writers interested in sociological and political consequences, was scant. The implementation of widespread competition control sprang from general dissatisfaction with the present state and structure of the economy, rather than from a carefully developed theoretical framework. With the inauguration of the first Roosevelt administration in March 1933 a series of large-scale efforts to overcome the economic crisis was initiated in order to restore profitability and investment on the one hand and purchasing power on the other. Not an easy task, as the two objectives were partly contradictory.

The National Industry Recovery Act of June 1933 was designed to give America's industry an essentially corporatist structure. This was all the more remarkable as competition and antitrust legislation had hitherto been hallmarks of the American way of doing business. Its far-reaching goals were to be achieved by de facto cartelization of 95 percent of American industry. The cartels were to be run according to so-called codes to which employer organizations, unions, and consumer organizations were to contribute. These cartels would assign quotas and fix minimum prices. Employment was to be increased by the introduction of the forty-hour week and additional measures were to promote basic elements of labor legislation such as work safety, collective bargaining, and minimum requirements for working conditions.

Despite big propagandistic and bureaucratic efforts, the NIRA was already a failure due to business resistance, lack of enforcement, and inadequate planning before it was declared unconstitutional by the Supreme Court in May 1935. This spelled the end of actively interventionist policies concerning the competitive structure of American industry. Nevertheless, the NIRA remains the biggest and most coherent attempt to introduce elements designed to improve the results of private laissez faire in a democratic society.

The Social Market Economy

The more indirect influences of monopolistic competition theory are connected with discourses about a social market economy. The case of West Germany, in which this discourse was promoted most explicitly, displays in exemplary manner structural developments that are significant also for the economic policies undertaken after World War II in Italy, Great Britain, the United States, and a host of other countries.

In Germany, a genuine debate took place, initiated by the neoliberals around Walter Eucken. Similarly, there was widespread discussion about the postwar economic order in Italy, yet without partisan voices of comparable stature. In Great Britain postwar economic policy brought big structural changes, largely without reference to theoretical or ideological questions. The United States constitutes something of a counterexample, since continuity with the successful wartime economy was to be preserved. Continental Europe saw a much more intense discussion for two main reasons: the collapse of the old regimes made new beginnings necessary, and despite its connection with these regimes, the corporatist discussion had a heightened awareness of the effects of potential shortcomings of laissez faire.

Despite the orientation of the reconstructed economies in Western Europe toward the American model of an essentially liberal economy, strong concerns remained about the possible pitfalls of competition and an increased tendency to assign responsibilities to national governments. It was agreed that some of the events of the 1930s had had their roots in social shortcomings, such as high unemployment, of the old capitalist system. The new or reemerging democracies designed different means to prevent similar events.

The conviction that labor could not be treated like any other commodity, bought and sold on an anonymous market, was part of this postwar consensus. Workers' rights to form independent unions were generally asserted and often (as in Germany and Italy) constitutionally guaranteed. These results were also influenced by the work on monopolistic competition, which had established on theoretical grounds that workers were partially exploited as long as extra profits were made and adequate representation and bargaining power were lacking. Nonunionized workers would receive only their marginal revenue product as factors of production, but would have to pay average cost plus eventual excess profits as consumers.

In Italy, the constitution of the new "Repubblica antifascista fondata sul lavoro" guaranteed the existence and political power of the labor movement. Protection of labor by law was continuously improved throughout the postwar years. Furthermore, the state controlled up to 40 percent of Italian industry through a variety of state holdings, most important among them the Istituto per la Ricostruzione Industriale (IRI). The state-owned enterprises were often in the forefront of the implementation of new social measures such as workers' representation on the shop-floor level.

Great Britain resisted the trend to heightened state interference in the economy during the 1930s. But after the wartime experience with planning, the mood was more propitious for an interventionist economic policy. In 1945 a Labour government under the premiership of Clement Attlee had come to power. With the 1942 Beveridge Report as a blueprint for social policy and with Keynesian demand-management theories as a theoretical foundation, it undertook the task of a restructuring of Great Britain's war-torn economy, which had become largely dependent on American lend-lease aid.

Their ambitious policies included the creation of the British welfare state (at its core, the National Health Service), the nationalization of the Bank of England and of several key industries, and the creation of development councils, which attempted to direct private investment according to the priorities of social planners and not of monopolistically competitive businesspeople. The results were mixed. In the short run, Labour policies managed to stabilize an economy in the face of huge international commitments; in the long run, it seems that too rigid a system of industrial organization prevented structural adjustments to changing demand and income patterns. The events in Great Britain owe more to a shift toward heightened state responsibility, stemming from an increase in the awareness of social shortcomings, than to a theoretical concern about monopolistic competition. But monopolistic competition theorists such as Joan Robinson and Nicholas Kaldor had for years emphasized in their circles of political and academic discussants the unlikeliness of perfect competition and thus the unlikeliness of its desirable optimality results.

The United States was indeed fairly free from major state interference after the war. Its successful war economy, in combination with military victory, gave its liberal economy the character of a model for Europe, victors and vanquished alike. But even in the United States, the government retained some important means of furthering its objectives. There was first the government sector, with around a quarter of the gross national product (considerably higher during wartime), which allowed discretion in macroeconomic variables and resource allocation. Second, there was the extensive antitrust legislation designed to enforce a competitive order aimed at bringing maximum benefit to consumers. Based on the Sherman Act (1890) and the Wheeler-Lea Act (1938), the Celler-Kefauver Act (1950) tried to limit the possible damage of the market power of industrial conglomerates. But the effectiveness of these laws was and is hampered by the reluctance of various administrations to pursue them and of courts to implement them. The legacy of monopolistic competition theory in the United States is small, at best.

The case of Germany was quite different. There, an organic development from monopolistic competition theory to the theory and practice of a social market economy took place. Heinrich von Stackelberg was an integral part of this process. The most influential theoretician of the social market economy was the head of the Freiburg school of German neoliberalism and founder of the yearbook *Ordo*, Walter Eucken. Like Stackelberg, he took the lessons of monopolistic competition theory and integrated them into the basic principles of the new economic order. Taking a middle stand between the German historical and the Anglo-Saxon and Austrian neoclassical schools, Eucken's chief concern was with the accumulation of economic power, whether in private or in public hands. The ultimate objective of economic policy is to assure by an integrated legal and societal framework a competitive order that comes as close as possible to the ideal of perfect competition: "The problem of economic power can only be solved by an intelligent coordination of all economic and legal policy. Laws relating to joint stock companies, for instance, should avoid anything that encourages growth of undertakings to proportions beyond what is compatible with technical efficiency; and patent legislation, all too often used in support of monopolies, should once again be made to serve only its true purpose" (Eucken 1951, 54). Eucken develops an institutional framework in order to keep the losses from monopoly elements in the economy to an absolute minimum. Barriers to entry were to be severely limited. In addition, the state was to engage in structural measures for the enhancement of competition, such as facilitating transportation, the technical development of substitutes, and an increased flexibility of capital. The state was not to engage in the economic process itself, but would determine and guarantee the form of this process.

Another important theoretician, and the creator of the expression "social market economy," is Alfred Müller-Armack. He emphasized that the neoliberal school, to which he, Eucken, and Stackelberg belonged, is based on the principles of classical liberalism but widened by a strong emphasis on social problems. The market is still the reference point for all economic activity, with the crucial restriction that labor is not a commodity like any other. State interference in the economic process is not shunned per se (which is a slight shift in emphasis from the general principles outlined by Eucken), but the important criterion for its acceptance is *Marktkonformität* (conformity with the market). As an example, consider housing rents. Rent ceilings are to be rejected, but rent subsidies for the needy are acceptable (Müller-Armack 1956, 12:391).

In West German policy after World War II, these theoretical elaborations were largely implemented. The state limited its direct intervention in the economy to the planning and execution of fiscal and monetary policy. The West German welfare state included relatively high unemployment benefits. Moreover, the state encouraged capital formation for low- and middle-income families. Workers' codetermination at the enterprise level and factory councils at the shop-floor level allowed the participation of the labor force in the decision-making processes of the economy. Unions were important not only in collective bargaining, but also as partners in the *konzertierte Aktion* (concerted action), in which government, capital, and labor tried to build consensus on economic policy issues. This consensus-based policy has been essentially carried over into the new postunification Germany.

Competition control was regulated by the law against limitations on competition, which regulated all markets except the labor market. The law prohibited any market concentration higher than 33 percent for a single firm. Cartel authorities reviewed every important merger and referred their judgment to the minister of economics, at whose discretion action would be taken. Recent experience shows that the actual handling of this procedure might still conform to the letter of the law, but runs counter to its spirit.

All in all, even the phenomenon of the social market economy cannot be reduced simply to a direct result of monopolistic competition theory, since a host of different considerations of an ethical and political nature played a role in its creation. Also, the concern with monopolistic competition was primarily a theoretical endeavor, and, despite the political and social awareness of its participants, not a blueprint for interventionist policies. Nevertheless, it is on the social market economy that the work of a generation of theoretical economists left its most visible and successful mark. It remains to be seen whether the resurgent theoretical interest in monopolistic competition theory will yield policies beyond those described above. Trade, research, and industrial policy at large have become highly sensitive areas due to the presumed existence of increasing returns. If historical precedent is any guideline, then the emerging awareness of new problems goes hand in hand with the theoretical attempts to provide new answers.

CHAPTER 19

Theoretical Legacy

The theoretical legacy of the work on monopolistic competition is difficult to assess. The symptoms of and the reasons for the demise of monopolistic competition theory have been discussed above. After the attacks of the Chicago school and the triumph of Keynesianism, monopolistic competition theory proper was largely sustained by the persistence of Edward Chamberlin. Yet his work during the 1950s was far from innovative, remaining mainly an exposition, clarification, and reassertion of existing results. Apart from that, there was little or no theoretical work in thirty years following 1941 that could rightly claim to be an extension of monopolistic competition theory, in the sense of a coherent research project. Monopolistic competition theory survived only as an affair for specialists in different camps.

The situation today is markedly different, as monopolistic competition is again an object of interest in several areas in theoretical economics. But the different research agendas are taking place without any reference to the attempts to construct a comprehensive alternative framework to perfect-competition microeconomics as envisaged in the 1930s. The approaches outlined below are largely independent of each other and only rarely refer to each other.

The specialists concerned with monopolistic competition may be grouped into four different streams of research—the classic, the game-theory, the general-equilibrium, and the near-rationality approaches. In addition, there is renewed interest in a variety of fields in the subject of increasing returns to scale and its implications. The classic approach provides the closest continuity with the original research. Having experienced a period of extremely limited attention confined mainly to Chamberlin's almost single-handed defense, it received new and intense notice in the 1970s and is continued today mostly in the form of research on spatial competition.

Endogenous growth theory and trade theory are two of the areas in which the interest in increasing returns has prompted researchers to make extensive use of concepts originally developed in the first quarter of the century. Research in endogenous growth theory has even revitalized the old Marshallian concept of the effects external to the firm and internal to the industry allowing for downward-sloping competitive supply schedules due to positive spillover effects in technology and knowledge, thus following Arrow's insight into the economics of "learning by doing" (Sala-i-Martin 1990, 8). The New International Economics instead centers on product differentiation between large international firms to explain trade under increasing returns without the complete specialization of either country.

The near-rationality approach has gained considerable interest among macroeconomists in recent times. From a historical point of view, it comes close to the original intentions of earlier monopolistic competition theorists because of two factors: first, its concern with a general model of behavior of the firm that exhibits clearly definable welfare implications; and second, its concern with policy questions. Clearly, these approaches are not yet fully developed. They deserve a more coherent formulation, which would include, for instance, aspects of product differentiation and interfirm relationships under increasing returns to scale. The latter point especially should—in principle—greatly facilitate the achievement of Keynesian results as intended by Mankiw, Akerlof and Yellen, and Hart.

During the period of academic and intellectual exile beginning in the 1940s, the most vigorous vein of research fed by problems of monopolistic competition was (until recently) game theory. It was the only area of note in which problems of increasing returns and competition between firms with limited monopoly power were discussed. It takes up the theoretical arguments of the interaction of oligopolistic competitors begun by Cournot, Bertrand, Hotelling, and Stackelberg. The classic text on game theory, John von Neumann and Oskar Morgenstern's *Theory of Games and Economic Behavior*, appeared at a time when monopolistic competition theory seemed to have exhausted itself. In a limited way, game theory was a product of the decline of general monopolistic competition theory; it took certain clearly defined problems of monopolistic competition and refined them to a high degree.

No assessment of the vast literature on games between strategically interacting competitors can be undertaken in this context. By its very nature the theory of games is linked to the idea of monopolistic competition, since under perfect competition no strategic interdependence exists. The argument that game theory is not concerned with the construction of a comprehensive theory is gratuitous, since its research is geared toward the elucidation of unique constellations. Although game theory has taken up some important features of monopolistic competition, it is regrettable that it has little to say about the claim of monopolistic competition theory to be a general representation of economic behavior.

With regard to the analytical determination of a point after which taking strategic interaction into account becomes sensible for profit-maximizing firms, d'Aspremont, Gabszewicz, and Thisse elaborate an important result in "On Hotelling's 'Stability in Competition,'" their 1979 reevaluation of Hotelling's 1929 paper. They showed that there is a quantitatively definable measure of closeness (product differentiation) at which strategic interaction of the Bertrand type takes over, replacing monopolistic competition of the usual nonstrategic Cournot-Nash type. Thus there seems to be a definable point at which firm interaction becomes strategic. If firms are too close to each other their specific actions become subject to game theory; if they are close, yet not too close, their behavior would be the subject of a more general theory of monopolistic competition.

Game theory, with its purified concepts of profit-maximizing agents in frictionless environments, moves away from the intentions of researchers for whom general economic reality had at all times constituted the benchmark for economic theory. There is another significant difference between game-theory research and what has been called monopolistic competition theory proper. The latter had in mind a series of interconnected firms with a potentially unlimited number of competitors who were all to a small degree affected by the decisions of any one firm. Thus only in particular cases would it be worthwhile to develop conjectures about rivals' behavior and to adjust one's own output accordingly. The treatment of the demand curve (and thus of rival behavior) was hardly explicit at the time. Much more important were questions of welfare and policy, which are treated in game-theory research only in passing, if at all. Thus game theory can only in an abstract sense be seen in theoretical continuity with research on monopolistic competition. Significantly, despite their close succession in time, there is no personal continuity whatsoever between the two areas of research.

Thus only the general-equilibrium approach and the classic approach can be truly considered continuations of the theory of monopolistic competition as envisaged by Sraffa and his followers in the 1930s. They are witness to the fact that monopolistic competition theory is a subject worthy of research beyond an arbitrarily formulated downward-sloping demand function or some assumption, not of increasing returns to scale.

The Classic Approach and Spatial Economics

The classic approach is mainly a development of Chamberlin's continuing work in the theory of monopolistic competition. It was taken up with refined techniques and renewed analytical ambition in the late 1970s and received a general formulation by Kelvin Lancaster in 1979. Recent research in spatial economics has also clarified this line of inquiry. It continued the concepts and issues that had characterized the original research and so can claim continuity with the events of the 1930s and their extension by Triffin. The emphasis on descriptive realism connected with the Chamberlinian approach led in the late 1950s and early 1960s to an inquiry into the economic aspects of advertising and selling costs. This research involved a series of economists, among them Lester Telser, George Stigler, Nicholas Kaldor, and Edward Chamberlin. Despite some important insights into the effects of advertising (such as its potential enhancement of competition due to the wider distribution of knowledge), no general results were reached. The complicated interplay of unpredictably manipulated consumer preferences and increased average costs allowed either only the most abstract general statements or case by case ad hoc reasoning, but no broadly testable formulation.

In 1959, Harold Demsetz developed an extension of this approach by showing that the efficiency results from Chamberlin's model are ambiguous and that excess capacity is not a necessary implication. His main advance was the integration of selling costs as a third parameter besides price and quantity into the profit-maximizing decisions of the firm, with the help of price/selling-cost isoquants for given quantities. His argument relies on an initially upward-sloping demand curve due to the effectiveness of advertising at low outputs. Combined with the homogeneity of products and the absence of indivisibilities, firms will indeed produce at the lowest average cost point, although not necessarily at the lowest average production cost point. For all its ingenuity, Demsetz's construction suffers from serious disadvantages by not accounting for product differentiation or indivisibilities, two main features of monopolistic competition.

Advertising makes his firms behave as perfect competitors at a higher total average cost.

Chamberlin's lame and belated "Nature of Equilibrium in Monopolistic Competition: Reply to Mr. Demsetz," published in 1964, restricts itself to a defense that points out that similar results had been mentioned as a chance possibility in *The Theory of Monopolistic Competition*. After the death of Chamberlin, the main proponent of the classic approach, in 1965, there was a definite gap. These are the years of Milton Friedman and Robert Lucas, and monopolistic competition theory was most definitely outmoded. Surprisingly, in the mid-1970s a series of papers appeared that explored the problems defined by the work of Chamberlin in a new and creative fashion. "Product Selection, Fixed Costs, and Monopolistic Competition," by Michael Spence, published in 1976, and "Monopolistic Competition and Optimum Product Diversity," by Avinash Dixit and Joseph Stiglitz, published in 1977, are the two most important examples of a new line of research, which not only took up the technical features of monopolistic competition, but also addressed one of its most pressing underlying concerns—the question of efficiency (Pareto optimality) in general and the related trade-off between product diversity and increasing returns in particular. The final question turned out to be: is it better to produce many goods with many small firms and few economies of scale, or few goods with few large firms and large-scale economies?

Spence begins his analysis with a benchmark case in which a monopolistic competitor of the Chamberlinian type is able completely to discriminate in prices and is thus able to appropriate the entire consumer surplus of his goods. Clearly in such a case a market equilibrium would also be optimal, since any good for which total utility is higher than total production cost would be produced. This starting point conditions his subsequent analysis. He writes: "since revenues accurately reflect social benefits under price discrimination, there is some reason to believe that revenues without price discrimination will *not* reflect social benefits and may not cover costs for socially valuable products" (Spence 1976, 220; emphasis in original). His subsequent analysis is driven by the underlying assumption that a higher number of goods automatically achieves a higher level of welfare. Thus the existence of fixed costs implies a general tendency toward too few goods. In particular, he argues, this holds for goods that have difficulty extracting the entire consumer surplus, such as complementary goods (which cannot extract the additional marginal utility they impute to the use of other goods) and for goods with a low elasticity of demand, where a tangency solution implies a relatively larger proportion of nonextractable consumer surplus.

The analysis suffers from one major drawback: the idea of a fully extractable surplus biases Spence toward considering product variety a uniquely positive feature, much in the tradition of Chamberlin. Unfortunately, his elaborate demand functions do not contain variety as an argument, except through the mechanism of complementarity, yet this is fully outweighed by corresponding substitutability. This does not allow him to compare eventual gains from increased variety to gains from increased scale use in fewer firms. His producer-centered analysis also does not allow him to think of a pooling of resources by consumers in order to finance large-scale production units through the mechanism of lump-sum subsidies. But Spence's paper allowed Dixit and Stiglitz to proceed one step further.

They try explicitly to remedy the shortcomings of Spence's paper by avoiding its complete price discrimination. Their model shows that the market equilibrium of monopolistic competitors producing at the point of tangency between the average-cost curve and the demand curve is also socially optimal (in the sense of a second-best solution), as long as no subsidies are available. In this case also the product diversity is optimal, since it enables the resulting number of firms to fulfill their budget constraints given *arbitrary* fixed costs. Again they avoid the crucial point by not comparing their results to other possible equilibria with redistributed fixed investments. The equilibrium conceived by Dixit and Stiglitz contains the maximum number of firms with a minimal fixed investment. Their underlying a priori assumption that product variety is positive in every case in which it is feasible is now more explicit than in the case of Spence, yet it is still displayed in the form of an absolute qualitative bias—more is better—and not in a form that would allow the optimal quantitative trade-off between variety and scale economies: "We therefore take a direct route, noting that the convexity of indifference surfaces of a conventional utility function defined over the quantities of all potential commodities already embodies the desirability of variety. Thus a consumer who is indifferent between the quantities (1, 0) and (0, 1) of two commodities prefers the mix (½, ½) to either extreme" (Dixit and Stiglitz 1977, 297). True enough, yet hardly relevant. Their remark displays a surprising nonchalance about the phenomenon of scale economies. In order to assess the effects of the desirability of variety, the pure existence of convexity of preferences is not enough, but the degree of convexity is relevant, as convexity is contrasted with nonsatiation. The desire for variety has to be weighed against the desire for increased quantity. In other words, will their hypothetical consumer prefer (½, ½) or (3, 0) as resources are pooled to enable greater scale economies? They do not provide an answer. Like Spence's, their implications follow certain initial assumptions: "when variety is desirable, i.e. when the different products are substitutes, it is not in general optimal to push the output of each firm to the point when all economies of scale are exhausted . . . Thus our results undermine the validity of the folklore of excess capacity" (ibid., 301). It is correct that convexity and the ensuing desirability of variety act as a counterforce to the desirability of an exhaustion of scale economies, yet it leaves the determination of the optimal use of capacity open. Dixit and Stiglitz are at their most compelling not in their general results but in a magisterial discussion of several asymmetric (heterogeneous) cases. For instance, they confirm Spence's result of a tendency of the market toward goods with elastic demands; they argue convincingly that in certain cases a banishment of the production of good A (elastic) would raise total welfare as it would enable the profitable production of the substitute B (inelastic), which displays a higher consumer surplus, yet lower profit possibilities. Clearly these cases already depend on the specific forms of the demand and production functions.

Due to the unwillingness to conceptualize product variety in a meaningful way, both papers ultimately do not provide satisfactory answers to the questions they set out to answer. Nevertheless, all three authors deserve enormous credit for having provided a formalization of the model world of Chamberlin, Robinson, and their colleagues beyond an equilibrium of the firm with subsequent ad hoc conjectures. It was left to Kelvin Lancaster to provide answers to their questions. Lancaster understood that the question of optimal product differentiation had to be explicitly linked to some measurable argument of the utility function reflecting the appreciation of variety, and at the same time to the technical determinants of the production function reflecting the possibilities of large-scale production of fewer commodities.

Lancaster's analysis in *Variety, Equity, and Efficiency* is long and cumbersome, and its modeling requirements are satisfied only through a large effort of abstraction, yet it remains the only research so far that derives clear-cut conditions for optimum diversity. It has the ambitious aim of studying an economy of monopolistic competition in all its aspects. Lancaster assumes a preset welfare level at which each consumer receives his or her most preferred good in any "segment" of the product market. If the preferred good is not produced, the consumer will be compensated through additional quantities of the produced goods in the same segment. The size of the segments, in each of which only one good is produced, is defined by the number of segments over the whole continuous preference spectrum. The corresponding equilibrium condition states that the elasticity of the compensating function (depending on the average distance from the good actually produced, and thus on segment size) must be equal to the elasticity of the production function. Thus outside equilibrium, it is either profitable to increase scale production and increase segment size (bigger outputs, but also bigger compensation payments) or vice versa. On the point that there still will be excess capacity at the optimum, Lancaster writes: "To a considerable extent the debate has been rendered moot by the analysis given here, which shows that there will be 'excess capacity' at the optimum configuration . . . and thus that no normative significance can be attached to production at minimum average cost" (Lancaster 1979, 214). This confirms Dixit and Stiglitz by giving their conjecture a firm analytical basis.

Despite this important result, Lancaster's model of "segments" is not of unlimited use. Stability requires specific boundaries on the substitutability of the good inside a segment and outside goods once the general model attempts to integrate the decisions of profit-maximizing agents. Lancaster's work is not the definite formulation of monopolistic competition, yet it is clearly the most comprehensive and thorough attempt to provide a general model. As such, it lends itself quite naturally as a bridge to another area of monopolistic competition research that has recently received increasing attention: spatial economics.

Having arisen out of the work of von Thünen, the problems connected with the spatial differentiation of economic activities received a first abstract formulation in Harold Hotelling's seminal 1929 paper "Stability in Competition." Since then, spatial economics has held an intrinsic interest for the researcher of monopolistic competition, as many features of monopolistic competition receive an intuitively more approachable formulation when characteristics' surfaces can be thought of as geographical planes. Not only can spatial distance be a useful metaphor for distance in product characteristics, but transport costs can be conceptualized as the compensation payments in Lancaster's model, yielding equivalence between goods of otherwise different utility per unit. The location theorist David Starrett points out that there is an even more fundamental link between the two approaches, namely the existence of increasing returns to scale:

"in a world of uniform exogenous resources, all the essentials of location theory are tied to the presence of non-convexities (more specifically, to the presence of economies of scale)" (Starrett 1973, 418). In the light of the preceding discussion about optimal product choice and issues of equilibrium and optimality, "zoning" provides a convenient way for the social planner to conceptualize attempts to improve on inefficient market outcomes. Price discrimination according to geographical distance is not only more easily accomplished than the usually discussed form of discrimination according to individual marginal utility, but also far more frequently encountered in practice (Scotchmer and Thisse 1992, 278).

There are also clear differences. In product characteristics, space substitutability between products is usually assumed as smooth; in geographical space, substitution is discontinuous as soon as transport costs are lower than price differences and firms are thought of as being located along a straight line. (This relates to the point that d'Aspremont and his colleagues found faulty in Hotelling's original analysis.) These discontinuities are made possible because—technically speaking—spatial economics has no immediately equivalent concept to that of the convexity of preferences in general economics, since products are usually assumed to be identical except for their differences in transport costs. Similarly, concerns of spatial theory such as capitalization of land values and the optimal provision of local public goods are not primary concerns of the original research project, although they could rather easily be integrated into monopolistic competition theory.

The somewhat contradictory result must be noted: monopolistic competition theory in its classic form is, after a period of near-extinction, alive again. Yet despite Lancaster's admirable efforts, the formalization of a sufficiently rich general model, robust enough to be applicable to a large number of constellations, still eludes researchers. Even though spatial economics does not contribute any distinctive concept that could not also be integrated into the analysis with the help of alternative formulations, it seems to provide at this point the ideal allegory for problems of monopolistic competition—abstract enough to derive general results, concrete enough to allow the conceptualization and even quantification of some of the problems of monopolistic competition that prove elusive as soon as they are formulated in a completely general fashion. It would not be surprising if spatial economics were to prove the more fertile ground for the imagination of researchers in monopolistic competition in the near future. Monopolistic competition theory has always made its greatest progress when striking a balance between abstract analysis and descriptive realism, and spatial economics corresponds to this dichotomy. The classic approach—and with it the main legacy of the original research, after periods of repetition, neglect, revival, and transformation—is alive.

The General Equilibrium Approach

The general-equilibrium approach in monopolistic competition theory often sees itself, in its presentation and formulation, as continuing the issues debated in the 1930s. It refers frequently to the work of Edward Chamberlin. One of the most important contributions by Oliver Hart, for example, is called "Monopolistic Competition Theory in the Spirit of Chamberlin: A General Model." Despite the debatable foundation of some of these claims, it is the one field of research that strives to provide monopolistic competition with an analytical framework of equivalent conceptual importance to that of perfect-competition theory, namely the proof of the existence of a general equilibrium. The latter is of paramount importance, since it would make possible the fulfillment of the theoretical postulate of positivist economic science—that is, the capability of formulating predictions on the basis of an existing equilibrium.

The approach taken by the researchers in general-equilibrium theory frequently starts from an implicit framework of perfect competition, which is subsequently extended to include elements of monopolistic competition. This tends to obscure the fundamental dichotomy between the two, which had been insisted on by the original monopolistic competition theorists. Absent in this brief overview is work by Takashi Negishi, Kenneth Arrow, and Frank Hahn on monopolistic competition with firms acting according to subjective or "perceived" demand curves—mainly because it lacks any theoretical justification for agents forgoing real profit opportunities by not acting according to their real or objective demand curves. Concerning such models, Roberts and Sonnenschein comment: "Of course, these perceived curves are completely ad hoc, although one might attempt to construct a theory to explain them. Within such a theory, however, one would presumably want to allow for learning leading to the perceived curves more and more closely approximating the true relationships. In this case, one is confronted again with the original problem of non-existence [as in the case of objective demand curves]" (Roberts and Sonnenschein 1977, 111).

General-equilibrium theorists sometimes wrongly transfer results from perfect competition theory to a theory of monopolistic competition, as defined in chapter 2. This is demonstrated, for instance, in William Novshek's 1980 article "Cournot Equilibrium with Free Entry." After proving in his Theorem 2 the correctness of the Folk theorem (the approximate validity of the assumptions of perfect competition as firm size shrinks with respect to market size), he states with regard to monopolistic competition: "It should be noted that Theorem 2 is true even when average cost is always decreasing, so long as marginal cost is not decreasing for all sufficiently large outputs (e.g., with a fixed cost plus marginal cost)" (Novshek 1980, 484). While falling short of direct error, Theorem 2 nevertheless becomes meaningless under those amended conditions. As was well known to Sraffa in 1926 (not to mention Cournot in 1838), the ratio of the size of the firm to that of the market will stay bounded away from zero as long as firms compete under increasing returns to scale in homogeneous markets. Furthermore, the postulated concept of free-entry equilibrium becomes meaningless for a case in which fixed costs are necessary for production, for fixed costs are a barrier to entry.

The difficulties of a general-equilibrium theory of monopolistic competition were first explicitly formulated by John Roberts and Hugo Sonnenschein in 1977 in "On the Foundations of the Theory of Monopolistic Competition." In brief, their argument runs as follows: the usual existence proof for general equilibrium involves the application of the Kakutani fixed-point theorem. This requires the upper-hemicontinuity of the response correspondence (or the continuity of the reaction function for single-valued functions) of the agents. This condition is met only so long as a firm does not face several disjoint profit-maxima at different outputs for a given rival behavior. (Continuous profit-maxima over a range of outputs do not pose a problem, since they only constitute the step from reaction function to response correspondence.) In more usual economic formulations, the concavity of a firm's profit function in its own outputs is required. Only this makes unequivocal optimization of the profit function possible and yields continuous reaction functions in the case of Cournot competition between firms. Roberts and Sonnenschein show that the continuity of the reaction function (and thus the existence of equilibrium) might not be guaranteed in the case of two firms with costless production.

Roberts and Sonnenschein's counterexamples have been rightly criticized by Oliver Hart for their assumption that firms are maximizing profits, even when this is not in the interest of owners who are the only consumers of the goods produced (Hart 1984, 112n). It is not clear whether the discontinuity of the reaction functions depends on these "feedback effects." For a large class of profit functions the objections of Sonnenschein and Roberts do not hold so long as Cournot behavior is assumed. In any case, the problem of assuring concavity of the profit function and thus a nonpositive second derivative lies solely with the demand function. Taking the second derivative of a generic profit function (as total revenue minus total cost), it becomes clear that the second derivative of total cost is positive (after the minus sign) so long as marginal cost is not decreasing.

Even if Roberts and Sonnenschein's examples should eventually reveal themselves to be inconsistent, their objections focus on a critical point in the general-equilibrium theory of monopolistic competition. It remains to be decided whether the class of demand functions to be excluded due to the continuity requirements of the reaction functions is indeed large enough to warrant the abandonment of the research project. One possibility for rescue, the application of mixed strategies in the case of several disjoint profit-maxima, was explored by Dasgupta and Maskin in 1986.

The most prominent researcher in the field of monopolistic competition in general equilibrium has undoubtedly been Oliver Hart, with a series of papers all of which attempt (in various ways) to satisfy the continuity requirements formulated by Roberts and Sonnenschein, and thus to continue research on the existence of monopolistic competition equilibria. His paper "A Model of Imperfect Competition with Keynesian Features" was discussed in chapter 15. His assumption of a decreasing-returns technology is precisely motivated by the need to guarantee the existence of a Nash equilibrium, since he is reluctant to put stronger conditions on the demand function in order to ensure concavity of the profit function (Hart 1982a, 136–37).

In order to prove the uniqueness of a profit maximum, his procedure is as follows: If there is a profit maximum at price p (in the sense that marginal cost equals marginal revenue), then it is unique because marginal revenue is strictly increasing in prices and marginal cost is strictly falling in prices (due to reduced output). Thus no other profit maximum will be achievable, concavity of the profit function is assured, and profit maximization will yield Nash equilibrium. With the postulation of decreasing returns to scale (increasing costs), the mathematical needs of proof override any attempt at coherence with what is usually understood by monopolistic competition. To put conditions on the demand function in order to guarantee uniqueness of a profit maximum would have been closer to the spirit of monopolistic competition.

In at least three more instances, Hart has elaborated on monopolistic competition in a general-equilibrium setting. In the 1979 article "Monopolistic Competition in a Large Economy with Differentiated Commodities," he (like Novshek) had already claimed that monopolistic competition tends eventually to resemble perfect competition as the size of the firm becomes small relative to the market. Assuming U-shaped cost curves from the outset, he avoids the fallacy of Cournot's dilemma, yet his assumption that the market for each firm grows homogeneously, neither affecting substitutabilities nor leading to a finer grid of more differentiated commodities, is clearly not compatible with monopolistic competition. The original Chamberlinian concept had always emphasized that output was limited by demand, not by technology. In Hart's paper every differentiated firm gives rise to a whole competitive industry, in which his initial claim holds, but much of the inherent interest and relevance of the analysis of the position of that firm has been lost.

Hart addresses these conceptual questions in a slightly different and more attractive way in two papers from 1985, "Monopolistic Competition in the Spirit of Chamberlin: A General Model" and "Monopolistic Competition in the Spirit of Chamberlin: Special Results." Here an elaborate treatment of demand allows for cross-price effects, though they are spread uniformly over all firms and thus exclude different degrees of substitutability. In addition, the approximative concept of E-equilibrium allows for positive profits. At the end, the limitations of the two papers are openly acknowledged by Hart himself: "[the] analytical advantages must be weighed against the disadvantages that the assumptions underlying monopolistic competition (e.g. the absence of neighboring brands) are quite strong and severely limit the range of markets to which the model applies" (Hart 1985b, 903). Again, the idea of product differentiation with limiting demand curves is made an arbitrary corollary of an essentially competitive industry with small firms.

The difference between Hart's work and what has been presented here as monopolistic competition hinges crucially on the treatment of the downward-sloping demand curve of the monopolistically competitive firm. In Hart's work the market power of the individual firm is motivated neither by product differentiation nor by fixed costs, which would result in increasing returns to scale and barriers to entry. It stems solely from the idea that the firm satisfies a given portion of the total demand of an industry of which it is a "significant" part. Hart's procedure is clearly, and in the 1985 papers explicitly, based on the Chamberlinian concept of the large group. The approximation of larger and larger groups to a competitive industry is then not a result that would contradict intuition. Yet it should be kept in mind that the large-group concept, with its effective absence of cross-price effects between firms, played only a minor role in monopolistic competition theory, and any research solely based on it cannot claim to be a general representation of the spirit of Chamberlin or any other of the main researchers of the 1930s (see chapters 10 and 11).

Hart's analysis also leads to the idea that a monopolistically competitive economy corresponds in welfare terms to the norm set by a Pareto-optimal perfectly competitive one. For Hart this is because with increases in demand, U-shaped cost curves will lead to average-cost pricing, clearly at odds with Chamberlin's idea that real welfare losses due to excess capacity are only offset by the advantages of a greater variety of products.

Ultimately, all criticism stems from of the following conviction: Any attempt to construct a general theory of monopolistic competition on the basis of a theory of perfect competition runs counter to the original research project on monopolistic competition. The decision must be made whether to treat it as an abnormality whose affinities with the "normal" case of perfect competition must be stressed wherever possible, or whether it is worthwhile to explore monopolistic competition theory further, as a radical alternative requiring quite new approaches in order to capture its peculiarities within a model of general equilibrium.

A final verdict on monopolistic competition theory must be postponed. Only fifteen years ago, one could have argued convincingly that the attention it received was so limited that the original research project had to be deemed unsuccessfully concluded. That monopolistic competition theory has so far proved intractable to mathematical analysis beyond a certain level has undoubtedly contributed to its lack of attraction for modern theorists. This intractability stems not from internal inconsistencies but from the essential complexities of the problem. It is possible that a development of the Roberts-Sonnenschein line of reasoning will one day establish definitively that this intractability of monopolistic competition to mathematical reasoning is inherent. But this would constitute a valid argument against a more intensive treatment of the subject only for those who equate economic theorizing with mathematical analysis.

Recent work in general-equilibrium theory, with its foundations in the large-group concept and its implicit normative and conceptual benchmark of perfect competition, does not constitute a wholly convincing successor to monopolistic competition theory. It often seems concerned more with extending the existing theory of general equilibrium than with extending monopolistic competition theory. The emphasis on mathematical tractability clashes with the complexities of firms producing an infinite variety of substitutes under increasing returns to scale. In some cases researchers such as Novshek, Roberts, and Sonnenschein seem implicitly to advocate shelving the whole project of monopolistic competition in general equilibrium. In this they are inheritors of a point of view originally expressed by Hicks in his survey article (Hicks 1935a).

The question why renewed work on monopolistic competition theory is of interest for economists other than historians of thought thus must be given additional support. Here, it is argued that in fact monopolistic competition theory was abandoned in the 1940s not because of a lack of either inherent interest or internal consistency, but because of an exogenous shift in preferences among economists. It is only now that this shift has begun to reverse itself. There are several good reasons for this reversal: first, Cournot's dilemma, and Marshall's gloss thereon, remain unsolved. Empirically, both increasing returns and monopolistic competition appear to prevail. The assumption of perfect competition, on the other hand, requires nonincreasing returns to scale at the level of the firm. Modern economic theory based on perfect competition thus buys consistency at the price of excluding internal economies and increasing returns to scale.

Second, although Keynesianism is still very much alive (albeit on the defense), it will continue to lack microfoundations so long as monopolistic competition is not taken into account. Some research in this field is active, and it may well constitute another case in which monopolistic competition in its original form still could play a role in modern research. Third, and closely connected with the preceding two points, is the Sraffian claim from 1926 that a firm's output is limited not by technology but by demand. Moderate excess capacity due to fixed capital outlays still seems an empirical reality in most Western economies, while horizontal demand curves are for most firms easier to disprove than to verify.

The trade-off between mathematical tractability and realism arises because research in economics has subjected itself to increasingly stringent methodological requirements. Monopolistic competition theory is closer to the original conception of economics, or political economy, as a social science halfway between description and quantitative analysis. Monopolistic competition theory started out by pushing economic science away from purely descriptive realism. But the subsequent gain in logical consistency did not translate into increased mathematical tractability of any general model of monopolistic competition. Unless the profession develops a new interest in Lancaster's general model and attempts to bridge the gap to traditional theory, it will remain a fascinating yet ultimately sterile synthesis. Monopolistic competition theory is most vigorously alive where it is employed eclectically with limited, yet clearly visible, references to the original research project. The methodology of scientific positivism, which managed to create barriers to the continuing acceptance of monopolistic competition theory, is increasingly being questioned as a sensible procedure in a social science. The vision of a "centralized," all-encompassing, consistent theoretical foundation for economic research is slowly being supplemented by more flexible approaches. The future of monopolistic competition theory is again wide open. This, after a period of disregard and near-oblivion, is proof of its continuing ability to address vital economic questions.

CHAPTER 20

Epilogue

The new research presented above establishes the latest period in the development of monopolistic competition theory, which is characterized by its cautious reestablishment in some of the most interesting and policy-sensitive areas of economic theory. So far this has been accomplished without reigniting the methodological debates of the postwar era. One reason is that the paradigm of positive economic science is itself increasingly being questioned as the only useful framework for a social science such as economics. This period of cautious reestablishment follows a period of willful and almost complete disregard, which, in turn, succeeded the period 1926–41, when monopolistic competition theory was the area of research dominating professional interest. The banishment of monopolistic competition theory from the economic mainstream was the consequence of the de facto impossibility of constructing a testable model of comparative statics. But this impossibility was never conclusively proven on theoretical grounds. During this period, Keynesian macroeconomics also provided a more attractive field of activity for those economists whose main concerns remained economic policy and practical relevance. The close and contradictory relationship between these two theoretical fields has been widely discussed.

Scientific progress is being driven by a complex interplay of external and internal forces. In the case of monopolistic competition theory, the effects of external and internal forces coincided to create a fast and forceful rise to the center of scientific and popular interest and an equally swift exit from the scene. Sharp divisions can be discerned that distinguish it from its precursor, the Marshallian competitive industry with all its loopholes for dynamics and increasing returns, and from its successors, Keynesian macroeconomics and general-equilibrium theory based on perfect competition. Throughout the first half of the twentieth century, the development of economic theory was characterized by a conscious movement toward greater consistency in a theoretical edifice established on commonly agreed-upon "laws," such as the marginal principle, which amount to a thorough formalization of the assumption of "economic man"—utility maximization through consumption of marketable goods. This goes hand in hand with a movement toward greater mathematical tractability, with the ultimate aim of being able to make testable predictions, thus elevating economic theory to the status of a true science in the positivist sense.

The central irony of monopolistic competition theory is that at the beginning it was itself part of this movement toward greater theoretical consistency, and subsequently was overtaken by it, since the theory was unable to satisfy the next step of the very same movement—the development of a testable model. Monopolistic competition theory began when economists, many of them at Cambridge University, looked for logically satisfying ways out of Marshall's inconsistencies concerning the compatibility of empirically observed increasing returns and theoretically elegant perfect competition. This impetus was seconded by a contemporaneous movement toward greater concern with practical realism, mainly among American economists, who wanted to integrate the new aspects of modern capitalism into their theories. This concerned the observation that single productive establishments search to increase their output and raise their prices by attempting to influence consumer demand with the help of new tools such as advertising, marketing of brand names, and sales forces. These efforts, which are unexplainable in a perfectly competitive world, lead to product differentiation and limited monopoly power for each firm.

It has been argued that it was no coincidence that both strands of theory yielded the same basic results when they combined the concept of competition (contemporaneous profit maximization by a number of firms in the same market) with behavior compatible only with limited monopoly power. The point is moot whether the monopoly power is created by limited demand, increasing returns, product differentiation, or frictions such as transport costs. The last two are analytically equivalent, and all of these phenomena will always and necessarily occur together. The fascination exerted by the theory of monopolistic competition in the late 1920s and 1930s was due in large part to its combination of theoretical progress and increased realism, in the sense of being able to integrate and to explain hitherto unexplainable phenomena.

The exposure, mainly in the writings of Milton Friedman and George Stigler, of the idea that monopolistic competition theory was ultimately unable to conform with the new positivist requirement of testability clearly marked the end of this fascination. The theory had already lost much of its luster through petty squabbles between theorists of imperfect and monopolistic competition and through the advent of Keynesianism, which had captured the imagination of economists interested in policy. In this climate, the empirical observation that businesspeople usually took "average cost plus markup" as their pricing rule assumed a completely disproportionate and ultimately unjustified role in eroding the credibility of the marginal-revenue concept and thus contributed to the declining interest in monopolistic competition theory.

Suddenly, monopolistic competition theory itself, which only a few years before had appeared to be the embodiment of modernism, seemed hopelessly outmoded and, in fact, utterly Marshallian. Its incompatibility with comparative statics brought it again closer to Marshall's motto: *Natura non facit saltum.* Although theorists had long struggled to emancipate themselves from the grand old man's tendency to patch over theoretical inconsistencies with acute ad hoc observations of "reality," suddenly monopolistic competition theory itself seemed to prize realism more highly than analytical rigor. The methodological requirements had been further toughened in the meantime, and monopolistic competition theory was unable to fulfill them. There is, however, a fundamental difference between the initial rejection of Marshall's theory and the loss of interest in monopolistic competition theory. In the former case actual logical flaws could be and were discovered, whereas in the latter factors outside monopolistic competition theory itself, such as the ever-increasing formalization of economic analysis, made it unattractive for further research, even though no internal contradictions were revealed.

Despite this important difference, in the clash with modern economic theory monopolistic competition theory shows its Marshallian roots. Partial equilibrium was its starting point, and at the time it was considered a fully satisfying framework—despite Sraffa's short initial foray into general-equilibrium reasoning. Questions of exit and entry were discussed in a dynamic context that was not fully specified. A premium was placed on questions that would yield answers relevant for practical economics, whether for the businessperson or for the economic planner. Monopolistic competition theory displayed Marshall's concern with welfare, policy, and realism. Considering the purpose and scope of economic theory, the monopolistic competition theorists of the 1930s remained closer to Marshall and his predecessors than to modern general-equilibrium theorists.

These theoretical considerations are complemented by political and ideological considerations that reinforced the rise and decline of monopolistic competition theory. The link between perfect-competition theory and its necessary policy prescription of laissez faire brought the theory into disregard when this policy prescription was widely perceived as having failed. Not only was capitalism seen to be in need of new remedies, but its very existence was called into question by new systemic arrangements. In the light of the stock market crash of 1929 and the ensuing worldwide economic crisis, Soviet communism and Italian corporatism, soon to be complemented by German National Socialism, seemed viable alternatives. In particular, Italian corporatism and its claim to be searching for a "third way" encouraged the interest of theoreticians and policymakers, even when they rejected its nationalist and revolutionary overtones. Clearly, its fascination was also due to its compromise character, which allowed an ad hoc approach in which each researcher concentrated on those elements most to his or her liking. The consensus evolved that state intervention was necessary to complement market forces. The only theory that was able to deliver convincing rationales for this consensus was monopolistic competition theory.

The demand for greater state intervention went hand in hand with an increased concern for those less fortunate, in particular for industrial workers. "Monopolistic exploitation," a concept developed by Joan Robinson, was an added rationale for complementing, in this case, the forces of the labor market. Research based on the assumption of monopolistic competition delivered results very much in line with what was politically necessary. It is no coincidence that most important researchers in monopolistic competition theory belonged, in various and widely differing forms, to the political left. This does not hold for Edward Chamberlin, yet even his research has its roots in the institutional economics of Richard Ely and its subsequent transformations by Allyn Young. Monopolistic competition theory thus delivered results much appreciated by a large group of committed individuals in academia, politics, and the public at large. This does not in the least diminish the validity of any of the results derived by theorists of monopolistic competition, yet it explains to some extent the interest the theory generated and the eagerness with which its results were received.

The beginning of World War II brought an end to experiments, whether in thought or practice, aiming to introduce greater stability and fairer distribution into market systems, since all economic activity was organized according to the priorities set by the war effort. After the war, with the advent of the systemic conflict between the Soviet block and the United States and its allies, theories implying the unquestioned superiority of free markets were again much more in tune with the general mood. Nevertheless, monopolistic competition theory retained much of its relevance for actual policy making, since antitrust laws, a far-reaching welfare state, and progressive taxation were introduced in Western Europe and to a lesser extent in the United States. Yet this legacy was continued behind the cover of official rhetoric and much theoretical work in economics, whose only possible implications were in both cases the undisputable superiority of free markets. The exterior developments reinforced the theoretical shortcomings exposed in monopolistic competition theory. Nothing can be derived from this to judge any of the points enlisted above. It does, however, further explain the theory's extraordinarily swift fall into a state of disregard after World War II, when the results and policy implications of monopolistic competition theory were not supported by any vocal constituency.

These historical factors, which reinforced the interior development of economic theory so dramatically, are clearly of little importance today. Today it seems possible to judge the advantages and limitations of a theory built on the idea of limited monopoly power of the single firm on its own merits. This does not mean that economic theory now proceeds in a political and ideological vacuum. This essay has offered some evidence that the implications of research results and the conditioning methodological prescriptions cannot be seen as completely independent from a priori value judgments, political necessities, and ideological sympathies. Yet in the absence of great systemic conflicts or ideological disputes, the emphasis can rest even more strongly on the intrinsic contributions of an economic theory. There is no reason for debates about theory and methodology to assume the characteristics of a religious war. Indeed, economic theory and economic theorists are released from the pressure, whether consciously perceived or not, to take expediency into account, and the theory can redefine itself according to its own preferences. This redefinition will include the question of the validity of the legacy of monopolistic competition theory for today's research.

The opposition between economic theories built on perfect competition and those built on monopolistic competition remains valid today. A closed theory based on the assumption of perfect competition retains the benefits of logical consistency and mathematical tractability, but struggles in its models to provide a recognizable picture of reality or to yield policy implications other than laissez faire. On the other hand, the theory of monopolistic competition allows the integration and explanation of myriad real-world phenomena and interesting policy proposals, yet fails to satisfy methodological demands modeled on the natural sciences.

As the pressure has grown to provide more insights into the workings of the real economy, monopolistic competition has reestablished itself in various forms. This has not yet led to a resumption of the original research project, when researchers were actively trying to establish a general economic theory based on monopolistic competition. Undoubtedly, the insight by Cournot and Sraffa that output is limited by demand and not by technology proves to be a fruitful assumption in some of the most productive and promising areas of research. Yet it is unclear whether new research exploring the various views will be able to unite them into a complete vision of economic behavior based on firms with limited monopoly power. The question whether the legacy of the period 1926–41 will merely provide stimulating suggestions or will indeed bring the development of economic theory full circle remains open. Ultimately, the validity of the assumption of monopolistic competition as the relevant microeconomic structure for economic theory will hinge on the methodological conventions the community of economic theorists decides to give itself.

· BIBLIOGRAPHY

For further references, see the extensive "Bibliography on Monopolistic Competition Theory" in the appendix of the 8th edition of Edward H. Chamberlin's *Theory of Monopolistic Competition* (1962), which contains 1,497 entries. It should, however, be treated with caution, as it is not without bias. Most importantly, it completely excludes any reference to the literature on increasing returns.

Akerlof, George A., and Janet L. Yellen. 1985. "A Near-Rational Model of the Business Cycle, with Wage and Price Inertia." *Quarterly Journal of Economics* 100:823–38.

Alchian, A., and H. Demsetz. 1972. "Production, Information Costs, and Economic Organization." *American Economic Review* 62:777–95.

Aldcroft, Derek H. 1986. *The British Economy*. 2 vols. Brighton: Harvester.

Allen, R. G. D. 1932. "Decreasing Costs: A Mathematical Note." *Economic Journal* 42:323–26.

Amoroso, Luigi. 1909. "La teoria dell' equilibrio economico secondo il Professore Vilfredo Pareto." *Giornale degli economisti* 39:353–67.

———. 1911. "La teoria matematica del monopolio trattata geometricamente." *Giornale degli economisti* 43:207–37.

———. 1926. "Ciò che è scienza e ciò che è fede nel campo della dottrina economica." *Giornale degli economisti* 66:364–77.

———. 1928. *Lezioni di economia matematica*. Bologna: Zanichelli.

———. 1930. "La curva statica di offerta." *Giornale degli economisti* 70:10–46.

———. 1932. *Critica del sistema capitalista: Corsno nell'anno accadèmico 1931–1932*. Rome.

———. 1935. "La produzione in regime di concentrazione industriale." *Rivista italiana di scienze economiche* 7:157–63.

———. 1938a. *Principi di economia corporativa*. Bologna: Zanichelli.

———. 1938b. "Vilfredo Pareto." *Econometrica* 6:1–21.

———. 1942. *Meccanica economica: Lezioni tenute nell'anno accadèmico 1940–1941*. Bari: Macri.

———. 1949. *Economia di mercato*. Bologna: Zuffi.

———. 1954. "The Static Supply Curve." Trans. G. Forrest and W. M. Shepard. *International Economic Papers* 4:39–65.

———. 1959. "Onoranze al Prof. Luigi Amoroso." *Annali dell' Istituto di Statistica* (University of Bari) 30.

Amoroso, Luigi, and A. de' Stefani. 1932. "Lo stato e la vita economica." *Rivista di statistica, economia, e finanza* 4:353–67.

———. 1933. "La logica del sistema corporativa." *Rivista internazionale di scienze sociali e discipline ausiliarie*, 3d ser., 41:393–411.

Andrews, P. W. S. 1951. "Industrial Analysis in Economics, with Especial Reference to Marshallian Doctrine." In *Oxford Studies in the Price Mechanism*, ed. Wilson T. Andrews and P. W. S. Andrews, 139–72. Oxford: Clarendon.

Archibald, G. C. 1961. "Chamberlin versus Chicago." *Review of Economic Studies* 29:2–28.

———. 1963. "Archibald's Reply to Chicago." *Review of Economic Studies* 30:68–71.

———. 1987. "Monopolistic Competition." In Eatwell, Milgate, and Newman 1987.

Arndt, H. W. 1944. *The Economic Lessons of the Nineteen-Thirties*. Oxford: Oxford University Press.

Arnold, Thurman W. 1937. *The Folklore of Capitalism*. New Haven: Yale University Press.

Arnott, Richard. 1987. "Spatial Economics." In Eatwell, Milgate, and Newman 1987.

Arrow, Kenneth J. 1959. "Toward a Theory of Price Adjustment." In *The Allocation of Economic Resources: Essays in Honor of Bernard Francis Haley*, ed. Moses Abramovitz et al., 41–51. Stanford: Stanford University Press.

Backhouse, Roger. 1985. *A History of Modern Economic Analysis*. New York: Blackwell.

Beckerath, Erwin von. 1932. "Die Wirtschaftsverfassung des Faschismus." *Schmollers Jahrbuch* 56:347–97.

Berle, Adolf A., and Gardiner C. Means. 1940. *The Modern Corporation and Private Property*. 12th ed. New York: Macmillan.

Bernheim, Alfred L., ed. 1937a. *Big Business: Its Growth and Its Place*. New York: Twentieth Century Fund.

———. 1937b. *How Profitable Is Big Business?* New York: Twentieth Century Fund.

Blaug, Mark. 1968. *Economic Theory in Retrospect*. Homewood, Ill.: Irwin.

Blitch, Charles, ed. 1928–29. "Kaldor's Lecture Notes in Allyn Young's London School of Economics Class, 1928–1929." Manuscript.

Blum, Fred H. 1947. "Marginalism and Economic Policy." *American Economic Review* 37:645–52.

Boulding, Kenneth E. 1948a. *Economic Analysis*. 2d ed. New York: Harper.

———. 1948b. "Professor Tarshis and the State of Economics." *American Economic Review* 38:92–102.

Bowen, Ralph H. 1947. *German Theories of the Corporative State.* New York: Whittlesey.

Bowley, Arthur L. 1924. *The Mathematical Groundwork of Economics.* Oxford: Clarendon.

Breglia, Alberto. 1935. "Su alcuni concetti di economia corporativa." *Giornale degli economisti* 75:281–98.

Broadberry, S. N. 1986. *The British Economy between the Wars: A Macroeconomic Survey.* Oxford: Blackwell.

Brook, Werner F. 1962. *Social and Economic History of Germany from William II to Hitler, 1888–1938.* New York: Russell and Russell.

Brown, Douglass V., et al. 1934. *The Economics of the Recovery Program.* New York: Whittlesey.

Brown, Henry Phelps. 1980. "Sir Roy Harrod: A Biographical Memoir." *Economic Journal* 90:1–33.

Burns, Arthur R. 1933. *The Decline of Competition.* New York: McGraw-Hill.

Capozza, Dennis R., and Robert van Order. 1987. "Spatial Competition." In Eatwell, Milgate, and Newman 1987.

Castronovo, Valerio. 1980. *L' industria italiana dall' ottocento a oggi.* Milan: A. Mondadori.

Chamberlin, Edward H. 1929. "Duopoly: Value Where Sellers Are Few." *Quarterly Journal of Economics* 44:63–100.

———. 1933. *The Theory of Monopolistic Competition.* Cambridge, Mass.: Harvard University Press.

———. 1937. "Monopolistic or Imperfect Competition?" *Quarterly Journal of Economics* 51:557–80. Reprinted in Chamberlin 1962 (page references are to original publication).

———. 1938. "Reply." *Quarterly Journal of Economics* 52:530–38.

———. 1947. Review of *The Theory of Price,* by George Stigler. *American Economic Review* 37:414–18.

———. 1948. "Proportionality, Divisibility, and Economies of Scale." *Quarterly Journal of Economics* 62:229–62. Reprinted in Chamberlin 1962 (page references are to original publication).

———. 1949. "Proportionality, Divisibility, and Economies of Scale: Reply." *Quarterly Journal of Economics* 63:137–43.

———. 1957. *Towards a More General Theory of Value.* Oxford: Oxford University Press.

———. 1958. "The Economic Analysis of Labor Union Power." Washington, D.C.: American Enterprise Association.

———. 1961. "The Origin and Early Development of Monopolistic Competition Theory." *Quarterly Journal of Economics* 75:515–43. Reprinted in Chamberlin 1962 (page references are to original publication).

———. 1962. *The Theory of Monopolistic Competition: A Reorientation of the Theory of Value.* 8th ed. Cambridge, Mass.: Harvard University Press.

———. 1964. "The Nature of Equilibrium in Monopolistic Competition: Reply to Mr. Demsetz." *Journal of Political Economy* 72:314–15.

Clapham, J. H. 1922a. "The Economic Boxes: A Rejoinder." *Economic Journal* 32:560–63.

———. 1922b. "On Empty Economic Boxes." *Economic Journal* 32:305–14.

Clark, J. M. 1913. Review of *Wealth and Welfare*, by A. C. Pigou. *American Economic Review* 3:623–25.

Classen, Wolfgang-Dieter. 1987. "Fascism." In Eatwell, Milgate, and Newman 1987.

Clough, Shepard B. 1932. "The Evolution of Fascist Economic Practice and Theory." *Harvard Business Review* 10:302–10.

Clower, Robert W. 1984. "The Keynesian Counter-revolution: A Theoretical Appraisal." In *Money and Markets: Essays by Robert W. Clower*, ed. D. Walker, 34–59. Cambridge: Cambridge University Press.

Coase, R. H. 1934. "The Problem of Duopoly Reconsidered." *Review of Economic Studies* 2:137–43.

———. 1952. "The Nature of the Firm." In *Readings in Price Theory*, ed. G. Stigler and K. Boulding, 331–51. Chicago: Irwin. First published in *Economica*, n.s., 4 (1937): 386–405.

Cole, Margaret I. 1949. *The Webbs and Their Work*. London: Muller.

Committee on Price Determination for the Conference on Price Research. 1943. *Cost Behavior and Price Policy*. New York: National Bureau of Economic Research.

Cournot, Antoine Augustin. 1960. *Researches into the Mathematical Principles of the Theory of Wealth*. Trans. Nathaniel T. Bacon. 1928. Reprint, New York: Kelley.

———. 1980. *Recherches sur les principes mathématiques de la théorie des richesses*. 1838. Reprint, Paris: Vrin.

Dalton, Hugh. 1923. "Pantaleone fascista." *Economic Journal* 33:66–69.

Dasgupta, P., and E. Maskin. 1986a. "The Existence of Equilibrium in Discontinuous Economic Games, I: Theory." *Review of Economic Studies* 53:1–26.

———. 1986b. "The Existence of Equilibrium in Discontinuous Economic Games, II: Applications." *Review of Economic Studies* 53:27–42.

d'Aspremont, C., J. Jaskold Gabszewicz, and J.-F. Thisse. 1979. "On Hotelling's 'Stability in Competition.'" *Econometrica* 47:1145–50.

Davidson, Paul. 1987. "User Cost." In Eatwell, Milgate, and Newman 1987.

Dean, Joel. 1941. "The Relation of Cost to Output for a Leather Belt Shop." National Bureau of Economic Research, Technical Paper no. 2. New York: National Bureau of Economic Research.

de Michelis, Paolo. 1940. *Le rôle économique des corporations fascistes en Italie*. Geneva.

Demsetz, Harold. 1959. "The Nature of Equilibrium in Monopolistic Competition." *Journal of Political Economy* 67:21–30.

de Vito, Francesco. 1934. "Le basi teoriche dell' economia corporativa." *Giornale degli economisti* 74:467–78.

———. 1935. "Sui fini dell' economia corporativa." *Giornale degli economisti* 75:429–37.

Dewey, Donald. 1950. "Professor Schumpeter on Socialism." *Journal of Political Economy* 58:187–210.

Dixit, Avinash K., and Joseph A. Stiglitz. 1977. "Monopolistic Competition and Optimum Product Diversity." *American Economic Review* 67:297–308.

Durbin, Elizabeth. 1985. *New Jerusalems: The Labor Party and the Economics of Democratic Socialism*. London: Routledge.

Eatwell, John, and Murray Milgate. 1983. *Keynes's Economics and the Theory of Value and Distribution*. New York: Oxford University Press.

Eatwell, John, Murray Milgate, and Peter Newman. 1987. *The New Palgrave: A Dictionary of Economics*. 4 vols. London: Macmillan.

Edgeworth, Francis Ysidro. 1922. "The Mathematical Economics of Professor Amoroso." *Economic Journal* 32:400–407.

Edwards, Corwin D. 1934. Review of *The Theory of Monopolistic Competition*, by Edward Chamberlin, and *The Economics of Imperfect Competition*, by Joan Robinson. *American Economic Review* 24:683–85.

Erbe, René. 1958. *Die nationalsozialistische Wirtschaftspolitik 1933–1939 im Lichte der modernen Theorie*. Zurich: Polygraph.

Eshag, E. 1963. *From Marshall to Keynes*. Oxford: Basil Blackwell.

Eucken, Walter. 1947. *Die Grundlagen der Nationalökonomie*. Godesberg: Küpper.

———. 1948a. Obituary of Heinrich von Stackelberg. *Economic Journal* 58:132–35.

———. 1948b. "On the Theory of the Centrally Administered Economy: An Analysis of the German Experiment." *Economica* 15:79–100, 173–93.

———. 1951. *This Unsuccessful Age; or, The Pains of Economic Progress*. Edinburgh: Hodge.

Feiwel, George R., ed. 1989a. *The Economics of Imperfect Competition and Employment: Joan Robinson and Beyond*. New York: New York University Press.

———. 1989b. *Joan Robinson and Modern Economic Theory*. New York: New York University Press.

Felderer, Bernhard, and Stefan Homburg. 1989. *Makroökonomik und neue Makroökonomik*. 4th ed. Berlin: Springer.

Fellner, William J. 1960. *Competition among the Few: Oligopoly and Similar Market Structures*. 2d ed. New York: Kelley.

Fischer, Wolfram. 1968. *Deutsche Wirtschaftspolitik, 1918–1945*. Opladen: Leske.

Florinsky, Michael T. 1936. *Fascism and National Socialism: A Study of the Economic and Social Policies*. New York: Macmillan.

Forget, Evelyn L., and Sharam Manouchehri. 1988. "Keynes's Neglected Heritage: The Classical Microfoundations of *The General Theory*." *Journal of Post-Keynesian Economics* 10:401–13.

Friedman, James W. 1977. *Oligopoly and the Theory of Games*. Amsterdam: North-Holland.

———. 1983. *Oligopoly Theory*. Cambridge: Cambridge University Press.

Friedman, Milton. 1953. *Essays in Positive Economics*. Chicago: University of Chicago Press.

———. 1963. "More on Archibald versus Chicago." *Review of Economic Studies* 30:65–68.

Frisch, Ragnar. 1933. "Monopole-Polypole: La notion de force dans l'économie." In *Til Harald Westergaard, 19. April 1933*, Festschrift, *Nationaløkonomisk Tidsskrift* 71:241–59.

———. 1951. "Monopoly-Polypoly: The Concept of Force in the Economy." Trans. W. Beckerman. *International Economic Papers* 1:23–36.

Gandolfo, Giancarlo. 1987a. "Amoroso, Luigi (1886–1965)." In Eatwell, Milgate, and Newman 1987.

———. 1987b. "Ricci, Umberto (1879–1946)." In Eatwell, Milgate, and Newman 1987.

Gordon, R. A. 1948. "Short-Period Price Determination in Theory and Practice." *American Economic Review* 38:265–88.

Gramsci, Antonio. 1965. *Lettere dal carcere*. Ed. Sergio Caprioglio and Elsa Fubini. Turin: Einaudi.

———. 1975. *Quaderni del carcere*. Ed. Valentino Gerratana. 4 vols. Turin: Einaudi.

———. 1986. *Nuove lettere di Antonio Gramsci: Con altre lettere di Piero Sraffa*. Ed. Antonio A. Santucci. Rome: Editori Riuniti.

Gregory, Paul R., and Robert C. Stuart. 1985. *Comparative Economic Systems*. Boston: Houghton Mifflin.

Hahn, Frank. 1949. "Proportionality, Divisibility, and Economies of Scale: Comment." *Quarterly Journal of Economics* 63:131–37.

———. 1959. "The Theory of Selling Costs." *Economic Journal* 69:293–312.

Halevi, Joseph. 1987. "Corporatism." In Eatwell, Milgate, and Newman 1987.

Hall, R. L., and C. J. Hitch. 1939. "Price Theory and Economic Behaviour." *Oxford Economic Papers* 2:12–45.

Hall, Robert E. 1986. "Market Structure and Macroeconomic Fluctuations." *Brookings Papers on Economic Activity* 2:285–338.

Harcourt, Geoffrey C. 1972. *Some Cambridge Controversies in the Theory of Capital*. Cambridge: Cambridge University Press.

Harrod, Roy F. 1930. "Notes on Supply." *Economic Journal* 40:232–41. Reprinted in Harrod 1952 (page references are to original publication).

———. 1931. "The Law of Decreasing Costs." *Economic Journal* 41:566–76. Reprinted in Harrod 1952 (page references are to original publication).

———. 1932. "Decreasing Costs: An Addendum." *Economic Journal* 42:490–92.

———. 1933a. "A Further Note on Decreasing Costs." *Economic Journal* 43:337–41. Reprinted in Harrod 1952 (page references are to original publication).

———. 1933b. Review of *The Theory of Monopolistic Competition*, by Edward H. Chamberlin. *Economic Journal* 43:663–67.

———. 1934a. "Doctrines of Imperfect Competition." *Quarterly Journal of Economics* 48:442–70. Reprinted in Harrod 1952 (page references are to original publication).

——. 1934b. "The Equilibrium of Duopoly." *Economic Journal* 44:335–37. Reprinted in Harrod 1952 (page references are to original publication).

——. 1936a. "Imperfect Competition and the Trade Cycle." *Review of Economic Statistics* 18:84–88.

——. 1936b. *The Trade Cycle: An Essay.* Oxford: Clarendon.

——. 1939. "Price and Cost in Entrepreneurs' Policy." *Oxford Economic Papers* 2:1–11.

——. 1952. *Economic Essays.* London: Macmillan.

——. 1967. "Increasing Returns." In Kuenne 1967, 63–76.

Hart, Oliver. 1979. "Monopolistic Competition in a Large Economy with Differentiated Commodities." *Review of Economic Studies* 46:1–30.

——. 1982a. "A Model of Imperfect Competition with Keynesian Features." *Quarterly Journal of Economics* 97:109–38.

——. 1982b. "Monopolistic Competition in a Large Economy with Differentiated Commodities: A Correction." *Review of Economic Studies* 49:313–14.

——. 1984. "Imperfect Competition in General Equilibrium: An Overview of Recent Work, with comments by J. J. Gabszewicz and H. Sonnenschein." In *Frontiers of Economics*, ed. K. Arrow and S. Honkapohja, 100–177. Oxford: Blackwell.

——. 1985a. "Monopolistic Competition in the Spirit of Chamberlin: A General Model." *Review of Economic Studies* 52:529–49.

——. 1985b. "Monopolistic Competition in the Spirit of Chamberlin: Special Results." *Economic Journal* 95:889–908.

Hayek, Friedrich A. von. 1946. "The London School of Economics, 1895–1945." *Economica* 13:1–31.

Heim, Carol E. 1983. "Industrial Organization and Regional Development in Interwar Britain." *Journal of Economic History* 43:931–52.

Heimann, Eduard. 1945. *History of Economic Doctrines: An Introduction to Economic Theory.* Oxford: Oxford University Press.

Hicks, J. R. 1935a. "Annual Survey of Economic Theory: The Theory of Monopoly." *Econometrica* 3:1–20.

——. 1935b. Review of *Marktform und Gleichgewicht*, by Heinrich von Stackelberg. *Economic Journal* 45:334–36.

——. 1937. "Mr. Keynes and the 'Classics.'" *Econometrica* 5:147–59.

——. 1939. *Value and Capital.* Oxford: Clarendon.

Hollander, Paul. 1981. *Political Pilgrims: Travels of Western Intellectuals to the Soviet Union, China, and Cuba, 1928–1978.* New York: Oxford University Press.

Hotelling, Harold. 1929. "Stability in Competition." *Economic Journal* 39:41–57.

Howson, Susan, and Donald Winch. 1977. *The Economic Advisory Council: A Study in Economic Advice during Depression and Recovery, 1930–1939.* Cambridge: Cambridge University Press.

Hutchison, T. W. 1964. *Positive Economics and Policy Objectives.* Cambridge, Mass.: Harvard University Press.

———. 1968. *Economics and Economic Policy in Britain, 1946–1966.* London: Allen and Unwin.

James, Harold. 1986. *The German Slump.* Oxford: Clarendon.

———. 1989. *A German Identity, 1770–1990.* Oxford: Clarendon.

Kahn, Richard F. 1932. "Decreasing Costs: A Note on the Contributions of Mr. Harrod and Mr. Allen." *Economic Journal* 42:657–61.

———. 1935. "Some Notes on Ideal Output." *Economic Journal* 45:1–35.

———. 1937. "The Problem of Duopoly." *Economic Journal* 47:1–20.

———. 1983. *L'economia del breve periodo.* Trans. Pier Luigi Cecioni. Turin: Borghieri.

———. 1984. *The Making of Keynes' General Theory.* Cambridge: Cambridge University Press.

———. 1989. *The Economics of the Short Period.* London: Macmillan.

Kaldor, Nicholas. 1934a. "The Equilibrium of the Firm." *Economic Journal* 44:60–76.

———. 1934b. "Mrs. Robinson's *Economics of Imperfect Competition.*" *Economica,* n.s., 1:335–41.

———. 1935. "Market Imperfection and Excess Capacity." *Economica* 2:33–50.

———. 1936. "Heinrich von Stackelberg's *Marktform und Gleichgewicht.*" *Economica* 3:227–30.

———. 1938. "Professor Chamberlin on Monopolistic and Imperfect Competition." *Quarterly Journal of Economics* 52:513–29.

———. 1984. "Piero Sraffa." *Cambridge Journal of Economics* 8:2–5.

Kalecki, Michael. 1939. *Essays in the Theory of Economic Fluctuations.* London: Allen and Unwin.

———. 1954. *Theory of Economic Dynamics.* London: Allen and Unwin.

———. 1966. *Studies in the Theory of Business Cycles, 1933–1939.* New York: Kelley.

Kellenbenz, Hermann. 1981. *Deutsche Wirtschaftsgeschichte.* 2 vols. Munich: Beck.

Keynes, John Maynard. 1924. Obituary of Alfred Marshall. *Economic Journal* 34:311–72.

———. 1930. "Increasing Returns and the Representative Firm: A Symposium." *Economic Journal* 40:79–116.

———. 1939. "Relative Movements of Real Wages and Output." *Economic Journal* 49:34–51.

———. 1971–83. *The Collected Writings of John Maynard Keynes.* Ed. Donald Moggridge. 29 vols. London: Macmillan for the Royal Economic Society.

———. 1973. *The General Theory of Employment, Interest, and Money.* 1936. Vol. 7 of Keynes 1971–83.

———. 1989. *Keynes' Lectures, 1932–1935: Notes of a Representative Student.* Edited by Thomas K. Rymes. Ann Arbor: University of Michigan Press.

Khan, M. Ali. 1992. "On the Irony in/of Economic Theory." Paper presented at the Colloquium on Intercultural Comparisons, Johns Hopkins University.

———. 1993. "On Economics and Language: A Review Article." *Journal of Economic Studies* 20.

Kirby, M. W. 1973. "Government Intervention in Industrial Organization: Coal Mining in the Nineteen-Thirties." *Business History* 15:160–73.

Knight, Frank Hyneman. 1921. *Risk, Uncertainty, and Profit.* New York: Houghton Mifflin.

———. 1976a. "The Ethics of Competition." In Knight 1976b. First published in *Quarterly Journal of Economics* 37 (1923): 579–624.

———. 1976b. *The Ethics of Competition and Other Essays.* Chicago: Chicago University Press.

Kregel, Jan. 1976. "Economic Methodology in the Face of Uncertainty: The Modelling Methods of Keynes and the Post-Keynesians." *Economic Journal* 86:209–25.

Krelle, Wilhelm. 1987. "Stackelberg, Heinrich von (1905–1946)." In Eatwell, Milgate, and Newman 1987.

Kreps, David M. 1987. "Nash-equilibrium." In Eatwell, Milgate, and Newman 1987.

Kuenne, Robert E., ed. 1967. *Monopolistic Competition Theory: Studies in Impact: Essays in Honor of Edward H. Chamberlin.* New York: Wiley.

———. 1987. "Chamberlin, Edward H. (1899–1967)." In Eatwell, Milgate, and Newman 1987.

Kuhn, Thomas. 1967. *The Structure of Scientific Revolution.* Chicago: University of Chicago Press.

Laidler, Harry W. 1931. *Concentration of Control in American Industry.* New York: Crowell.

Lambrecht, Matthias. 1988. "Heinrich von Stackelberg: Leben und Werk." Hamburg. Manuscript.

Lancaster, Kelvin. 1979. *Variety, Equity, and Efficiency: Product Variety in an Industrial Society.* New York: Columbia University Press.

Laski, K. 1987a. "Kalecki, Michael (1899–1970)." In Eatwell, Milgate, and Newman 1987.

———. 1987b. "Steindl, Josef (1912-)." In Eatwell, Milgate, and Newman 1987.

Layard, P. R., and Alan A. Walters. 1978. *Microeconomic Theory.* New York: McGraw-Hill.

Leontieff, Wassily. 1936. "Stackelberg on Monopolistic Competition." *Journal of Political Economy* 44:554–59.

Lerner, A. P. 1933–34. "The Concept of Monopoly and the Measurement of Monopoly Power." *Review of Economic Studies* 1:157–75.

Lester, Richard A. 1946. "Shortcomings of Marginal Analysis for Wage-Employment Problems." *American Economic Review* 36:63–83.

———. 1947. "Marginalism, Minimum Wages, and Labor Markets." *American Economic Review* 37:135–48.

McCloskey, Donald N. 1985. *The Rhetoric of Economics.* Madison: University of Wisconsin Press.

Machlup, Fritz. 1946. "Marginal Analysis and Empirical Research." *American Economic Review* 36:519–54.

———. 1947. "Rejoinder to an Antimarginalist." *American Economic Review* 37:148–54.

McLeod, A. N. 1949. "Proportionality, Divisibility, and Economies of Scale: Comment." *Quarterly Journal of Economics* 63:128–31.

Makowski, Louis. 1987. "Imperfect Competition." In Eatwell, Milgate, and Newman 1987.

Mancini, Ombretta, Francesco Parillo, and Eugenio Zagari. 1982. *La teoria economica del corporativismo.* Naples: Edizioni Scientifiche Italiane.

Maneschi, Andrea. 1986. "A Comparative Evaluation of Sraffa's 'The Laws of Returns under Competitive Conditions' and Its Italian Precursor." *Cambridge Journal of Economics* 10:1–12.

———. 1988. "The Place of Lord Kahn's *The Economics of the Short Period* in the Theory of Imperfect Competition." *History of Political Economy* 20:155–71.

Mankiw, N. Gregory. 1985. "Small Menu Costs and Large Business Cycles: A Macroeconomic Model of Monopoly." *Quarterly Journal of Economics* 100:529–37.

Mankiw, N. Gregory, and David Romer. 1991. *New Keynesian Economics.* 2 vols. Cambridge, Mass.: MIT Press.

Marris, Robin L. 1991. *Reconstructing Keynesian Economics with Imperfect Competition.* Aldershot, Hants, England: Edward Elgar.

———. 1992. "R. F. Kahn's Fellowship Dissertation: A Missing Link in the History of Economic Thought." *Economic Journal* 102:1235–43.

Marshall, Alfred. 1961. *Principles of Economics.* 9th ed. Ed. C. W. Guillebaud. London: Macmillan.

Marwick, Arthur. 1964. "Middle Opinion in the Thirties: Planning, Progress, and Political 'Agreement.'" *English Historical Review* 79:285–98.

Means, Gardiner C. 1931. "The Growth in the Relative Importance of the Large Corporation in American Economic Life." *American Economic Review* 21:10–42.

Möller, Hans. 1949. "Heinrich Freiherr von Stackelberg und sein Beitrag für die Wirtschaftswissenschaft." *Zeitschrift für die gesamte Staatswissenschaft* 105:395–428.

———. 1956. "Heinrich Freiherr von Stackelberg." In *Handwörterbuch der Sozialwissenschaften.* 12 vols. Stuttgart.

Mueller, Klaus O. W. 1965. *Heinrich von Stackelberg: Ein moderner bürgerlicher Ökonom.* Berlin.

Müller-Armack, Alfred. 1956. "Soziale Marktwirtschaft." In *Handwörterbuch der Sozialwissenschaften.* 12 vols. Stuttgart.

Mussolini, Benito. 1935. *Four Speeches on the Corporate State.* Rome: Laboremus.

Nathan, Otto. 1944. *The Nazi Economic System: Germany's Mobilization for War.* Durham, N.C.: Duke University Press.

Negishi, Takashi. 1979. *Microeconomic Foundations of Keynesian Macroeconomics.* Amsterdam: North-Holland.

———. 1987. "Monopolistic Competition and General Equilibrium." In Eatwell, Milgate, and Newman 1987.

Newman, Peter K. 1960. "The Erosion of Marshall's Theory of Value." *Quarterly Journal of Economics* 74:587–601.

———. 1986. Review of *The Economics of the Short Period*, by Richard F. Kahn. *Contributions to Political Economy* 5:113–18.

———. 1987. "Young, Allyn Abbott (1876–1929)." In Eatwell, Milgate, and Newman 1987.

———, ed. 1968. *Readings in Mathematical Economics*. Baltimore: Johns Hopkins University Press.

Newman, Peter K., and J. N. Wolfe. 1961. "A Model for the Long-run Theory of Value." *Review of Economic Studies* 29:51–61.

Newman, Peter K., and Spyros Vassilakis. 1988. "Sraffa and Imperfect Competition." *Cambridge Journal of Economics* 12:37–42.

Nichols, A. J. 1934. "Professor Chamberlin's Theory of Limited Competition." *Quarterly Journal of Economics* 48:317–37.

Novshek, William. 1980. "Cournot Equilibrium with Free Entry." *Review of Economic Studies* 47:473–86.

Oliver, Henry M. 1947. "Marginal Theory and Business Behavior." *American Economic Review* 37:375–83.

Overy, R. J. 1982. *The Nazi Economic Recovery, 1932–1938*. London: Macmillan.

Oxford University Institute of Statistics. 1946. *The Economics of Full Employment*. Oxford: Basil Blackwell.

Pasinetti, Luigi L. 1987. "Robinson, Joan (1903–1983)." In Eatwell, Milgate, and Newman 1987.

Patinkin, D., and J. C. Leith, eds. 1978. *Keynes, Cambridge, and the General Theory*. Toronto: Toronto University Press.

Peacock, Alan T. 1950. "Recent German Contributions to Economics." *Economica* 17:175–87.

Pigou, Arthur C. 1912. *Wealth and Welfare*. London: Macmillan.

———. 1922. "Empty Economic Boxes: A Reply." *Economic Journal* 32:459–65.

———. 1927. "The Laws of Diminishing and Increasing Cost." *Economic Journal* 37:188–97.

———. 1928. "An Analysis of Supply." *Economic Journal* 38:238–57.

Pré, Roland. 1936. *L'organisation des rapports économiques et sociaux dans les pays à régime corporatif*. Paris: Librairie Technique et Economique.

Rauch, Basil. 1944. *The History of the New Deal, 1933–1938*. New York: Creative Age Press.

Ricci, Umberto. 1926. *Dal protezionismo al sindacalismo*. Bari: Laterza.

Roberts, John, and Hugo Sonnenschein. 1977. "On the Foundations of the Theory of Monopolistic Competition." *Econometrica* 45:101–13.

Robertson, D. H. 1924. "Those Empty Boxes." *Economic Journal* 34:16–31.

Robertson, D. H., Piero Sraffa, and Gerald Shove. 1930. "Increasing Returns and the Representative Firm: A Symposium." *Economic Journal* 40:79–116.

Robinson, E. Austin G. 1931. *The Structure of Competitive Industry.* London: Nisbet.

Robinson, Joan. 1932. "Imperfect Competition and Falling Supply Price." *Economic Journal* 42:544–54.

———. 1933. "Decreasing Costs: A Reply to Mr. Harrod." *Economic Journal* 43:531–32.

———. 1934. "Euler's Theorem and the Problem of Distribution." *Economic Journal* 44:398–414. Reprinted in Robinson 1980 (page references are to original publication).

———. 1935. "What Is Perfect Competition?" *Quarterly Journal of Economics* 49:104–20. Reprinted in Robinson 1980 (page references are to original publication).

———. 1941. "Rising Supply Price." *Economica* 8:1–8. Reprinted in Robinson 1980 (page references are to original publication).

———. 1948. *The Economics of Imperfect Competition.* 8th ed. London: Macmillan.

———. 1953. "Imperfect Competition Revisited." *Economic Journal* 63:579–93.

———. 1962. *Economic Philosophy.* Chicago: Aldine.

———. 1980. *Collected Economic Papers.* 6 vols. Cambridge, Mass.: MIT Press.

Roncaglia, Alessandro. 1978. *Sraffa and the Theory of Prices.* Trans. Jan Kregel. New York: Wiley.

———. 1983. "Piero Sraffa and the Reconstruction of Political Economy." *Banca Nazionale del Lavoro Quarterly Review* 147:337–50.

Roos, Charles F. 1937. *NRA Economic Planning.* Bloomington, Ind.: Principia.

Sala-i-Martin, Xavier. 1990. "Lecture Notes on Economic Growth (I): Introduction to the Literature and Neoclassical Models." National Bureau of Economic Research, Working Paper no. 3563. Cambridge, Mass.: National Bureau of Economic Research.

Samuelson, Paul A. 1967. "The Monopolistic Competition Revolution." In Kuenne 1967, 105–38.

———. 1976. *Foundations of Economic Analysis.* 1947. Reprint, New York: Atheneum.

———. 1987. "Sraffian Economics." In Eatwell, Milgate, and Newman 1987.

Sarti, Roland. 1971. *Fascism and the Industrial Leadership in Italy, 1919–1940.* Berkeley and Los Angeles: University of California Press.

Schneider, Erich. 1932. *Reine Theorie monopolistischer Wirtschaftsformen.* Tübingen: Mohr.

———. 1948. "Zur Konkurrenz und Preisbildung auf vollkommenen und unvollkommenen Märkten." *Weltwirtschaftliches Archiv* 48:399–419.

———. 1949. "Heinrich von Stackelbergs Grundlagen der theoretischen Volkswirtschaftslehre." *Schweizerische Zeitschrift für Volkswirtschaft und Statistik* 85:54–59.

———. 1967. "Milestones on the Way to the Theory of Monopolistic Competition." In Kuenne 1967, 139–44.

Schumpeter, Joseph A. 1927. Obituary of Friedrich von Wieser. *Economic Journal* 37:328–30.

———. 1928. "The Instability of Capitalism." *Economic Journal* 38:361–86.

———. 1949. "Science and Ideology." *American Economic Review* 39:345–59.

———. 1954. *History of Economic Analysis*. New York: Oxford University Press.

Scotchmer, Suzanne, and Jacques-François Thisse. 1992. "Space and Competition: A Puzzle." *Annals of Regional Science* 26:269–86.

Shackle, G. L. S. 1967. *The Years of High Theory: Invention and Tradition in Economic Thought, 1926–1939*. Cambridge: Cambridge University Press.

Sherard, Alfred. 1951. "Advertising, Product Variation, and the Limits of Economics." *Journal of Political Economy* 59:126–42.

Shove, Gerald F. 1928. "Varying Costs and Marginal Net Products." *Economic Journal* 38:258–66.

———. 1930. "Increasing Returns and the Representative Firm." *Economic Journal* 40:94–116.

———. 1933a. "The Imperfection of the Market: A Further Note." *Economic Journal* 43:113–24.

———. 1933b. Review of *The Economics of Imperfect Competition*, by Joan Robinson. *Economic Journal* 43:657–63.

———. 1942. "The Place of Marshall's *Principles* in the Development of Economic Theory." *Economic Journal* 52:294–329.

Smithies, A. 1940–41. "Equilibrium in Monopolistic Competition." *Quarterly Journal of Economics* 55:95–115.

———. 1942. "The Stability of Competitive Equilibrium." *Econometrica* 10:258–74. Reprinted in Newman 1968 (page references are to original publication).

Sombart, Werner. 1927. *Der moderne Kapitalismus*. Munich: Duncker und Humblot.

———. 1934. *Deutscher Sozialismus*. Berlin: Buchbolz und Weisswange.

Sonnenschein, Hugo. 1987. "Oligopoly and Game Theory." In Eatwell, Milgate, and Newman 1987.

Spence, Michael. 1976. "Product Selection, Fixed Costs, and Monopolistic Competition." *Review of Economic Studies* 43:217–35.

Spirito, Ugo. 1932. "Individuo e stato nella concezione corporativa." *Nuovi studi di diritto, economia, e politica* 5:85–93.

Sraffa, Piero. 1925. "Relazioni fra costo e quantità prodotta." *Annali di economia* 2:277–328.

———. 1926. "The Laws of Returns under Competitive Conditions." *Economic Journal* 36:535–50.

Stackelberg, Heinrich von. 1932. *Grundlagen einer reinen Kostentheorie*. Vienna: Julius Springer.

———. 1933. "Zwei kritische Bemerkungen zur Preistheorie Gustav Cassels." *Zeitschrift für Nationalökonomie* 4:456–72.

———. 1934. *Marktform und Gleichgewicht*. Vienna: Julius Springer.

———. 1935. "Der typische Fehlschluß in der Theorie der gleichgewichtslosen Marktformen: Ein Beitrag zum Seinsgebundenheitsproblem der Wissenschaft." *Zeitschrift für die gesamte Staatswissenschaft* 95:691–708.

———. 1938. "Probleme der unvollkommenen Konkurrenz." *Weltwirtschaftliches Archiv* 48:95–141.

———. 1939. "Theorie der Vertriebspolitik und Qualitätsvariation." *Schmollers Jahrbuch* 63:43–85.

———. 1940. "Die Grundlagen der Nationalökonomie: Bemerkungen zu dem gleichnamigen Buch von Walter Eucken." *Weltwirtschaftliches Archiv* 51:245–86.

———. 1941. "Kapital und Zins in der stationären Volkswirtschaft." *Zeitschrift für Nationalökonomie* 10:25–61.

———. 1947. "Entwicklungsstufen der Werttheorie." *Schweizerische Zeitschrift für Volkswirtschaft und Statistik* 83:1–18.

———. 1948. *Grundlagen der theoretischen Volkswirtschaftslehre.* Bern: A. Francke.

———. 1949. "Geistige Möglichkeiten und Grenzen der Wirtschaftslenkung." *Ordo: Jahrbuch für die Ordnung von Wirtschaft und Gesellschaft* 2:193–206.

———. 1952. *The Theory of the Market Economy.* Trans. Alan T. Peacock. New York: Oxford University Press.

———. 1992. *Gesammelte Wirtschaftswissenschaftliche Abhandlungen.* Ed. Norbert Kloten and Hans Möller. 2 vols. Regensburg: Transfer Verlag.

Starrett, David A. 1973. "Principles of Optimal Location in a Large Homogeneous Area." *Journal of Economic Theory* 9:418–48.

Steindl, Josef. 1945. *Small and Big Business.* Oxford: Basil Blackwell.

———. 1976. *Maturity and Stagnation in American Capitalism.* 1952. Reprint, with a new introduction by the author, New York: Monthly Review Press.

Stigler, George J. 1946. "The Economics of Minimum Wage Legislation." *American Economic Review* 36:358–65.

———. 1947a. "Professor Lester and the Marginalists." *American Economic Review* 37:154–57.

———. 1947b. *The Theory of Price.* 2d ed. New York: Macmillan.

———. 1949. *Five Lectures on Economic Problems.* London: Longmans and Green.

———. 1963. "Archibald versus Chicago." *Review of Economic Studies* 30:63–68.

Stigler, George J., and Kenneth E. Boulding, eds. 1952. *Readings in Price Theory.* Chicago: Irwin.

Stolper, Gustav. 1940. *German Economy, 1870–1940: Issues and Trends.* New York: Reynal and Hitchcock.

Sweezy, Paul M. 1939. "Demand under Conditions of Oligopoly." *Journal of Political Economy* 47:568–73.

Suranyi-Unger, Theo. 1940. "Korporative Wirtschaftstheorie." *Weltwirtschaftliches Archiv* 51:149–50.

Sylos-Labini, P. 1987. "Oligopoly." In Eatwell, Milgate, and Newman 1987.

Tarshis, Lorie. 1983. "Post Keynesian Economics: A Promise that Bounced." In *John Maynard Keynes, Critical Assessments*, ed. John Cunningham Wood, 4 vols., 4:525–31. London: Croom Helm.

———. 1987. "Keynesian Revolution." In Eatwell, Milgate, and Newman 1987.

Thomas, Hugh. 1973. *John Strachey*. New York: Harper and Row.

Tirole, Jean. 1989. *The Theory of Industrial Organization*. 2d ed. Cambridge, Mass.: MIT Press.

Tobin, James. 1981. Review of *Keynes's Monetary Thought: A Study of Its Development*, by Don Patinkin. *Journal of Political Economy* 89:204–7.

Toniolo, Gianni. 1980. *L' economia dell' Italia fascista*. Rome: Laterza.

Triffin, Robert. 1941. *Monopolistic Competition and General Equilibrium Theory*. Cambridge, Mass.: Harvard University Press.

Varian, Hal R. 1984. *Microeconomic Analysis*. New York: Norton.

Viner, Jacob. 1952a. "Cost Curves and Supply Curves." In Stigler and Boulding 1952, 198–226. First published in *Zeitschrift für Nationalökonomie* 3 (1931): 23–46.

———. 1952b. "Supplementary Note." In Stigler and Boulding 1952, 227–32. First published in *Readings in Economic Analysis*, ed. R. V. Clemence, 2:31–35 (Cambridge: Addison-Wesley, 1950).

von Neumann, John, and Oskar Morgenstern. 1953. *Theory of Games and Economic Behavior*. 3d ed. Princeton: Princeton University Press.

Weintraub, E. R. 1979. *Microfoundations: The Compatibility of Microeconomics and Macroeconomics*. Cambridge: Cambridge University Press.

White, Horace G. 1936. "A Review of Monopolistic and Imperfect Competition Theories." *American Economic Review* 26:637–49.

Wicksell, Knut. 1958. "Mathematical Economics." In Wicksell, *Selected Papers on Economic Theory*, ed. Erik Lindahl. London: Allen and Unwin.

Yntema, Theodore O. 1928. "The Influence of Dumping on Monopoly Price." *Journal of Political Economy* 36:686–98.

Young, Allyn A. 1913. "Pigou's Wealth and Welfare." *Quarterly Journal of Economics* 27:672–86.

———. 1928. "Increasing Returns and Economic Progress." *Economic Journal* 38:527–42.

Zeuthen, Frederik. 1930. *Problems of Monopoly and Economic Warfare*. London: Routledge.

Library of Congress Cataloging-in-Publication Data

Keppler, Jan.
  Monopolistic competition theory : origins, results, and implications / Jan
Keppler.
    p.   cm.
  Includes bibliographical references and index.
  ISBN 0-8018-4813-X (acid-free paper)
  1. Monopolistic competition.   I. Title.
HB238.K46 1994
338.8'2—dc20   93-48382